❧ PRAISE FOR *Paramhansa Yogananda, A Biography* ❧

"This new biography of Paramhansa Yogananda will pave the path to perfection in the spiritual journey of each individual. . . . It is a masterpiece that serves as a guide in daily life. Through the stories of his life and the unfolding of his destiny, Yogananda's life story will inspire the reader and flower a spiritual awakening in every heart."

—**Vasant Lad, BAM&S, MASc,** Ayurvedic Physician, author of *Ayurveda: Science of Self-Healing, Textbook of Ayurveda* series, and more

"Through this biography of Paramhansa Yogananda, people will discover their divine nature and potential."

—**Bikram Choudhury,** Founder of Bikram's Yoga College of India, author of *Bikram Yoga*

"A deeply insightful look into the life of one of the greatest spiritual figures of our time, by one of his most accomplished, yet last-remaining living disciples. Like the life it depicts, this book is a gem!"

—**Walter Cruttenden,** author of *Lost Star of Myth and Time*

"Swami Kriyananda's biography is a welcome addition to the growing literature on Paramhansa Yogananda. . . . Yogananda was a true seer and indeed, his words 'shall not die.'"

—**Amit Goswami,** PhD, quantum physicist and author of *The Self-Aware Universe, Creative Evolution,* and *How Quantum Activism can Save Civilization*

"In this wonderful new work, we are treated to an intimate portrait of Yogananda's quick wit and profound wisdom, his challenges and his triumphs. We see his indomitable spirit dealing with shattering betrayals and his perseverance in his goal of establishing a spiritual mission that has enriched the world. All seekers of enlightenment owe a great debt to Swami Kriyananda for giving them the biography of Yogananda that could only have been written by one who studied under the master and served him faithfully and who continues his work in the Ananda communities."

—**Brad and Sherry Steiger,** authors of *Real Miracles, Divine Intervention, and Feats of Incredible Survival*

"Swami Kriyananda masterfully presents and illumines Yogananda's life and teachings. Hundreds of new stories about Yogananda will enthrall you."

—**Joseph Cornell,** author of the *Sharing Nature* book series, and Founder of Sharing Nature Worldwide

"Swami Kriyananda's *Paramhansa Yogananda: A Biography* is a unique look at one of the greatest spiritual masters ever to live in America. The book is filled with hundreds of new stories and alive with luminous insights. It is not just a biography, but a window onto the nature of reality, the spiritual quest, and the life and teachings of Paramhansa Yogananda."

—**Jyotish Novak,** Spiritual Director of Ananda Worldwide,
author of *How to Meditate*

"On the face of the earth, there exists no one else more qualified to write the biography of Paramhansa Yogananda than Swami Kriyananda. . . . I consider *Paramhansa Yogananda: A Biography with Personal Reflections and Reminiscences* to be the second volume of *Autobiography of a Yogi.*"

—**Manuel Freedman,** Filmmaker, Founder, Max Freedman Media

"An extraordinary biography of an extraordinary life. A perfect complement to *Autobiography of a Yogi.* Kriyananda gives us stories and insights into the life of Yogananda that only a close disciple could have experienced. It provides deeply moving glimpses of what it would have been like to live with a spiritual master."

—**Joseph Selbie,** co-author of *The Yugas*

"*Autobiography of a Yogi* is already a sourcebook of inspiration for all of us. This new biography of his holiness by an eminent disciple like Swami Kriyanandaji will add to the inspirational treasure of Yogananda's life."

—**Dr. Ram Karan Sharma,** author of *Researches
in Indian and Buddhist Philosophy*

"Swami Kriyananda is surely one of Paramhansa Yogananda's most serious and dedicated disciples. Here he has given us the missing link to that great master's life, the link which that ego-free being could not himself provide: a book about himself. Swami Kriyananda has brought his guru once again to life! Congratulations for a courageous, honest, and inspiring work!"

—**Dr. Jurgen Klein,** biochemist, naturopath, Founder of Jurlique Company,
and author of *Unearthing Nature's Secrets*

"This is a monumental classic. In this enthralling dedication to his guru, Kriyananda has once again grasped our Zeitgeist and given us the incredible story behind the man, the great avatar, Paramhansa Yogananda."

—**Selima Gurtler,** Founder, East Meets West Peace Foundation

"Kriyananda's biography of Yogananda is more revealing of its towering subject than any merely factual account could be. Yogananda comes to life in this book in luminous, full view: generous, joyful, and unswerving in his mission to bring souls to God."

—**James Surendra Conti,** Co-Manager of East West Bookstore

"I devoured Swami Kriyananda's . . . biography of Paramhansa Yogananda . . . . I highly recommend this book to all spiritual seekers."

—**Dr. Swami Ramananda Maharaj,** President of the Nevada Institute of Asian Study, author of *Bliss Now* and *From India with Love*

"*Paramhansa Yogananda: A Biography* presents the most intimate account of Yogananda's life, illuminating the multifaceted nature of his life and mission. Swami Kriyananda's work enriches our understanding of Yogananda with revealing narratives told here for the first time. Here is a loving biography of a spiritual teacher, written by a disciple attentive to historical accuracy."

—**Anantanand Rambachan,** Professor and Chair, Religion Department, Saint Olaf College

"Swami Kriyananda helps us to appreciate Yogananda anew—and with great clarity and depth grasp this spiritual teacher's thoughts, intentions, and world-changing mission. I believe that this book will move as many as Yogananda's own *Autobiography of a Yogi*, and that millions will find inspiration in its pages."

—**Richard Salva,** author of *Walking with William of Normandy: A Paramhansa Yogananda Pilgrimage Guide*

"This delightful book recounts the story of Paramahamsa Yogananda from a fresh perspective. It includes details and adventures not found in the *Autobiography*. The reader gains a deeper sense of the robust greatness of this spiritual pioneer. Packed with history, anecdote, and wisdom, this honest examination of Paramahamsa Yogananda's accomplishments and legacy helps further our understanding of yoga in America."

—**Christopher Key Chapple,** Doshi Professor of Indic and Comparative Theology, Loyola Marymount University

"What a blessing to be gifted with a whole new insight into the magical world of Paramhansa Yogananda! Thank you, Swami Kriyananda, for your efforts!"

—**Deva Premal and Miten,** musicians, composers of *The Essence, Soul in Wonder,* and other works

PARAMHANSA YOGANANDA

A Biography

Paramhansa Yogananda at Niagara Falls, 1927.

PARAMHANSA YOGANANDA

A Biography

WITH PERSONAL REFLECTIONS
AND REMINISCENCES

Swami Kriyananda

Crystal Clarity Publishers
Nevada City, California

Crystal Clarity Publishers, Nevada City, CA 95959-8599

Copyright © 2011 by Hansa Trust
All rights reserved. Published 2011

Printed in China

ISBN: 978-1-56589-264-4
ePub ISBN: 978-1-56589-507-2

1 3 5 7 9 10 8 6 4 2

Cover and interior designed with love, by: Amala Cathleen Elliott

  Library of Congress Cataloging-in-Publication Data

Kriyananda, Swami.
  Paramhansa Yogananda : a biography, with personal reflections and reminiscences / Swami
Kriyananda.
     p. cm.
  ISBN 978-1-56589-264-4 (pbk.) -- ISBN 978-1-56589-507-2 (ebook)
1. Yogananda, Paramahansa, 1893-1952. 2. Yogis--India--Biography. I. Title.

  BP605.S43Y635 2011
  294.5092--dc23
  [B]

                               2011041122

  www.crystalclarity.com
  clarity@crystalclarity.com
  800-424-1055

Master chanting "AUM," 1950.

Paramhansa Yogananda playing an esraj (musical instrument of India).

Contents

 # Foreword

by Shri D.R. Kaarthikeyan

positions held in India: Director, Central Bureau of Investigation;
Director General, National Human Rights Commission;
Special Director General, Central Reserve Police Force

Autobiography of a Yogi is the most celebrated autobiography of all time. It was written by one of the great and all-too-rare spiritual masters that appear from time to time to bless our earth. This biography of Paramhansa Yogananda by his favourite disciple may become equally popular.

It is most fitting that this biography should be written by the master's most celebrated direct disciple—J. Donald Walters—who is now widely known in the world as Swami Kriyananda. Walters met his Master in 1948, after reading *Autobiography of a Yogi*. He has continued to be his loyal disciple for over six decades.

This book was born of firsthand knowledge. It is not, as the author himself states, a book of *hagiography*. In other words, it contains solid facts, not fulsome praise.

Every chapter—indeed, every page makes absorbing reading. The reader feels he is sitting with Swami Kriyananda, listening to him narrate his personal experiences in the most natural way.

In one unusual chapter, number 17, Swami Kriyananda describes beautifully the Salient Characteristics and qualities of his Master, citing many real episodes from his life.

As Swami Kriyananda himself says, "One reason I am writing this book on Yogananda's life is to set the record straight on the greatest man I have ever known, and known well (at least outwardly), in my life."

I heartily recommend this book to all readers. Further than that, I can do no better than quote a few passages from the book itself:

"The foremost of all such qualities was his [Yogananda's] concern for the upliftment of all mankind, and his ever-blissful outlook on life. He wanted nothing from others except their own highest happiness."

"My guru, as an avatar, had both a qualitative and a quantitative work to do. Seeing my own zeal for bringing everyone in the world to God, he had assigned me to this kind of activity also, in addition to my own meditations. 'Your duty in this life,' he told me, 'will be one of intense activity, and meditation.' I could not help noting that he had put activity first, even before meditation."

"Toward the end of his life, Master said to a group of us monks, 'Respect one another, as you respect me.'"

"People are a very important part of any life of spiritual service. Our first duty is to love and respect them, as images of God."

"The world will become a better place, because he lived."

In short, I believe this book—of the more than 140 books he has authored—will be widely welcomed throughout the world.

New Delhi
June 24, 2011

PARAMHANSA YOGANANDA

A Biography

The author presenting his guru with a box of Indian savories
at Mt. Washington, three days before Yogananda's *mahasamadhi*.

Introduction

*W*hy a biography of Paramhansa Yogananda, when he himself wrote a world-famous account of his own life in the book, *Autobiography of a Yogi*? The answer is, quite simply, that he wrote his book in a spirit of such humility that the reader could only intuit the author's spiritual greatness from his perfect attitude toward every life situation. I myself read *Autobiography of a Yogi* in 1948, and was so overwhelmed by that perfection that I took the next bus across the country: New York to Los Angeles. I had already been seeking God almost desperately. The first words I addressed to Yogananda when we met were, "I want to be your disciple." He accepted me at that very meeting, and I was blessed to live with him as a close disciple for the last three and a half years of his life.

Will this book be a hagiography (the biography of a saint, often expressed in idealizing or idolizing terms)? That depends. I will spare no pains to share with you the very real greatness that I beheld in my guru. But if, to you, *hagiography* implies a work of fulsome praise, filled with glowing adjectives and numerous legends that might more properly be assigned to the category of myth, then this work will definitely not be such. I will share with you what I know, what I heard from the Master's own lips (yes, he was indeed a spiritual master, and he himself would never use that word lightly), what I myself experienced, and what I sincerely believe because I heard it from others who were close to him, and whose words were, in my opinion, believable.

The advantage of this book is that it will be written from first hand knowledge. I am not a historian. No doubt real historians will get into the act someday, as the world-impact of Yogananda's life becomes increasingly known to the world. This book will lack the historian's perspective, but it will be much more intimate than anything he could offer.

My sincere opinion is that Yogananda's life will have a major impact on the world—that, indeed, it will change the very course of history. I hope by the end of my account to have convinced you that I have at least sound cause for this belief.

I will not repeat here stories that appear in *Autobiography of a Yogi*, though I may refer to some of them. I omit them because the charm with which Yogananda tells them deserves to stand alone: To retell them would be to do him an injustice. There are many other stories, however, that never found their way into his book—stories about himself that he would not tell publicly because he couldn't, and simply wouldn't, speak glowingly about himself. Indeed, although his book was an autobiography, it was in some ways almost more about other people than about himself. His book, too, is mostly a book of reminiscences about others.

The purpose of this book, then, is to tell you how Yogananda was perceived by others, and especially by me. I want to show you that Paramhansa Yogananda's life was much more than that of a humble devotee who had had the good luck to meet many great saints, and to "stumble," so to speak, onto the highest levels of realization. The truth is, not every devotee, on entering the spiritual path, can expect to be blessed with anything like such lofty spiritual experiences!

Yogananda was a towering giant among saints—one of those few who come from age to age, having been sent by God with the divine mission of guiding mankind out of the fogs of delusion into the clear light of divine understanding. In the best-known Indian scripture, the Bhagavad Gita ("The Lord's Song"), the statement appears, "O Bharata (Arjuna)! Whenever virtue (dharma, or right action) declines and vice (*adharma*, or wrong action) is in the ascendant, I (the Supreme Lord) incarnate Myself on earth (as an *avatar*, or divine incarnation). Appearing from age to age in visible form, I come to destroy evil, and to reestablish virtue." (IV:7,8) I might add that this is not the first time that this great soul, whom we know as Paramhansa Yogananda, appeared on earth.

Often and often he told us, "I killed Yogananda many lifetimes ago. No one dwells in this temple now but God." And the incredible depth of his compassion for suffering mankind is evident in these lines from a poem he wrote, named, "God's Boatman":

Oh! I will come back again and again!
Crossing a million crags of suffering,
With bleeding feet, I will come,
If need be, a trillion times,
As long as I know that
One stray brother is left behind.

That compassion is what I saw in his eyes every time I gazed into them deeply. It was no mere sentiment. It was the expression of his soul, as he reached out with yearning to help everyone who came to him with a desire to be lifted toward final liberation in God.

Mukunda Lal Ghosh (Paramhansa Yogananda) at the age of six.

CHAPTER ONE

His Beginning Years

O n January 5, 1893, a baby boy was born to a Bengali couple in Gorakhpur, a city in the north of India. Mukunda Lal was the name they gave him. His family name was Ghosh. He was the second of four sons and the fourth of eight children. From early childhood his mother knew his life's destiny was to live for and to serve God. He once told me that she saw him one day talking with a few little girls. "Mukunda," she called to him, "come away from there. That is not for you." He understood, and came away.

He was a child of extraordinary will power. The following episode must have occurred when he was not much beyond the age of two. Late one evening he woke his mother to say, "Mother, I want some *sandesh* (a Bengali sweetmeat)."

"The shops are closed, Dear," was her reply.

"But I want *sandesh*! And I want it now!"

"What are we to do?" she asked her husband.

"I don't think it is good to thwart this little one's will," was his reply.

"I don't think we *can* thwart it!" she said.

The two of them went out into the night. Reaching the candymaker's shop, they called out to him in his quarters above.

Grumbling, he at last came down, opened the shop, and sold them a few cuts of *sandesh*. Mukunda was satisfied, and so also were his parents—to be able to go back to sleep! (It is, I might add, a practice in India to allow little children up to the age of two to have their own way whenever possible. Discipline usually begins at the age of three.)

Gorakhpur was the home of a sage known as Gorakhnath. My guru told us the following story about him. Gorakhnath, by his yogic powers, lived to the ripe old age of 300 years. In that long space of time he developed all the eight *siddhis* (spiritual powers) mentioned by Patanjali, the ancient and supreme authority on the science of yoga. When Gorakhnath saw that the time had come for him to leave his body, he gazed through the spiritual eye to find someone fit to receive from him the gift of those powers. He saw a young man, in yoga pose, seated on the banks of the Ganges. Here, he thought, was a fit recipient. Gorakhnath materialized before the young man and declared, "I am Baba Gorakhnath!" No doubt he expected to be greeted with awe and wonder.

"Indeed," said the youth, not greatly impressed. "And what may I do for you?"

"I have realized that the time has come for me to leave this body. Before I do so, I want to give to someone I consider worthy the eight *siddhis* of yoga I have developed. Will you accept them?"

The young man said nothing, but Gorakhnath gave him eight pellets of mud. "I have condensed my powers," he explained, "into these eight pellets. All you need to do is hold them in your right hand, and meditate on what you feel emanating from them. The powers will then become yours."

The youth took the pellets in his right hand, gazed at them a moment, and then asked, "Are these mine to do with as I please?"

"Certainly," the old sage replied. "I have given them to you. They are yours now to use as you like."

Turning toward the river, the young man threw into its flowing water all the eight pellets, which dissolved and disappeared.

"What have you done!?" cried the old man. "It took me three hundred years to develop those powers!"

The young man gazed at him calmly. "In delusion yet, Gorakhnath?"

At these words the old man suddenly realized that, in his search for yogic powers, he had to that extent forgotten God. Offering himself up wholly now to the Lord, he merged back into the Infinite, a free soul.

Mukunda was not interested in powers. He was a complete *bhakta* (saint of devotion). His brother Sananda once told me, "When Mukunda merely heard the word, God, tears of longing would stream down his cheeks."

Once, when the child was old enough to have learned how to write at least rudimentary Bengali, Mukunda wrote a letter to God, telling the Lord of his love for Him. Addressing the letter to "God, in Heaven," he posted it trustingly. Thereafter, day after day, he waited for a reply. "Lord," he prayed daily, "why haven't You answered me?" At last he was granted a vision. Shining before him in letters of light was God's answer. It filled the child's heart with deep satisfaction and gratitude.

Always, throughout his life, Mukunda tried to get people to understand that God is not some mere abstraction. Though the Lord has created billions of universes, He is also very human in the way he relates to His human children. And He likes above all to see in them an attitude of childlike trust. One time, many years later, and not long before his death, Mukunda—who by that time was known by his monastic name, Paramhansa Yogananda—spoke of one of his disciples, Horace Gray, a very simple monk who found it difficult even to speak: he was spastic. "Horace will get there in this life," the Master remarked. "His devotion has pleased God." Another disciple, trying to reconcile this prediction with Horace as he knew him, remarked, "But it must be a very simple kind of devotion isn't it, Sir?"

With a blissful smile the Master replied, "Ah, that is the kind which pleases God!"

Childlike though Mukunda certainly was, he also had a strong sense of justice, and a strong will. His will power inspired his companions to do what was right even when it took great courage to do so.

In his school there was a boy, Mukunda's senior by several years, who found pleasure in bullying those smaller and weaker than himself. One day, as this boy was inflicting a brutal beating on a child much smaller than himself, Mukunda marched up to him and cried, "If you want to fight, fight me!"

"Why, gladly!" replied the bully with a leer. He turned from the little one and sprang at Mukunda.

The other boys gathered in a circle to watch this unequal battle. Privately they sided with Mukunda, but they didn't dare say so out loud.

The bully lifted his adversary above his head, then dashed him to the ground, momentarily stunning him. He stooped over and lifted him up again. This time, however, Mukunda saw his chance. With both arms he grasped the bully about the neck and squeezed. The much bigger boy, finding it difficult to breathe, did everything he could to shake Mukunda off. Repeatedly, he beat the smaller boy's head against the ground until he'd rendered him almost unconscious. Still Mukunda held firm.

"Do you give up?" Mukunda demanded between clenched teeth.

At last the bigger boy had to cry, "Yes! Yes! Let go my throat! I give up!"

Mukunda released his hold. The other stood up and inhaled great lungsful of air. Once he had regained his breath, however, he broke his word and leapt a third time at Mukunda. This time, the other boys intervened.

"Mukunda has beaten you fairly!" they cried. "If you try again to beat him, we will all jump on you."

From then on, realizing he'd only be outnumbered, the bully never tried to beat Mukunda again. But from Mukunda's courage the boys received a bracing lesson on the importance of standing resolutely for the cause of justice.

Another time, in Bareilly, a large group of boys surrounded him menacingly. He himself, in telling me the story, said "Fifty boys." Laurie Pratt, however, his chief editor, said to me, "Fifty boys is inconceivable. He must have said fifteen." Well, fifty is the number I heard, but I agree that, under the circumstances, even fifteen would have been a difficult number for him to count at that moment. Surely, then, he gave whichever number he did only to indicate a large group.

Their leader challenged Mukunda: "Why have you been avoiding our company?"

"Frankly," Mukunda answered, "I don't like the language you use."

"We speak as we are!" retorted the leader angrily. "Who are you to be uppity with us? We're going to teach you a good lesson!"

A second boy shouted, "Yeah! We'll massacre you."

A third joined in, "We'll break every bone in your body! When you crawl home to your mother, she won't even recognize you!"

Mukunda backed against a tree and cried fiercely, "How brave of you all, to menace me in this number! And, yes, in these numbers, you can do all that you say. But I tell you this: I'll 'massacre' the first boy who dares to lay a hand on me!"

Much foot shuffling ensued. Finally their leader said, "We didn't really mean it, Mukunda. We'd rather be friends."

Mukunda then concluded, "If it's friendship you want, then friends let us be." He and their leader walked off, arms about each others' shoulders.

Mukunda (Yogananda) standing behind his elder brother, Ananta.

CHAPTER TWO

His Teenage Years

Mukunda's father held a high position with the Bengal-Nagpur Railway Company. Owing to that position, he could give his son free passes even to distant cities. Mukunda sometimes took advantage of this offer, traveling with a small group of friends.

Dr. Nagendra Das, a boyhood friend of his, told me, "Wherever we stopped, groups of boys would gather around Mukunda in a very short time, drawn by his magnetism." Indeed, Mukunda's—and later, of course, Yogananda's—power to win friends wherever he went was extraordinary.

Mukunda used to meditate in the attic room of the family home, at 4 Gurpar Road in Calcutta. The male cook teased him one day that he would tell Mukunda's older brother, Ananta, on him. Mukunda replied quite seriously, "Don't tease me about a thing like that. If I wish, I can discipline *you*."

"Oh, sure!" mocked the cook. "So tell me, little one, what can you do to me?"

"I can stick your hand to the wall."

"Just try it!" laughed the cook.

Mukunda took the cook's left palm and placed it against the wall, extending the attached arm out from the body. Suddenly the cook found that his hand wouldn't move. Try as he would, it remained stuck to the wall.

He pleaded to be released, but Mukunda answered gaily, "You'll have to stand there awhile. That is your punishment for making fun of my spiritual practices!"

It was some time before Mukunda, returning, released the cook, who at once fell to his knees and begged for forgiveness.

Mukunda's meditations were not what one might expect of a little boy. For one thing, he would often meditate for long hours—seven, eight at a time. As he told me, "I would practice *Hong-Sau* (a meditation technique) for seven hours at a time, until I went breathless." For another, he often had extraordinary visions.

He told himself, however, "Some day I must have a really *long* meditation. After all, what are seven or eight hours—out of a twenty-four hour day? Don't people work that long merely to supply their material needs?"

One morning Mukunda awoke with the thought, "A whole year has passed. And *still* I haven't fulfilled the promise I made to myself! Will a long meditation always wait until 'tomorrow'? Why not *today*? Why not this very morning?"

He sat down for meditation. Forty-eight whole hours passed. To Mukunda, they seemed more like forty-eight minutes. During a part of that ecstatic period, his body rose above the ground in levitation.

At last he returned to the pandemonium of this bustling world: the sounds of servants at their household chores; the voices of family members in the rooms below; the hubbub of people's voices in the streets, and the noise of traffic outside. This cacophony invaded his ears discordantly, though it could not disturb his inner peace. In the passageway to the kitchen he met the cook—the same one, perhaps, whose hand he had stuck to the wall. This faithful servant had for many years been suffering from a pain in his back. Mukunda touched him, and the man was instantly healed.

It was lunchtime. Mukunda's family members were seated Indian fashion on straw mats around the dining room floor. They had paid scant attention to Mukunda's absence of two days. They knew he liked to meditate, and left it at that.

Mukunda now joined them. While he ate, he was conscious of a transcendent detachment from everything. Looking up at one point, he noticed Bodi, the wife of Ananta (Mukunda's older brother), regarding him curiously. Bodi, like Ananta, had never approved of what they both considered Mukunda's "religious fanaticism." Smiling inwardly, Mukunda thought, "Let me have a little fun with them all, especially with Bodi!"

Withdrawing his consciousness partially from the body, he returned a little bit to the complete inwardness he had experienced scarcely half an hour earlier. His body, suddenly deprived of energy, fell silently backward to the floor. Bodi uttered a frightened cry. Quickly she stepped over and felt his pulse. There was no heartbeat. The rest of the family, terrified, gathered around the inert form.

The family doctor, frantically summoned, requested that the boy's body be carried to a couch. After careful examination, he pronounced the dreaded verdict: "He's dead."

Bodi looked around her solemnly. "This," she declared, "is what comes of too much yoga practice!"

The rest of the family uttered loving encomiums for this dear child, now lost to them forever.

Present in the room was a maidservant who was much loved by the family; they used to call her "Maid Ma." Maid Ma had served them for many years with an almost motherly devotion. But she would sometimes argue hotly with Mukunda for bringing his friends to the house, in ever-increasing numbers. Now she added her encomiums to those of the rest.

"Alas! though it's true he was mischievous, for all that he was a good boy." Then, disconsolately, she cried, "O Bhagavan (Lord)! now I won't have anyone to fight with anymore!"

Mukunda could contain himself no longer. "Oh, yes you will!" he cried.

"You!" shouted Maid Ma. "I *knew* you were only playing!" She picked up a broom and, in mock anger, threw it at him.

On another occasion Mukunda remarked to a friend, "People never see God because they never try to see Him."

"Never try! But thousands go every day to the temples. Don't *they* try?"

"Never *sincerely* try," Mukunda returned, his smile remote from this world.

"But if God longs to come to mankind, as you've so often told us, can't He quite easily do so when they at least pray to Him, even if not with deep concentration?"

"It isn't that He *won't* come," Mukunda replied. "Rather, it's that they won't meet Him on His level. Instead, they insist that He come down to theirs. But why *should* He come to them? He knows that most people only want to argue with Him! There is no room in worldly hearts for His perfect bliss. People are more concerned with their worldly desires than with the pure longing for His love."

"Are you saying, then, that if we sat down this very night and called to Him from our hearts, He would come?"

"Why not? Of course He would!" was the firm reply. "Why should He refuse us, whose only 'ulterior' motive is our love for Him?"

"Tonight!" his friend cried. "Why not tonight?"

"Agreed," said Mukunda.

Later, they went to Mukunda's attic room and sat on little mats in lotus posture.

"Do you think we might see God as Lord Krishna?" Mukunda's friend asked.

"Again, why not? Sri Krishna will surely come to us tonight!"

They began to chant. Later, chanting done, they practiced Kriya Yoga, then *Hong-Sau* (watching the breath), then simply called to Krishna in the silence, summoning him with their hearts' love to appear before their inward gaze. Hours passed. The night sky grew dim. They chanted, then meditated some more. Still Krishna had not appeared.

"I'm afraid he won't come now," Mukunda's friend finally said.

"He *will* come!" was the adamant reply.

Still later: "Mukunda, the dawn is breaking. He hasn't come yet. I'm growing sleepy!"

"You sleep if you like," Mukunda whispered reproachfully, "but if I die trying I will call to him until he comes!"

Suddenly, within his inner temple, he beheld a wondrous vision: Krishna walking on soft clouds of gold! Krishna, his sweet smile a gift of heavenly peace!

"I see him!" cried Mukunda. "I see him, the moon of Gokula!"

"It can't be true. You're imagining it."

"You shall see him for yourself!" Mukunda reached out and gently struck his friend on the chest over the heart.

"I see him too!" his friend cried. "Oh, I see him too!"

What bliss welled up in both their hearts that wondrous morning!

Mukunda's education was somewhat different from the norm. That is to say, though he went to class, he received more revelations inwardly than from his teachers. Usually he preferred to sit at the back of the classroom, where he could close his eyes without the teacher's notice, and listen to the truths that came to him from within. In one classroom, however, the teacher ordered him to keep his eyes open and pay attention. Mukunda tried, but didn't always succeed.

"Come sit in the front row before me!" the teacher ordered.

"I did so," Yogananda told me many years later. "But now the teacher took it for granted that I'd keep my eyes open. Right in front of him, I found it actually easier to close my eyes and meditate."

One day in school he slipped a note to the boy seated next to him. God had instructed him to write this note, so he did.

"I am your guru," said the note.

"The boy looked over at me reproachfully," Yogananda told me. "'Bad boy!' was his only comment, whispered under his breath.

"I smiled. That night, this classmate had a divine visitation. God showed him the truth of what I had written him. Thrilled, he tried to seek me out the next day. But I hid from him. Hours passed before we met again."

Mukunda worshiped God especially in the form of Mother. Westerners have scoffed at Hindus for what they consider "idol worship." In reality, it is not idol worship, but *"ideal* worship." Idol worship means to seek the things of this world: wealth, power, fame, and the like. None but the completely ignorant in India imagine that God is anything but infinite. Still, as God is everywhere, so a spiritual image is a part of that great reality, and can help us to focus our attention on Him. Infinity is a difficult concept to bring into focus. In fact, there are many instances in India's long history of God actually enlivening a stone image. There is an account, for example, from the life of Trailanga

Swami, a great saint of Benares who also, like Gorakhnath, lived for centuries. He had an image in his temple—it may have been of Kali, but I no longer remember. A devotee of his begged him repeatedly to bless him through that image.

One evening the two of them were seated together in the next room. The image itself walked in, sat down, and conversed with them on lofty topics. After some time, the "idol" left the room and returned to its customary position. The divine power left it.

Trailanga looked at the devotee calmly and asked, "And now, what have you got?" That passing phenomenon had been inspiring, certainly, but had it changed the devotee to the extent of giving him God? As my guru was wont to say, "The path to God is not a circus!" The important thing is that we change ourselves. In this respect especially, Buddha was completely right.

Nevertheless, visions can be a consolation, certainly, though they are no guarantee that the visionary is a saint.

Mukunda, as I said, worshiped God especially in the form of Mother of the Universe. Because his friends knew this was the focus for his devotion, they would happily bring him news of any new Kali temple they found in the vicinity. One day they came to him bearing tidings of a new temple.

Mukunda smiled. "You all go, if you like. This evening I prefer to stay home."

"Stay home! But why?"

Mukunda only smiled. His friends went to the temple, prostrated themselves before the image it held of the Divine Mother, and chanted a few devotional songs. Their hearts were uplifted, but the upliftment lasted only for that evening.

At home, Mukunda went up to his attic room. Temples, too, have value, primarily as aids to bringing people's devotion to a focus. But Mukunda's devotion had long since achieved that focus at the point of superconscious ecstasy in the forehead—that is to say, in the frontal lobe of the brain *behind* that point.

"Mother with lotus feet!" he prayed. "Mother with hair spreading out over all creation! O Mother, come to me! Mother, your smile twinkles in a million stars. O Divine Mother, tear asunder this veil of darkness which hides You from me!"

Long he called to Her. Years earlier, when he had lost his earthly mother, his aching love for her had been redirected to the Divine Mother of the Universe. (Wise Child! Instead of grieving over our earthly losses, we should direct our love to God, where every pain becomes a blessing.) And now at last that Mother of all mothers appeared to him!*

"Kali!" he whispered. "Mother Kali, You have come! Oh, how beautiful You are! Mother, may my life be a song of constant love for Thee!"

The Divine Mother smiled. "Your prayer is granted, My child. Though you shall have to travel far, and bring many souls to My all-sheltering arms, in your heart of hearts you will always be at rest in My formless presence. And as often as you call to Me, whenever you desire it, so often shall I appear before you in this form."

Mukunda (Yogananda) called Kali, when seen in vision, "beautiful." But certainly the images presented of Her are anything but that. She is depicted with four arms, a garland of skulls, Her hair unkempt and straggling out in all directions, Her tongue lolling out of Her mouth, standing (as if in triumph, as the Westerner would perceive Her) on the prostrate form of Her husband, Shiva. All this, however, is deeply symbolic. The English thought of Her as the goddess of death, the form worshiped by Thuggees (a band

---

* In his autobiography, in the chapter, "The Blissful Devotee and His Cosmic Romance," Master described an early vision he had of the Divine Mother. I do not know which of these two appearances came first.

of criminal assassins). Yogananda explained this symbolism to us:

"Kali represents Mother Nature. Her four arms symbolize Creation, Preservation, and Destruction, the fourth depicting the gift of salvation to those who go beyond Nature to the heart of Infinity. The garland of skulls signifies Her divine omnipresence in all human minds. Why skulls? Because all human life is temporary. Her hair streaming outward signifies God's energy reaching out through all Creation. In Her dance, the rhythmic steps signify the vibratory nature of Creation. Her husband Shiva is depicted as lying prostrate, because God the Father, the Eternal Spirit, is beyond Creation, beyond all vibration, alive in the vibrationless void of Brahman (Spirit).

"Kali's dance ceases when Her light footsteps touch the breast of the Infinite. The reason She is shown with Her tongue out is that She suddenly realizes She has gone too far! Finitude cannot penetrate into the heart of Infinity."

In India, one bites his tongue, sticking it out a little beyond the teeth, when he is conscious of having made a mistake. Even in Western countries, this is a common, instinctive gesture.

Needless to say, many Indians, too, fail to understand this deep symbolism, and assume that Kali's tongue is lolling out in blood lust; that Her streaming hair suggests almost a harridan raging about to find whom She may devour next. The garland of skulls suggests to them, again, blood lust. And the four arms seem to serve no purpose at all. Her position, standing on Shiva's breast, is taken for a posture of victory.

Indian images of God are often deliberately not beautiful, in order that the devotee may not be deluded into thinking that any image can ever define the Infinite. The images of Kali are certainly not beautiful. Yet She has been worshipped by many great saints and masters, including Yogananda and Sri Ramakrishna.

Ram Proshad, a great poet-saint of the seventeenth century, worshipped Kali also. One day he was mending a fence on his property, when his daughter came and helped him. He'd been singing. His daughter asked him, "To whom are you singing, Daddy?"

"I am singing to my Divine Mother Kali. But She's very naughty! Though I often sing to Her, She never comes to me."

"If She never comes, Daddy, why do you keep on calling? Isn't it all a useless waste of time?" With a light laugh, his daughter then ran away.

Later that day, his job finished, Ram Proshad went indoors. There he told his wife how their daughter had been helping him. The wife replied, "That isn't possible. She's spending the whole day on the other side of town with some friends."

When their daughter returned that evening, he questioned her. She answered, "Daddy, you can ask anybody. I wasn't here. I was far away, on the other side of town."

And then Ram Proshad realized that it had been his Divine Mother, coming to him in the form of his daughter, and teasing him by saying, "If She never comes, why do you keep calling to Her?"

So you see, Kali comes in many forms, and rarely, if ever, in the form one beholds in the temples. She can also be infinitely kind, friendly—even teasingly playful! Her eyes, however, though childlike, reveal also the deep, ego-free calmness of Infinity.

Lord Jagannath, depicted in the great Jagannath temple in Puri, is shown with both his arms truncated. The image itself is not at all beautiful, and has been deliberately marred by those truncated arms. The purpose of that disfigurement is to show that the Infinite Lord can never truly be captured in human form.

Interestingly, Bokhara rugs in Persia (Iran) always contain a flaw too, placed there deliberately. The purpose for this disfigurement is to state that perfection can never be captured in outward form.

Temples themselves are symbolic of the human body, wherein the devotee is counseled to sit in meditation and "go within." Otherwise, God is omnipresent; He cannot be localized in either space or time.

Paramhansa Yogananda with a tiger skin.

The Power of Delusion

*F*illed one day with the thought of God's omnipresence, Mukunda was walking down a street in Calcutta with a young
friend when he spied a little pile of putrid rice. As he was gazing
at it thoughtfully (after all, it is easy to think of God being present in a flower, but not so easy to think of Him as equally present
in filth), a cow came up to the little mound, extended its muzzle
toward it, then hastily backed away.

"Well," thought Mukunda, "that cow is ignorant. I can eat that
rice, if I remain firm in the thought that God is in the rice, too."

To his companion he said, "I can eat that rice."

Mockingly his friend replied, "Oh, sure! Well, if you eat it, so
also will I."

Mukunda answered, "Remember your promise!" Stooping
down, he put a handful of the putrid grain into his mouth, then
chewed and swallowed it with every evidence of relish. Seeing
what he'd done, his friend bolted.

"You promised!" Mukunda called after him. "When you make a
promise, you have to keep it." Taking another handful, he chased
after him. When he caught up with his friend, he insisted on

pushing some of the rice into the boy's mouth. Everything the boy had eaten that day came up in one great rush of revulsion!

So then, God is even present in putrid rice. Does this mean He is also present in evil? Yes, it does! As His pleasantness is present *behind* even putrid rice, and His beauty *behind* ugliness, so is His presence also *behind* evil. We should not seek Him in those things which don't remind us of Him, but we should know that there is but one God, everywhere, even as the Jews proclaim. God and Satan, ultimately, are one. Satan is merely that creative, and—yes—divine force which tries to take everything further into outward manifestation.

People sometimes say, "Oh, I can play with liquor, drugs, sex, and other ego-absorbing activities, but if I keep my mind inwardly free they won't touch me." Just as Satan's greatest triumph lies in persuading people that he doesn't exist, so is his greatest power demonstrated in that simple thought, "It won't catch me, if I don't allow it to." What people don't know is that any step they take, either toward God or away from Him, is an invitation to powers infinitely greater than their own, which influence them to continue moving in the same direction. Our very thoughts are not our own!

Many years ago on Cape Cod in Massachusetts, I was in a room with fifty or a hundred other young people. (For I myself was young, then.) Someone from New York was touting marijuana. He tried to reassure everyone, "It isn't habit-forming." I was the only person there who didn't test the cigarettes he passed around that day. The reason I wouldn't touch one was that I could feel an evil influence in the room.

I have felt the same evil presence on other occasions, when people were smoking dope. That presence prevented me from ever experimenting with such things. As Yogananda said, "Delusion has its own power. Never play with it." This is a very real, and very important, aspect of the spiritual path: Don't "shop around" too freely. You are playing with your own happiness, even for incarnations to come.

The safest way to remain on the "straight and narrow" is to serve others, never thinking of what you can get from them. Mukunda decided one day to feed two hundred poor people. At first, everyone thought he was crazy to attempt it. Bit by bit, however, as he attracted more donations, people's enthusiasm increased.

"We need money," said a friend, stating the obvious.

"We will get it," Mukunda said. "And it will come through you!"

"Me? Impossible!"

"Oh, yes it will. You have an aunt who will give it to us. Go ask her for it."

"But my aunt is completely against everything you stand for!"

"Nevertheless, go ask her."

The boy went to his aunt and asked her for a donation. She went into a tirade against the way Mukunda was spoiling her nephew. The nephew was about to leave the room when she called out to him: "Stop! I hear he is doing some good with this feast he is providing the poor. Here is some money. Ask him to use it for that purpose."

In the end, the boys served ten times the two hundred they had originally planned.

In a similar way also, Mukunda created a library for the neighborhood. He went from house to house, asking for books that people might be willing to donate to this project. I myself saw this library in Calcutta. It was still in existence in 1959.

Mukunda tried many different spiritual practices to make sure he was teaching the best methods. For a time he stood in water up to his neck, chanting to God. The water helped to make him feel lighter and less tied to the body, and the coldness of it (he stood in the Ganges) helped him to rise above body consciousness.

He meditated in cremation grounds to sharpen his sense of the fleeting nature of all life.

He tried tantric practices. These he later warned people against, for such practices can raise people's consciousness quickly, but they dash one's spiritual hopes just as quickly to the ground. They help people to raise the kundalini (the "serpent power, sleeping" at the base of the spine), but they don't prepare those morally or spiritually who practice them. In consequence, many practitioners fall, spiritually.

Tantra is a way also of indulging in delusion "a little bit," with a view towards freeing oneself from it ultimately. This is a dangerous practice, however. If one is already caught up in a delusion, it may indeed help him to escape it, at first, by removing his mind gradually from further indulgence in it. But he must then make the still-more difficult effort to renounce the action altogether. If one is already out of a delusion, it is better to stay out of it.

Mukunda once met a saint who asked him, "My boy, are you married?"

"No," was the reply.

"Better stay that way, then!" The saint himself was married to a very materialistic woman. "But I've fooled her," he said with a smile. "She doesn't know where I am." He meant, he had escaped from her into the inner, spiritual realms.

CHAPTER FOUR

The Beauty of Devotion

One's inner life is often best kept a secret from others. Yogananda told us the story of Meera, a queen who lived several centuries ago in India. She herself was a *bhakta* (one who follows the path of devotion), and many devotees would gather around her for blissful *sankirtans* (group singing to God). Her one grief in life was that her own husband never spoke of God.

He, meanwhile, was actually an even greater lover of God than she. But he had promised the Lord, "If ever anyone discovers my secret, I will leave this body, for I will feel that my devotion has been besmirched."

One night, lying beside him in bed, Meera awoke to hear him crying quietly, "Oh, my Beloved, how can I live without seeing You! This world of *maya* [delusion] means nothing to me! Help me to know You! Help me to merge in You!"

The next morning, with radiant face, she cried to him, "Aha! I have discovered your secret!"

"Don't say it!" he cried. "Please don't say it!"

"Oh, yes! I know now how much you love God."

"I am sorry you told me that. Now, I shall have to leave you, for

I promised God that I would no longer keep this body if anyone ever discovered the precious secret I've been keeping."

He sat on the floor in lotus pose, and forthwith left his body.

Mukunda's whole life was a devotional offering to the Divine Mother. Indeed, divine love is the active expression of divine bliss. As he pointed out to others, "Everyone in the world is seeking one thing only: Bliss." That is because all beings are the manifestations of God's Bliss. Most people, however, translate that soul-desire into human terms: they seek emotional happiness. They then translate happiness even further, into very human, and deluded, definitions: money, power, fame—or, still more darkly, revenge, destruction, and the suppression of others. Wherever eternal Bliss is brought down to the level of human emotions, it enters the realm of duality (without which the universe could not have been manifested). And wherever there is duality, everything is balanced out by its own natural opposite. Happiness alternates endlessly with unhappiness. Human love alternates with hatred; success, with failure. For there is only one reality in existence: The Supreme Spirit. The oppositions of Nature are ineluctable. Everything must be canceled out, eventually. No matter how hard a man works to succeed, any success he achieves will have to alternate with failure, just as failure leads back to success again. No state of perfection is possible in this world. Nothing lasts. Never can anyone rightly say: "I've arrived! I have everything I ever wanted."

The only thing to which there is no opposite is inner Bliss. And because divine love is the outward expression of Bliss, there is no opposite to selfless, self-giving love.

As Sri Yukteswar wrote in his book, *The Holy Science*, one cannot put one foot in front of the other on the spiritual path until one has developed the natural love of the heart. Anyone who thinks to find God without that love will, quite simply, fail. Dry theologians think to grasp truths by defining them to the last comma of exquisite precision. What does God care for their definitions? All He wants from all of us, His children, is our love and devotion.

With childlike faith, however, comes a power that is not rooted in egoic desire. During the years when Mukunda's family lived in Bareilly, a huge cyclone hit the city. Black clouds swirled everywhere, accompanied by heavy rains. The garden of their home became flooded.

At just that time, Mukunda's father was summoned to Calcutta with the order to appear within seven days.

"How can I go," he asked his family, "in these torrential rains? The newspapers say it's a cyclone. They predict it will last fifteen more days!"

"But it's important that you go!" cried Mukunda.

His father gestured helplessly. After he'd left the room, Mukunda turned to his sister Nalini. "Nalini," he said, "why is everyone afraid? It's important that Father go. I'll just have to stop this terrible storm!"

Sarcastically Nalini said, "Yes, and order the sun to burn those dark clouds away?"

"Well, why not?" He went to the back door and sat in the entrance, gazing out over the flooded garden. Then he turned to Gora, his younger brother.

"Gora," he said, "go fetch me a large stack of newspapers."

Gora brought the papers and offered them with a mocking smile. "So, what are you going to do with these?" he asked. "Scan them for a bit of good news to cheer us up?"

"You'll see," was the reply.

Mukunda made a paper boat, then cast it onto the water, muttering as he did so a seemingly incomprehensible *mantra* (a series of sacred Sanskrit words).

"This is silly!" cried Gora.

"Never mind. Just keep giving me more pages."

Thirty minutes later, Mukunda was still making boats and sailing them on the water. Gora finally complained, "You've been doing this for half an hour. Come on, Mukun. You may as well give up!"

Mukunda gave him a brief glance, then continued what he was doing. Suddenly Gora, looking up, cried, "It has stopped raining!"

Nalini then shouted, "The sky is clearing!"

Another family member gasped, "Mukun! What have you done?!"

They all gazed at the boy with undisguised awe. The whole family entrained the next day for Calcutta.

CHAPTER FIVE

With Renunciation Comes Great Inner Strength

There were other saints our guru told us about, besides those he'd described in his autobiography. One was a man who had a caustic critic, who made it a point to criticize him in front of his own disciples. One day a disciple came to the Guru and cried exultingly, "Master, your great enemy, the critic, is dead!"

"Oh, my best friend is dead!" lamented the Master. "He was the only one who would tell me my faults. I am heartbroken!"

Another saint my guru told me about was a naked sadhu who lived a life of complete nonattachment in the forest. "His genitals," my guru told me, "were the size of a baby's. I was so touched! He asked me, 'What if you were about to eat, and someone came to you complaining that he was hungry. What would you do?'

"'I would give him my meal,' I replied.

"'What, then, if you prepared another meal, and had just sat down a second time to eat when someone else came with the same complaint?'

"'I would give him my second meal.'

"'What if it happened a third time?'

"'I would give him half my meal, and eat the other half myself.'

"'Get out of here! Go on! You are no sadhu.'"

My guru told me this story without a breath of self-justification. In my opinion, however, it seemed to me that his third answer showed eminent good sense, and better attunement to the actual realities than that sadhu had shown.

Mukunda's life, to return to it, was spent not only in devotional practices. He also was a perfectly normal boy, and loved sports. He didn't like boxing, which involves hitting others, for he had no wish to hit or harm anyone. But he enjoyed wrestling as a means of exuberantly exercising the physical body. Years later, in America, he sometimes displayed his strength in public to show a practical benefit of yoga practice.

Once, in a large lecture hall in Boston, he invited anyone who cared to, to come up and pit his strength against him. Six burly policemen jumped up onto the platform. Everyone in the audience thought that the Master, this time, had met more than his match!

He backed against the rear wall, then invited the six men to press against his stomach, keeping their arms straight. "Are you ready?" he asked.

"Yeah!" they grunted fiercely.

He arched his back. In an instant, all six men tumbled backward into the orchestra pit.

The Master was also a very fast runner. As a boy, he beat everyone who ever ran against him. During his years at Ranchi (which I'll describe briefly later), the school was disturbed for a time by a pack of stray dogs. They chased after the horses (we tend to forget, nowadays, how very recently the motor car was invented) and created many disturbances. The young yogi chased after them with gunny sacks, put each dog into a sack, and secured it. Later, the dogs were taken miles away, and released.

Years later, on Catalina Island off the coast of California, he challenged a young college athlete to a race. By the time the young man had completed the first block, the Master was finishing the second.

And when Yogananda played tennis, he was so fast he seemed almost to be there already, wherever the ball landed. A friend of mine told me, "I used to wonder whether he didn't just materialize, playfully, at that spot!" One also wonders, however, whether using a spiritual power to win at a mere game would not have been to trivialize it. Still, the Master *was* playful!

After Mukunda's graduation from high school, and after he'd met his guru Sri Yukteswar, his father bought him a motorcycle with sidecar. Mukunda enjoyed his new toy, a symbol of his approaching manhood. Sometimes his guru would ride with him in the sidecar. As they went bouncing through the streets, laughing merrily, the breeze would blow their clothing, flapping it about their bodies as if with kindred enthusiasm. For a time Mukunda was known, jokingly, as "the motorcycle swami."

Mukunda was indeed pleased with his new acquisition. It was easily the nicest present he had ever received. He never entertained the thought, however, of being attached to it.

One day he parked his motorcycle on the street in front of his father's home, and went indoors. Later, as he was leaving the house, he saw a casual acquaintance gazing at the vehicle admiringly. "Isn't it beautiful?" exclaimed Mukunda.

"Oh, *yes!*" replied the other warmly. A note of longing entered his voice as he added, "If only I could have one like it!"

"But you *can*," Mukunda replied instantly. "Take it. It's yours."

"I—I—what do you mean?" his acquaintance faltered. Then, thoughtfully, "How much are you asking for it?"

"I wouldn't take anything for it," Mukunda replied with a smile. "I'm giving it to you."

The other was incredulous. "But—but you can't just *give* away something so valuable!"

"Of course I can! And I will. Seriously," Mukunda insisted, "I *want* you to have it. I couldn't enjoy it anymore, knowing that you'd like to have it. I'll be very pleased if you accept it." He added, "Just wait a minute. I'll get you the bill of ownership." He reentered the house, and returned moments later with that important piece of paper.

The other could barely stammer his gratitude. His eyes, however, bore eloquent testimony to his feelings.

Mukunda felt divinely contented. "I own nothing, beloved Divine Mother," he thought happily. "The things I use are Thine, not mine. I return them joyfully to Thee, their rightful owner, whenever I see Thee wanting them through others."

I'm not sure how it happened, but somehow Mukunda once acquired an Indian string instrument called an esraj. He loved to play it in accompaniment to his devotional singing.

One day, someone expressed a desire for an instrument "just like that one." Without hesitation, Mukunda gave him the esraj. "Whenever I see anyone who needs something of mine more than I do," he told us, "I give it away."

Sri Yukteswar and Paramhansa Yogananda in Calcutta, 1935.

CHAPTER SIX

He Meets His Guru

*A*fter graduation from high school, Mukunda went to an ashram in Benares called the Mahamandal Hermitage. While in that city, he discovered a hole in the floor of a nearby temple. Steps led downward from there.

"The opening was very small," he said. "Perhaps the authorities had once tried to close it. But I was thin, and found that I could squeeze through. I went down quite a distance below the ground level, and sat there in truly silent surroundings, in meditation. The mighty sound of *AUM* roared all around me. I would blissfully lose myself in that great vibration."

It was on an outing from that ashram that he met his guru, Swami Sri Yukteswar. Again, I will not repeat the wonderful account of that meeting, for it is already told beautifully in *Autobiography of a Yogi*. From the Benares hermitage, he wended a circuitous journey to the ashram of his guru in Serampore (Sri Rampur). What a relief to have left that "hermitage"! During his stay there, his fellow residents had utterly contemned his spiritual practices. They had wanted him to put in his daily quota of hours working in the office. Such is the problem with nearly all spiritual organizations: Their primary interest is what they can get out of you, not what they can give you, nor what they can give others through you.

In this world of delusion, the law of duality (*dwaita*), as I said earlier, rules supreme. For every plus there is a minus; for every emotional exaltation there is a compensating depression. The unhappiness Mukunda experienced at the hermitage provided a fitting backdrop for his joyful meeting of Sri Yukteswar in that narrow lane of Benares.

I won't tell the story of what followed—of his brother Ananta in Agra; of being sent penniless to Brindaban; of converting his older brother; of going to his guru in Serampore; and of living with him there. All these accounts are covered beautifully in *Autobiography of a Yogi*. I will say only that if you have not read that book, the reading treat of a lifetime awaits you. That chapter, "Two Penniless Boys in Brindaban," is one of the greatest chapters in the book. There are, however, a few stories I can add from this period of Mukunda's life that are not included in his account. Others are told there, but not fully.

One story that could stand "fleshing out" is this: Yogananda tells us about Sri Yukteswar's criticizing him to his father. Sri Yukteswar humbly apologized to him. Yogananda then goes on to write, "The only cause of Sri Yukteswar's displeasure at the time was that I had been trying, against his gentle hint, to convert a certain man to the spiritual path."

That "certain man" was someone who later betrayed him. This person's family name was Bagchi; his monastic name was Swami Dhirananda. Sri Yukteswar had wanted to protect his disciple from a very painful experience in the future, but he was certainly aware also that Mukunda himself knew perfectly well what would happen.

And during that same time period Mukunda confided to Tulsi Bose (as a sister disciple of mine who visited Calcutta many years later learned from Tulsi himself), a close friend, "Someday Bagchi will betray me, renounce his vows, and marry a white woman."

Why then, knowing all these things, did he insist on trying to help this man? There existed a close karmic connection between them. My guru felt it was his duty to try to help him, though well knowing this friend's true nature. The man had betrayed him, egregiously, in a former life also.

That was a lifetime that my guru told us about: He said he had been William the Conqueror. (I shall return to this subject in a later chapter, so will omit most of it here.) Bagchi (Dhirananda) had been Robert Curthose, his oldest son. For many years Robert tried to foment a rebellion against his own father. Even as William was lying on his deathbed, Curthose roamed the land seeking to stir people's hearts to rebellion.

Sri Yukteswar in that life was Lanfranc, William's close friend, priest, and advisor.

It is utterly fascinating to contemplate the interplay between great masters and their equally great disciples, as we see between Sri Yukteswar and Yogananda!

Another story my guru told me was of one time when his fellow disciples, fed up with the strictness of their guru's discipline, came to Mukunda and cried, "We're sick of his discipline! Come, let us leave this place. We'll follow you."

"You leave, if you like," he told them sternly. "I'll stay with my guru."

This isn't to say that Sri Yukteswar wasn't really strict. "He was even sarcastic!" Master once said to me with a deprecatory smile, "And very hard on me. One time we were on the balcony at his

Puri ashram, facing a large crowd. I went to fetch him a glass of water, and tripped a little on the corner of a small carpet, turning it over slightly.

"'Look at that oaf!' he cried as if with contempt.

"Everyone present laughed. I looked at them and thought, 'Not one of you has what I have!' But I knew Master was preparing me for ridicule in America, which I'd receive only because of superficial cultural differences, and not because I'd done anything foolish. One time in Boston some people actually threw apples at me! But nothing has ever troubled me."

Paramhansa Yogananda with a class of Minneapolis students
during the 1920s.

CHAPTER SEVEN

His Work with Education

After Sri Yukteswar had made Mukunda a swami (Mukunda took the name, Swami Yogananda), the disciple began the work he himself had been commissioned by God to do. He started a school at a place called Dihika. Education had always been a keen interest of his. A saying (perhaps Scottish?) goes, "As the twig inclineth, so doth the tree grow."* If society is to be uplifted, the crucial time to begin this transformation is during people's childhood, for that is when the mind is at its most malleable. Some people, at even as early an age as twenty, have already become what Yogananda called "psychological antiques." After the age of forty, he said, it is almost impossible for most people to change.

On the other hand, not to discourage people who are already in the upper age bracket, he told the story of a woman he'd met in Seattle who was in her eighties. She'd been an atheist all her life. After meeting Yogananda, she changed completely. She spent her few remaining years chanting his name and meditating. "She attained liberation in that life," he told me.

Proper childhood education is, then, of supreme importance. Yogananda's system began with the student himself, rather than

---

* This saying is attributed, originally, to the Roman poet Virgil. It is an image that springs so naturally to the mind that one wonders whether Virgil himself did not repeat it from some other, older source.

with the information to be shoveled into his head. Children need spiritual and moral values. These, therefore, should be made attractive by showing that adherence to them brings the happiness that all men are seeking. Without neglecting the importance of other information, Yogananda concentrated on developing the students' own abilities, above all the ability to concentrate and to absorb information; on their mental clarity; and on their courage to approach life itself with a positive attitude. Only with such grounding did he proceed to interest them in their studies.

For instance, later, at his school in Ranchi (Bihar), there were two boys who fought together constantly. At night, he had them sleep in the same bed! From then on it was constant, sleep-depriving warfare, or enforced peace. They began to show signs of a budding friendship.

Yogananda then, to make sure this new friendship had gone deep enough, tiptoed silently one night to the head of their bed, and stood there. Seeing that they were fast asleep, he reached down and rapped one of them on the forehead. The boy raised himself and spoke angrily to his bedmate.

"Why did you do that?" he demanded.

"What do you mean? I didn't do anything." This answer was so patently sincere that the first boy subsided, too sleepy to wonder how the episode might have occurred.

Once he was soundly asleep, Yogananda leaned down once again and rapped the other boy on the forehead. This boy then sat up and shouted angrily, "I *told* you I didn't do anything!" They both sat up then, ready to do battle, when they happened to glance at the head of the bed. There they saw Yogananda smiling down at them.

"Oh, *you!*" they cried. From that night on they became the best of friends.

Dihika, as I said, was where his school was first located. It proved to be a malarial place. Students were coming down with the disease. Swami Yogananda approached the Maharaja of Kasimbazar and asked him if he could help to provide them with school facilities in a more salubrious part of the country.

The Maharaja responded, "But I thought you were all yogis. What are your boys doing, contracting malaria?"

"A mother once wanted to give her little son more energy," Yogananda replied, "so she fed him some food. Immediately, she asked him solicitously, 'My boy, are you getting stronger?'

"'How can I tell, Mama?' the child responded. 'The food hasn't reached my stomach yet.'

"'The boys,' I concluded, 'have only begun their practice of yoga. It is hardly surprising that they've succumbed. But you don't see me ill!'"

The Maharaja was impressed with Yogananda's answer. But then he continued, "So you want to start a spiritual school? How can I know whether you yourself have the proper credentials to instill lofty teachings in others?"

He summoned a group of pundits (scholarly theologians) and asked them to grill this young man, in order to verify his credentials.

"When I entered the room," Yogananda said later, "I saw a group of dry old men ready to engage in a spiritual bullfight. I therefore said to them at the outset, 'Let's talk only from truths we ourselves have realized.'

"Well, that put them on the defensive! None of them had realized *any* of the great truths taught in the scriptures. All they could ever do was quote the statements of others.

"I then asked them a question for which, I knew, no scripture provided the answer. 'We've all read,' I said to them, 'that the four aspects of human consciousness are *mon* (mind), *buddhi* (intellect), *ahankara* (ego), and *chitta* (feeling). The scriptures say also that these four aspects have their corresponding locations in the body. In no scripture, however, do we find any explanation of where those locations are situated. Can any of you tell me where they are?'

"Well, the pundits were helpless to respond. I then explained to them: '*Mon* (mind) is located at the top of the head; *buddhi* (intellect) in the forehead between the eyebrows; *ahankara* (ego) at the back of the head, in the medulla oblongata; *chitta* in the region of the heart.' Of these four locations, *mon* may have to be taken on faith, but the other three are easily verified.

"When a person thinks deeply, he tends to knit his eyebrows. When one is excessively proud, tension at the back of the head and neck makes him draw his head backward. When a young man's girlfriend leaves him for another, he never cries, 'I have a broken knee!' but it is quite natural for him to say, 'I have a broken heart.' And when someone has an emotional shock, again, it is natural for the hand to fly to that part of the chest which is over the heart.

"I then explained to the pundits," the Master continued, "'The mind is like a mirror. If a horse is before one, the mirror will reflect it, but will not discriminate as to what that object is. The intellect then steps in to say: "Oh, that's a horse." The ego then chimes in and cries, "Why, that's *my* horse!" Feeling then gives the final verdict, saying, "How *happy* I am to see *my* horse!"

"'Delusion,' I finished, 'begins with the reactions of the ego, but its final nail is driven home by feeling.'"

Therefore Patanjali, the foremost, ancient exponent on yoga, gave as his definition of yoga the statement: "*Yogas chitta vritti nirodha* (Yoga is the neutralization of the vortices of feeling)."

Swami Vivekananda, and other scholars also, translated that

sentence to mean: "Yoga is the calming of the waves of mind-stuff."
Vritti, however, means vortex—a much more accurate rendition
of what really happens, since what both feeling and ego do is draw
impressions inward to themselves. *Chitta*, again, is not "mind-
stuff." Scholars, addicted as they are to intellectual understanding,
have not been able to grasp the higher role played by feeling in
one's life. They've also defined *chitta* as "the lower mind." Feeling,
however, is the very essence of awareness. *Adi* (the first) Swami
Shankaracharya defined God Himself as *Satchidananda*, which
Yogananda translated to mean, "ever-existing, ever-conscious,
ever-new Bliss." *Chid (chitta)* actually is the very essence of
consciousness.

There are two things which science will never be able to
duplicate: feeling, and self-awareness.

Of Yogananda's translation, learned scholars may complain,
"There is nothing in the original term that signifies 'ever-new.'"
Freely granted! This was Yogananda's supremely important
addition to the meaning of that term. Bliss is indeed ever new—
new from moment to moment in eternity, new (and in some way
unique) in every soul, new in every pinpoint of infinite space.

The scholars summoned by the Maharaja were impressed, and
gave the go-ahead for donating to this young man the property he
sought. The Maharaja then gave Mukunda his palace just outside
the town of Ranchi, in the state of Bihar. To this place it was that
Yogananda brought his students from Dihika. And here the school
flourished. In only two years, the enrollments far exceeded the
capacity to absorb them.

Yogananda tells the story in his book about a young boy, Kashi,
whose approaching death the Master had predicted. Kashi did die.
Before the dread event, he asked Yogananda to trace him in his next
life, and bring him back to the spiritual path. The Master did so.

I myself have a related story to add here. In 1959, I met an older man in an office in Calcutta, who told me that his brother Kashi had had some contact with my guru. He went on to tell me the story of Kashi's death, making it clear that he was actually speaking about the Kashi we know about at Ranchi! I then told him the full story, and he rose to his feet in excitement, especially when I told him about his brother's next incarnation. I told him to read the account in *Autobiography of a Yogi*. He said enthusiastically that he certainly would do so.

Yogananda called his school a *Brahmacharya Vidyalaya*. *Vidyalaya* means school: in this case, a school to which a child goes to receive knowledge (*vidya*). In ancient India, life was formally divided into four stages: the student, the householder, the person who is partially retired from life, and one who is fully retired and devoted to the quest for God. These stages are called *brahmacharya*, *grihastha*, *vanaprastha*, and *sannyas*. Persons who are already fully devoted from early life to the divine quest may remain *brahmacharis* (or, if women, *brahmacharinis*), passing directly from the first stage to the fourth, *sannyas*.

Brahmachari means, "schooled in the ways of Brahman." It is a stage intended to put the child from the very outset of life in tune with God and with godly attitudes. Because sex is the greatest temptation human beings face, the word, *brahmacharya*, has come to be associated primarily with sexual control. Indeed, it is very important for everyone's true happiness to achieve self-control in this aspect of life. After one has developed this virtue, it is safer for him to marry.

For the next thirty or forty years of his life, he is expected to devote himself to earning a living, raising a pious family, and offering to the world an exemplary life of *dharma*, or right action.

At the end of this phase of life, a person is supposed to withdraw partially from outward activity. He may remain sufficiently in touch with his family to guide it, but ever-decreasingly so, until he feels he can safely leave it to develop on its own.

He is then counseled, if he feels so inclined, to enter the phase of full renunciation, *sannyas*, no longer claiming any earthly identity as his own, but dedicating himself completely to offering his very ego into the fire of self-transcendence.

What Yogananda wanted to do was bring back the ancient values, translated realistically into modern terms. He began at the level of childhood.

In his commentary on the Bhagavad Gita, he explained also the deeper meaning of the four castes. This system, he said, was not meant to be repressive; rather, in its pristine form, it was offered as a guideline to the soul's natural development. The system as it was originally conceived was not hereditary as it has now become.

Yogananda placed great emphasis on the supreme virtues, always pointing out their importance to ultimate human fulfillment. One of those virtues was *ahimsa* (non-violence), taught and practiced in the last century by Mahatma Gandhi. A story showing perfection in this trait is the following: One day the Master hired a bullock cart and driver, and took a group of boys into the jungle near Ranchi. On their way deep into the woods, they came upon a saintly sadhu.

"Aren't you afraid of tigers," Yogananda asked, "living way out here in the jungle as you do?"

"Oh, no," the sadhu replied casually. "I think of them as my pussycats."

Later, the little group found it was getting late. Their driver ought to have turned back toward Ranchi hours ago. Now there was no time left to do so. Night was falling. By fortunate chance, the little group came upon an abandoned hut. Here they found some protection from the night air and from marauding animals. The little group went inside and secured the door.

As night deepened, the cries of nocturnal creatures began to be heard. Before long, these sounds came to include the roaring of tigers. Presently, one tiger roar began to sound ominously close to their cabin.

"H—He's going after our bullocks!" exclaimed the driver fearfully. Prudently he withdrew to the back of the room, putting the others between him and the door.

"Do you mean to say you didn't secure the stall door?" demanded Yogananda. The foolish fellow had forgotten! If their bullocks were killed, they'd be truly stranded in this wilderness.

"Will anyone accompany me to the stall?" asked the Master. Well, you can imagine the general chorus of volunteers! Alone, then, he went out into the night. Taking a lantern for safety, he closed the door behind him. As soon as the door closed, a gust of wind blew out the lantern. In darkness, he stepped out into the clearing. Just then, a large Royal Bengal tiger appeared on the far side of it. Yogananda was standing between the tiger and the open stall door!

Well, can you guess what the tiger did then? It simply transferred its attention from the bullocks to this intruder. Slowly it approached the Master, its tail twitching.

Yogananda looked at it. Uppermost in his mind was the thought, "God is coming to me in this form." He gazed at the tiger with divine love, seeing nothing of menace in its approach.

Suddenly, as the tiger reached Yogananda, the great beast lay down and rolled onto its back. Yogananda stroked and patted it a little, then went and secured the stall door. The tiger rose and walked calmly away. When Yogananda returned to the hut, you can be sure he reproached that neglectful driver!

Patanjali states that, when *ahimsa* is perfected, wild animals and ferocious criminals become tame in one's presence.

I know several stories from this era of the Master's life. Another one concerns a waterfall near Ranchi, called Hoodroo Falls. Yogananda would sometimes take a group out to visit these falls. They would cross the river above the falls by foot, stepping on rocks to reach the other side. It was dangerous, but Yogananda would call out to the boys, "Do you believe in God?" "Yes!" came back the shout. Thus armed with God's protection, they always passed to the other side in safety.

"A few years after I left there," the Master told me, "another teacher tried to do the same thing. He lacked spiritual power, however: one of the boys slipped off a rock, and fell to his death below. Thereafter, the practice was discontinued."

During my own years in India, a newcomer to Master's work, Binay N. Dubey, took over the management of the whole organization, including the school. One day he said to me, "You know, the government wants to promote schools. If we get government subsidy for our Ranchi school, we'll be able to grow four times as quickly!"

"Binay," I said, "if the government gives us so much as a paisa (in value, roughly a penny), it will from then on own and direct everything." He proceeded with his plan, however, and the Ranchi school did grow; it did so, however, at the expense of any ability to continue sharing Yogananda's teachings with the students—except in private, to a few outside the classroom.

Yogananda's innovative system has died out in India. He wanted to introduce it in America, but here he found he had to win the parents' interest before they'd send their own children to take part in such a novel experiment.

Fortunately, his ideals for a more consciousness-raising type of schooling have survived in the schools he has inspired me to found in his name: four so far in America, one in Italy, and one in India. All these schools are flourishing. Their system is based on a book of mine, *Education for Life*, which was inspired by Yogananda's ideals. For I, too, was disillusioned by most of the schools I had attended as a boy. And my experience of schooling was wider than that most children get: nine schools, in all.

Several delusions support the modern system of education. One of them is the false notion that happiness and fulfillment depend upon material success. Another is that the greater a person's knowledge, the greater his assurance of success in every field. A third delusion is that success of all kinds depends on how much money one earns.

Obviously it takes money to build anything, whether a home or a hospital. More important than owning money, however, is one's ability to *attract* it. The Education for Life system offers a far better way of achieving all of the above, and perfectly natural, ends. It is not a system based on woolly theories. It is based on well-proven facts—proved over the more than forty years of the system's existence so far.

Is the system idealistic? Yes, of course it is! One cannot be happy, nor can he achieve fulfillment of any kind, if his consciousness lacks a sense of high purpose.

Are happiness and fulfillment consequent upon material success? The world is full of rich people who have found little happiness in their lives. Howard Hughes, the richest man in the world at that time, was asked only a week before he died, "Are you happy?"

"Nah!" he replied sadly. "I can't say that I've found happiness."

Happiness and fulfillment are attitudes of mind. They depend on such intangibles as the ability to make friends; to be enthusiastic;

to be solution-oriented rather than problem-oriented; to be at peace with oneself.

The Education for Life system teaches *right attitudes*, for a truly happy and fulfilled life.

Is it true that success in all fields depends on knowledge of the relevant facts? To some extent, yes, of course it does! One cannot speak French if he doesn't know the vocabulary or the grammar of that language. There is another aspect of success, however, that very few people, and no educational system of which I am aware, takes into account. *Mental attunement* with a subject is essential, if one would truly master it. To speak French well, one must *feel* an affinity with French; indeed, one must feel himself almost to be a Frenchman. To be truly successful in business, one must enjoy business, and feel himself a part of the consciousness it takes to achieve success in that field—and to *enjoy* the process, rather than finding it stressful. He must tell himself, "For now, I am a *businessman!*"

The Education for Life system does not belittle the importance of knowledge. It teaches what one needs to know in order to achieve mastery in any field. One aspect of true success, however, is universally ignored in modern education: the human being himself, who will have to *use* that knowledge! If a person has not learned how to apply himself concentratedly to what he does, he will very likely fail no matter how much he knows. All people of outstanding success have been able to concentrate one-pointedly on whatever task is at hand.

There is another truth our system teaches: Very few people know *how to attract* money. They try to earn it by the sweat of their brow, but don't realize that what attracts money, success, and the very understanding of how best to succeed in every field is, above everything else, magnetism. Our present age is becoming growingly aware of energy as the underlying reality of the material universe. Just as a flow of electricity generates a magnetic field around it, so high energy, thought, and aspiration generate the magnetism needed to attract health, success, money, and fulfillment on all levels.

Education for Life as a system is deeply attuned to these realities in our present age. It stresses those aspects of human consciousness which will most surely satisfy every human need—yes, even the needs for love and happiness.

The proof lies in the trying. Students of our Ananda schools invariably find, when circumstances oblige them to transfer to more standard types of schooling, that, whether as students, or as leaders, or simply as human beings, they shine among their fellow students. In America, where it is a practice to conduct nationwide tests, our children usually place in the top five percent.

And—most important of all—they are *happy*!

Yogananda's basic ideals for proper schooling are alive and well in the Ananda communities worldwide. I will discuss these communities later on, in their proper place.

Yogananda en route to Alaska, 1924.

CHAPTER EIGHT

He Leaves for America

Soon Yogananda was to leave for America to begin what was no doubt the most important phase of his life. What was the Indian culture he represented? What were its values? To write a dissertation on this subject would require not only a few pages, but a whole library of books! Nevertheless, a few things might be said about it, simply and plainly.

India's culture has never been, as the English tried to make out, a foreign import from outside the borders of India, caused by a merely mythical race of Aryans in the West. It was indigenous. Many books have been written on the premise that the only greatness to be found in Indian culture came from outside India— so many that it is not altogether easy for anyone to claim anything to the contrary. Napoleon said, "History is a lie agreed upon." Max Müller even claimed that the source of the "Aryan race" was Germany. Hitler used this claim to insist that the German people (blond, blue-eyed—like himself? Actually, not so many Germans fit that description!) were the "master race (*Herrenvolk*)."

Assisting those who propagated these self-serving theories was the fact that history was never an absorbing interest among

Indians. Nevertheless, discoveries at Mohenjo Daro and Harappa (ancient ruins that are estimated to be thousands of years old) contain artifacts that point clearly to their being products of Hindu culture.

The chronology of history may not have been of major concern to the ancient Indians, but ancient events were certainly recorded, and were not mythical. Hinduism—the name itself is a foreign imposition, based on Western association of the entire culture with its placement "across the river Indus"—was known indigenously as *Sanaatan Dharma*, the "Eternal Religion." This religion was not to be confused with India's plethora of gods, which are only figurative representations of certain spiritual ideals; they are not idols. India's essential message proclaims the oneness of all religions, since all Creation is an emanation of the Supreme Spirit, and is only a dream. Creation's destiny, and therefore the destiny of every soul in it, is to be reabsorbed eventually into that Spirit. We are all nothing but waves on the ocean of Brahman. We derive our consciousness from That, and not from the mere fact that we have brains. Consciousness doesn't cease when we leave our bodies at death. In fact, we are, in a very real sense, as old as God Himself. The soul can neither be created nor destroyed. It is eternal.

I once asked my guru: "Can the soul ever be destroyed?"

"The soul," he replied, "is a part of God. How can you destroy God?"

Western concepts of an eternal hell are, quite simply, impossible. The thought of an eternal heaven, with angels flitting about endlessly, is equally absurd. Indeed, I can imagine no worse hell than to be incarcerated in a little body forever! Our destiny is, eventually, to be reabsorbed *consciously* into the Infinite. Not even our individuality will be lost, for, when we realize our oneness with

Omniscient Spirit, in that omniscience we will always remember that, for a long series of incarnations, we ourselves played a unique role as individualized manifestations of the Divine. Long before that supreme realization, moreover, the soul remembers all of its own—perhaps many million—incarnations.

When God (Brahman, in the aspect of Creator) manifested the universe, He didn't actually *create* anything: He merely dreamed it into existence. The material universe, we now know, is only a manifestation of energy. Someday, man will discover that energy is, in turn, only a manifestation of thought. And in the highest age, finally, it will become common knowledge that thought itself is only a manifestation of divine consciousness.

It is India's destiny to be the guru of this planet. In that country alone have the ancient truths been preserved. It would be good for representatives of other nations to heed India's ancient message, for therein lies our planet's ultimate salvation.

To return to Yogananda's own role in making that culture known to the world, it began (as I said) with his humble role as educator of children, whose purpose was to inspire people to live for high ideals during the stage of life before habits and attitudes become fixed, and to teach children how to live lives that are truly happy and fulfilled. Yogananda was headmaster for two years at his school in Ranchi, before God summoned him to America.

He had had constantly, during his life at Ranchi, to seek out new places where he might meditate—beyond the range, so to speak, of the noisy and inquisitive schoolboys he'd attracted. One day he went to meditate in the school's storeroom. There, suddenly, he had a vision: thousands of people passed before his gaze.

"America! Surely these people are Americans!" he exclaimed. Just then a little boy entered the room. The Master's new hideaway, like all the others, had been discovered!

"Come here, Bimal!" he cried gaily. "I have news for you. The Lord is calling me to America!"

Inwardly, then, he said to God, "So then, my work here is finished."

Bimal as a two-legged newspaper did his work well. By the time the youthful headmaster emerged from that storage room, the whole school had been apprised of the news. A few of the newer teachers said jokingly, "So, shall we carry lanterns ahead of you, to light your way into those dark regions?"

Yogananda replied, "Don't joke about it. I am going today, by the three o'clock train to Calcutta." Everyone wondered where he would find the necessary funding. He had been receiving no salary. He had no "counting house" full of gold coins. He was, in fact, more or less penniless.

That same day, however, he left for Calcutta. How amazingly sudden was this decision! That vision had come to him between ten and eleven o'clock in the morning. He entrained for Calcutta at three o'clock that same day! Before leaving he had to pack, appoint others to take his place, give them last-minute instructions and advice, then say goodbye to the whole student body.

Thus began the next, and most important, phase of his life: his mission to the West. After his arrival in Calcutta he told his latest news to everyone he knew. A college teacher named Bhajan came to him that very afternoon and said, "Do you know, the principal of my college, Haramba Maitro, will be going to a conference in Boston, Massachusetts, in September. It will be a congress of religious liberals, sponsored by the American Unitarian Association."

Yogananda replied, "You really must take me to him."

The principal selected him as the representative to that congress for the organization Yogananda had founded to create his school in Ranchi. And thus was the ball set in motion.

Yogananda went next to Serampore to see his guru. "Is this all true, Master?" he asked. "Am I really supposed to go?"

"Yes," replied the great guru. "It is now or never. All paths are open to you."

Yogananda returned to Calcutta. The next evening, a friend came over and told him of someone he knew who was also going to America. This person came over, and said, "I'll introduce you to a man at the shipping office."

At the shipping office, the man said, "There is no space available. Everything is fully booked for the next six months."

Yogananda said, "I'll be leaving anyway." The ship, *The City of Sparta*, was scheduled to sail the next month.

"There's simply no berth available," the clerk replied.

Yogananda's reply was the same: "I'll be sailing on it."

The clerk (an Englishman) now lost his temper. He shouted, "You can't even get a passport in so little time! The police will need a full six months to investigate you." India under the English had its own special difficulties.

"That's all right," the youthful swami replied. "I'll be sailing on that ship. Perhaps someone will cancel his booking."

"There's not a chance!" shouted the clerk angrily. He wrote Yogananda's name on his shirt cuff with a copying pencil. My guru commented later, "He didn't know it, but that action ruined his shirt!" Why the man wrote Yogananda's name at all I simply don't know. Perhaps it was to record Yogananda as an applicant, despite his assurance that there was no hope. Or perhaps he was just reminding himself to have nothing more to do with this human gadfly!

Two days later, Yogananda wanted to return there. "This time I won't join you!" his friend said. "You almost came to blows!"

"No," the young swami replied. "I was only asserting myself!"

Now, however, he went instead to the police, and there he requested a passport.

"Impossible!" they replied. "With the war so newly ended, everyone is under suspicion. To investigate you adequately will take us at least three months." *The City of Sparta* was the first steamer scheduled to depart from Calcutta since the end of World War I.

Later that very day, Yogananda's father said that a relative of theirs, an uncle, was in the next room. This man was a deputy magistrate. When the uncle understood his nephew's predicament, he said, "I'll see that you get your passport right away." And Yogananda thought, "As my guru said, all paths are open."

In a very short time, the passport was in his hands. He now returned to the shipping office. The clerk wouldn't even look at him. The young swami coughed to get his attention, then said to him, "Come here."

"Where is your passport?"

"Where is my berth?"

"Where is your passport?"

"Where is my berth?"

"All right, yes, we do have a cancellation, but it's for a berth you couldn't possibly afford. It's in first class."

"Who says I can't afford it? Write me down for that berth."

Yogananda hadn't the money. He possessed hardly a rupee. Confidently, however, he produced his passport. The man's jaw dropped. "All right," he said, "but you'll have to give me that advance deposit."

"I'll go back for it."

His father said to him, "Don't expect *me* to give you this money. I don't even *want* you to go!"

"But God wants me to go."

"Well, the money won't come from me!"

"That's all right. I didn't ask you."

The next day, his father, before he went out to work, left a check with another child of his, a daughter, telling her, "I was wrong to deny Mukunda that money. God has told me to give him this check." The check was enough to cover the cost of the cabin, leaving some for further expenses besides. When Yogananda next saw his father, he said, "Father, I can't take this money from you. I don't want you to feel coerced."

His father replied, "No, it was God who changed my mind. This money comes not from me as your father, but from a faithful disciple of Lahiri Mahasaya." He then wept. "Will you ever return?" he asked.

"I'll come back in three months," replied his son, "if the Americans don't need me. It all depends on their interest and need." Well, we all know the sequel to that.

The tests he faced throughout his life were many. What charmed me most about his autobiography was his perfect attitude under every imaginable circumstance. Always, he "came up smiling."

Paramhansa Yogananda with Luther and Elizabeth Burbank
in Santa Rosa, California, in the mid-1920s.

CHAPTER NINE

His First Years in America

He landed on American soil in Boston. A delegation met him from the Unitarian Church. His lecture at their congress was a great success. He had overcome his first hurdle: the need to lecture in the first place, and in what to him was a foreign language. As time passed he received other invitations to lecture.

Yogananda's reputation as an extraordinary man of God began to spread. One spiritual seeker asked him for a private interview on Christmas Eve, and the Master agreed. When the young man arrived at Yogananda's room, the Master asked him his name.

"Dr. Minott Lewis," was the reply. "I'm a dentist by profession."

Dr. Lewis then posed a question: "The Bible says, 'If thine eye be single, thy whole body shall be full of light.' Can you explain to me the meaning of that sentence?"

"I think I can," Yogananda replied with a smile. "Would you please sit on this mat, facing me?" The other man did so. Yogananda then reached out and touched him on the forehead. Suddenly Dr. Lewis saw a brilliant light in his forehead. Simultaneously with this vision he experienced a supernal bliss. He sat for a time, unmoving, immersed in deep meditation.

When he opened his eyes again, Yogananda asked him, "Will you always love me as I love you?"

"Yes," was the stunned reply. "Yes, I will!"

"Fine! I take charge of your life."

Dr. Lewis walked home from that meeting in a state of ecstasy. It was Christmas Eve. His wife, a little belligerent because it had taken him so long to return home (they still had the Christmas tree to decorate), was standing on the doorstep, in her hand a rolling pin. When she saw his face, however, she thought, "My husband can't have been up to any mischief. His face is that of an angel!"

Dr. Lewis was the Master's first Kriya Yoga disciple in America. He remained faithful to his guru to the end.

The Master spent time in the Lewises' home. Many were the experiences Dr. Lewis shared with us about those days.

One day, the doctor was in his dental office. His mind was disturbed. Someone had just told him heavily negative stories about Swami Yogananda. Doctor's belief in the Master was based on his own experience, but even so, his faith was a bit shaken.

Just then the office door flew open. Yogananda strode in, walked right up to Doctor, and gazed deeply into his eyes.

"Do you still love me, Doctor, as I love you?"

"Yes," Dr. Lewis said, his faith restored by love.

The Master had been on a streetcar many blocks away. Suddenly he had got off and walked the whole way—at least a mile—to his disciple's office out of concern for Doctor's spiritual well-being.

I myself, many years later, learned this important lesson: Doubts are best dispersed by selfless love.

One time, Dr. Lewis went out alone in a sailboat on Boston Harbor. A sudden storm blew up with great violence. It seemed to Dr. Lewis that he might drown. And then he remembered something the Master had told him: When you are in *AUM* (which includes the light), nothing can touch you.

Doctor therefore looked up into the light of the spiritual eye. At the same time, he held a tarpaulin over the hold, hoping the waves wouldn't swamp the boat. Suddenly he felt quite secure. When his boat finally made it back to land, his family welcomed him with tears of relief.

Later, on his return home, he had just entered the front door when the telephone rang. His guru was on the other end.

"You came pretty near getting wet, didn't you, Doctor?"

Yogananda had been with a friend, and had been reading aloud a story on the sea by Joseph Conrad. Suddenly he'd risen to his feet and paced the floor. "Doctor's in trouble—serious trouble, I tell you!"

Another time, the Master was far to the south, in New York City. Dr. Lewis had a sudden bout of a very painful illness. "About three in the morning," he said, "I heard the Master's voice in the driveway outside, calling my name." He had borrowed a car and driven all the way from New York to be with his disciple. He healed Dr. Lewis.

He also healed the Lewises' daughter, Brenda. She had been subject to occasional epileptic fits.

"She'll be all right now," the Master declared. "And she'll never have another seizure." Nor did she ever have another one.

During those early days, people became greatly concerned over the predicament a certain man was facing who, everyone believed, was innocent of a very serious crime. He was to be executed the next morning, and a reprieve could come only from the governor himself. It seemed to all a hopeless situation.

Dr. Lewis, along with many other people, grieved. When the Master heard of the matter from him, he became very grave.

Silently, he retired behind a screen. A few minutes later he emerged again, a big smile on his face, rubbing his hands.

The newspapers reported the next day that, at the last moment, reprieve had come from the governor himself.

Another time, late in the year, Dr. Lewis, his son, and Yogananda went down to the beach. "Shall we go for a swim, Doctor?"

"I'd be mad to do so!" Doctor exclaimed.

Master then stripped down to his swimming trunks, and walked out into the water. He remained there happily. Doctor's son asked his father, "How did he manage to do *that*?"

"All I can say," Doctor replied, "is that when he stepped into the water, I saw a great, blue light suddenly surround him."

Dr. Lewis saw that blue light again on another occasion, years later, when he was living with the Master in Encinitas, California. Yogananda had driven into Mexico. On the way back he had bought many mangoes. (Mexican mangoes are especially delicious.) It is strictly forbidden to bring fresh fruits into California from any direction, but particularly from Mexico. The whole car, moreover, reeked with the scent! Yet the Master's car sailed through customs with only a cursory glance by the customs officials.

"How did we manage *that*?" someone in the car asked Dr. Lewis.

"All I can say is, I saw a bright blue light around the whole car!" was Doctor's reply.

Yogananda had to endure many amusing situations during his early years in America. On one occasion he was at a flower exhibition, and wanted to go to the men's room. He approached a guard.

"Please tell me," he said. "Where is the men's room?" The guard looked at his long hair and smooth face, and pointed in a certain direction. Yogananda went into that room, and recoiled.

"My goodness!" he said later. "Ladies to the left of me! Ladies to the right of me!" He returned to the guard and said, "I said, the MEN'S ROOM!"

The guard this time pointed in another direction. And now the Master did finally enter the men's room.

"Not in here, lady! Not in here!" cried several voices urgently.

"I know what I'm doing!" came his reply in a deep voice.

The Master many times encountered people who weren't sure whether he was a man or a woman. The truth is, one who has overcome sexual desire often takes on the best qualities of both sexes: masculine impersonal wisdom, and feminine intuitive feeling.

He was traveling by train during those early years when a Negro porter, on seeing him, walked back and forth up and down the aisle, studying him from both angles. Finally, puzzled, he addressed the Master directly.

"Say," he demanded. "Is yo a man? or is yo a woman?"

"What do you theenk?" Yogananda responded in a deep voice. (His Bengali accent made the story all the more delectable to us!)

On another occasion he was walking on a street in Boston when a group of teenage girls walked behind him, giggling at this unusual spectacle. One of them reached out and tugged on a lock of his long hair. Yogananda stopped and looked behind him.

"I am a foreigner in your country. Is it strange that my clothing should be different? I would like to think that my people would receive you courteously, if you visited us. I have come here with respect for your people."

The girls were dumbfounded. They hadn't realized they might be received with such dignity.

"We're *so* sorry, Sir!" they exclaimed. "We'll never do it again."

On another occasion, Dr. Lewis was standing on a street with the Master, who was dressed in his orange robe. A man came by on a bicycle, saw the Master, and grimaced at him. A few yards further on, the man came to a large puddle of water. He had just reached the middle of it when the front wheel of his bicycle came off. He fell headlong into the water! The Master smiled impishly, but said nothing. Doctor Lewis, on the other hand, was convulsed with mirth.

On still another occasion, the Master received a letter telling him he was quite wrong in "sponsoring" Jesus Christ in America. "Don't you realize," the writer demanded, "that Jesus never even lived?" The letter was unsigned.

"I would like to meet the person who wrote it," Yogananda said. He prayed to be guided to him, or her.

A week later he entered the Boston Public Library. There, the first thing he saw was a man seated on a bench under a large window. He went over and, sitting next to him, inquired, "Why did you write me that letter?"

"Wh-wh-what do you mean? What letter?"

"The letter in which you stated that I was wrong in sponsoring Jesus Christ in this country."

"B-bu-but how could you possibly have known it was I who wrote that letter?"

"Let's just say I have my ways," the Master responded with a smile. "And I wanted you to know that by the same power that led me to you, I know Jesus *did* exist, and was everything the Bible says about him."

"I must admit that's impressive," said the man, amazed but still dubious. After a brief pause, he then said, "Well, all right, here's a question: How could Jesus—how could any human being—be the 'only' son of God?"

"That," Yogananda answered, "is a common misunderstanding.

Nowhere in the Bible is Jesus, the man, referred to as the Son of God. That epithet is reserved for the Christ consciousness: that aspect of the one God which is omnipresent throughout Creation, and with which the consciousness of Jesus was identified."

"So then, does the expression, 'God the Father, God the Son, and God the Holy Ghost' not refer to separate, individual entities?"

"Absolutely not! It refers to the three basic aspects of the One, Omnipresent God." The Master paused a moment, then continued, "You, too, are THAT! Everything in Creation is a part of God, for everything in cosmic manifestation is His dream. But most people are asleep in delusion. Jesus Christ was different from them only in the fact that he was awake in God!"

"Then is it true that, by his crucifixion, he took on the sins of the whole world?"

"For that question I can only say, 'Use your common sense.' Did the world improve after his crucifixion? If anything, it became worse! Consider the truly unholy glee expressed, centuries later, at the Roman 'circus' in the Colosseum! Even during the time of Jesus, we don't find the Roman soldiers gloating quite so gleefully at his crucifixion as people did, centuries later, as Christians were being fed to the lions. The lowest point in the cycle of human awareness was reached in 500 AD.

"We do find, however, that one group benefited from Christ's crucifixion: his disciples themselves. They changed greatly. By his death on the cross he took on their karma, and thereby brought them closer to God."

Yogananda, in the above story, was referring to the four *yugas* (ages of time), accepted as a fact since ancient times in India. (As a matter of record, over two hundred ancient civilizations propounded a very similar teaching. In Egypt, long ago, people believed in the four ages of gods, demi-gods, heroes, and men.

In ancient Greece, they believed in four descending ages of gold, silver, bronze, and iron. These are but two examples.) The *yugas* as described in India were Kali (dark); Dwapara (our present age of energy in a newly ascending cycle, when men discover that matter is only a vibration of energy); Treta (an age when men realize that everything is made of thoughts, or what the physicist Sir Arthur Stanley Eddington described as mind-stuff); and Satya, or Krita (an age when mankind generally realizes that everything is only a dream of God's).

Swami Sri Yukteswar made a deep study of this ancient teaching, and found that the timing, as taught in India today, is wrong. The error crept in during Kali Yuga, when men's minds were encased in relative darkness. In fact, he said, Kali Yuga doesn't last 432,000 years, as is now generally believed: it lasts only 1,200 years. Dwapara lasts 2,400; Treta, 3,600; and Satya, 4,800. Moreover, Kali Yuga does not end with a sudden leap into Satya Yuga—as, again, most people in India today believe.

Everything in nature is cyclic. Summer fades to autumn before it becomes winter; winter awakens through spring to become summer again. Day fades to twilight before again becoming the darkness of night; night brightens to dawn before once more becoming full daylight.

Kali Yuga's low point came, as Master said, in the year 500 AD. From then on, people's awareness began to rise. Kali Yuga ended in the year 1700, with the first glimmer of Dwapara Yuga. The last hundred years of Kali, which occurred during the seventeenth century, marked a gradual transition out of that period of darkness. During that period man saw the rise of modern science, and with it the birth of Isaac Newton and other scientific luminaries.

Dwapara began in the year 1700, bringing a transition period of two centuries. The eighteenth century saw a gradual awakening of people's consciousness to a sense of their own dignity. Hence, the Industrial Revolution, the urge to break open the limiting system of aristocracy in France, and the beginning of a truly new age in America.

That transition ended in the year 1900, when Dwapara Yuga began in earnest. Since then, people have been increasingly aware of the importance of energy. As early as 1905, Albert Einstein discovered the law of relativity. During the present 2,400-year Dwapara Yuga, man will conquer the illusion of space. He will go to distant planets. It is at least conceivable that he may even understand that space itself is only a mental concept, and that the farthest galaxy is really no farther away than one's own hand!

Right now, a little over a hundred years into Dwapara Yuga, we face a struggle between the old Kali Yuga consciousness and the new rays of Dwapara Yuga. This struggle will inevitably bring social upheaval. The next few years will be very stressful for mankind.

Yogananda came to these shores as, in a sense, the harbinger of this new age of Dwapara. A pivotal teaching of his, indeed, is contained in his energization exercises, which were designed to make one more aware of the energy in the human body.

After his first three years in America, he was poised to bring these revolutionary teachings to people everywhere. For that was why had he'd been sent to America. This country is a "new world" indeed, better adapted to new rays of consciousness that are destined to take mankind upward, into higher and higher ages. Europe, he once said, would be "devastated." Russia would be "annihilated." America would survive the coming hardships, battered perhaps, but not beaten.

In late 1923 or early in 1924, Yogananda began his amazing lecture "campaign" across America. He started, if my information is correct, at Symphony Hall in Boston, where he filled the hall.

I was present when Oliver Rogers, a fellow monk with me at Mt. Washington (Yogananda's international headquarters, which I'll discuss later), said to him, "I was there, at Symphony Hall, Sir. And you know, during your entire talk you kept looking straight at me."

"I remember," replied the Master with a quiet smile.

"I didn't stay with you then," Mr. Rogers continued. "Instead, I wandered far afield, through spiritualism and other teachings. Always, however, my mind was on you, wondering what had become of you."

On another occasion, the Master, while speaking with the monks, looked at Mr. Rogers and said, "Rogers, you will have clear sailing."

This happened, however, many years later. In 1924, the Master moved to New York, where his spiritual campaigns began in earnest.

Yogananda with his first African-American study group,
Washington, D.C., 1926.

CHAPTER TEN

His Spiritual Campaigns

O n the ship that had brought him to America, *The City of Sparta*, there had been a young Muslim by the name of Rashid, who may be mildly described as a prankster. At that time, Yogananda kept both his hair and his beard long. Rashid told him while they were approaching America, "In this country, people won't accept you if you have both your hair and beard long. You must either shave off the beard, or have a shorter haircut."

Because Sri Yukteswar had told his disciple to wear his hair long, Yogananda decided to sacrifice the beard. Rashid offered to shave it off for him.

He got Yogananda's face well lathered up, then shaved off the first half. That much accomplished, he left the scene. Yogananda still had half his face covered in foam. Some time later Rashid returned, laughing, and agreed to shave off the other half. The Master never got flustered, and therefore bore the prank with calm good humor. (Many years later, he told me to grow a beard. It had grown—shall we say?—luxuriant, when my parents wrote saying they were coming to Los Angeles to see me. I was with my guru at Twentynine Palms at the time. I planned to go from there and visit Los Angeles to see them. Master said to me, "I can't have you seeing your father looking like that!" At once he sent for a pair of scissors, had me sit down, and trimmed my beard himself, chuckling merrily all the while—perhaps in memory of Rashid, though in my case he refrained from playing any such prank. Since that day, I have kept my beard short, as he trimmed it himself.)

Somehow, Yogananda and Rashid were able to meet again in New York. They may have kept each other's addresses, or maybe they met by coincidence; I don't know. Anyway, from then on Rashid became the Master's secretary. Rashid was fairly efficient, though, just as alcoholics have a difficult time staying off the bottle, so Rashid had trouble—well, let's face it, he didn't even try—in staying off the women. Periodically, he would absent himself from his secretarial duties. Always his explanation was, "Well, you see, I met this person I know, and I couldn't just turn away and say, 'I have to go and work.'"

The Master knew what the true story was. One time he followed his secretary to one of his "appointments." The trail led into the park. Rashid sat down on a bench with a ravishing young woman. The Master parked himself behind a nearby bush. Just as Rashid was putting an arm around the woman and was about to kiss her, the Master called out in a deep bass voice: "Rasheeed!"

"He was so startled," our guru told us, laughing, "that for some time he came to work quite faithfully!"

Rashid it was who got the Master well known as a lecturer. He planned posters to which Yogananda objected (to him, they seemed fulsome), but they served their purpose. Yogananda became well known. In fact, he became, in time, quite possibly the best-known lecturer in America. And he became also a favorite among New York high society.

He was once invited to a dinner with people belonging to that social set. At the banquet, alcohol was served—perhaps only in the form of wine. Every time his glass was filled, Yogananda (who never drank alcohol in any form) passed it to the man on his right, who received it silently (not to say, gratefully!), and drank it down.

After the dinner, as the guests were rising to their feet, the hostess announced, "Swami Yogananda is a good sport. I saw him put away glass after glass of my wine."

"Divine Mother!" he prayed silently, "please help me out of this one!"

Just then, a man who had sat opposite to him announced, "Actually, the swami didn't drink a drop of it. I saw him, every time his glass was filled, pass it on to the man on his right."

At that moment, the happy recipient of the Master's bounty tried to rise to his feet, reeled uncertainly, then fell to the floor!

On another occasion Yogananda attended a formal high society banquet. About fifty people were present. As he sat in this company, he kept thinking, "What a waste of a good incarnation. These people have everything, yet they are simply throwing away this opportunity to improve their karma! Don't they realize what a good fortune it is even to incarnate in a human body?"

Later, the bejeweled hostess approached him.

"Swami," she said with a smile. "I'm sure our New York elite would just love to hear a few words from you."

"Forgive me," he replied, "but I really have nothing to say that anyone here would want to hear."

"Oh, please just say anything, Swami. You're a wonderful speaker. All my guests would be delighted to hear you."

To himself, Yogananda thought, "I will not be a social lapdog!"

Reluctantly then, he stood up, walked to the head of the table, and turned with a calm but fierce expression to face them.

"You call yourselves 'high society,'" he said. "What makes you that? 'High' ought to imply a heightened state of consciousness.

Is your consciousness high? Is it in any way uplifted? At least half of you are drunk. Your interests in life are shallow. If by 'high' you mean that your ponds are so shallow that the bottom of them is almost at the surface, then I agree with you! But from your conversation here this evening I have the impression that all any of you think about is money, profit, flattery, and chasing after one another's wives. Being in 'high' society ought to give you a sense of responsibility to those below you in the social scale. You should set them an example. You might act nobly, and stoop down to help them. Instead, what do you do? If you stoop at all, it is to empty their pockets of any pittance they may still have left. Shame on all of you! I hoped in coming here this evening at least to find people of culture. Instead, what I find is so many pigs at the trough, swilling, munching, and gulping as though life offered nothing higher to that supposedly noble creature, man, than whitewash for his sepulcher. No wonder Jesus Christ said, 'Let the dead bury their dead!'"

Many of the banquet guests were in tears. All of them looked shocked almost out of their senses. One woman exclaimed to him, "What a terrible picture you've painted of us! And the worst of it is, it's all true!"

The hostess was at first grim with rejection. "Can I thank you for this unfeeling indictment?"

Gazing around her, she saw in many eyes an expression of deep remorse. Then she continued, more humbly, "I am sorry. . . . All of us. . . . Well, we do our best. You have chastened us, but (she broke down) God forgive us all!"

Yogananda said inwardly to himself, "Satan! How often has he tried to win me. This time it was with the offer of social prestige!"

One evening, at Carnegie Hall, he inspired a full house to chant Guru Nanak's song, "He Hari Sundara," in English: "O God

Beautiful." For one hour and a half they chanted that song, uplifted by Yogananda's magnetism to a state that verged on ecstasy. Later, streaming out into the streets, their faces were wreathed in blissful smiles: a rare sight in that city!

The Master was in his interview room afterward, when a tough-looking gangster-type burst into the room and flung a revolver down on the desk. Emotionally he cried: "I could kill you for what you've done to me this evening! I can't go back to that way of life anymore!"

Yogananda looked at him kindly, then said, "No, you can't go back, because now you know why you committed yourself to that way in the first place: You thought the money you'd earn from crime would make you happy. Now you know it never will!"

The man began sobbing. "Oh! Let me feel that bliss you talked about! My heart has been a desert! Now, all I want is bliss!"

"Dear child of God!" Yogananda spoke compassionately. "Even if you turn your back on Him, He loves you always. Try now to see Him in all. When death comes, you will soar upward in His light!"

The man hunched over the desk, still sobbing. His whole life-direction had been changed.

Yogananda met other gunmen. In Philadelphia once, he was standing on a street corner when three men came before him brandishing pistols.

"Give us all your money!" they growled.

Yogananda reached into his pocket and pulled out a wad of dollar bills. "I'm happy to give you this," he said to them. "But I have another treasure inside me that you'll never be able to take from me."

The men glanced at one another sideways. "What's the matter with this guy? Is he crazy?"

"You'll never be able to rob me of my inner peace." He then looked at them penetratingly. Suddenly they began to tremble.

"Hey, listen! We don't want your money. We don't want nothing!" With those words they handed his money back to him and ran off as if for their very lives.

The Master's spiritual power was something many could feel, emanating from him. It was something that few ever really understood. One day he entered a hotel in Minneapolis, dressed in his orange robe. A man weaved his way up to him, drunk (as they say) "to the gills."

"Hello there, Jeshush Christ!" he said, then embraced the Master affectionately.

"Hello there," replied the Master affectionately. He was no sternly reproachful moralist. But then he gave the other man a little "shot" of bliss.

"Shay!" the man cried. "What're you drinkin'?"

"I can tell you this much," the Master answered. "It has a lot of kick in it!"

He left the other man sober, puzzled, and deeply reflective.

In Chicago once, he entered Lakeside Park after sundown. A burly policeman said to him, "I wouldn't go in there at this hour, if I were you. It'll very soon be dark. It won't be safe."

"Oh, I'm not worried," Yogananda replied. "Nothing can happen to me."

He went inside and sat on a park bench, planning to enjoy the moonrise. Just then, a large thug approached him menacingly and snarled, "Gimme a dime!"

The Master reached into his pocket and gave him a dime.

"Gimme a quatah!"

The Master gave him a quarter.

"Gimme fifty cents!"

The Master gave him fifty cents.

"Gimme a dollah!"

Finally the Master decided this could go on indefinitely. He'd come out here to enjoy the moonrise! With overwhelming power he leaped to his feet and shouted, "**GET OUT!**"

"I don't want your money! I-I don't want your money!" Hastily the man backed away, dropping what he'd already received from this dark stranger. Suddenly he turned and fled.

The Master sat down again and calmly enjoyed the moonrise. When he left the park a little later on, the same policeman came up to him and said, "Say, what took place between you two? We know that man. He's a very dangerous character."

"Oh, we came to a little understanding," Yogananda said, and left it at that.

On a long train journey, he always sat for his meals at the same table in the dining car. A Negro waiter served him at every meal with great love. For lunch one day, however, that waiter's tables were all filled; Yogananda had to sit elsewhere. The waiter was so disappointed, he actually wept.

Later, the man sought out the Master and asked him, "What is it you have, that I want?"

"I have God," the Master replied simply. "Let me teach you how you can experience Him for yourself." He taught the man something of meditation, and gave him a yoga technique for opening himself more fully to God.

In Los Angeles, Yogananda once went to a revival meeting. A woman was leading it. (I have always assumed that it was the famous woman evangelist Aimee Semple McPherson, but I don't really know.) During her harangue she shouted: "God has no use for sinners! In His eyes they are an abomination!"

Voices were raised everywhere in fervent response: "Hallelujah! Praise the Lord! Right on, Sister!"

"Unless you accept Jesus Christ, and live for his glory, you will end up in hell!"

Again the responses, with a few variations.

The woman continued: "Man is naturally sinful. He can be redeemed only by faith in our Lord, Jesus Christ!"

Once more the congregation intoned heartfelt replies.

"You are all sinners! Get down on your knees!"

In all that crowd, only Yogananda remained standing. Later, he commented, "I wouldn't accept her statement that I was a sinner! Nobody should ever say that. To call yourself a sinner is the greatest of all sins before God! Don't identify yourself with your mistakes. When you know God, you will become aware of His presence everywhere. And then you will never judge anyone."

On another occasion, in the Pacific Northwest, he stopped at a farmhouse hoping to buy some cherries, and got into a discussion on religion with the farmer. At a certain point this man, who proved to be a religious fanatic, shouted, "We are all sinners!— doomed to eternity in hell!"

The Master paused a moment before replying. Then he asked, as if irrelevantly, "You have a son, haven't you?"

The other answered dolefully, "Yes. I have a son."

"He gives you trouble, doesn't he?"

"Oh, my God, what trouble!"

"He drinks, I think?"

"Like a whale! You can't imagine the grief I go through on his account."

Yogananda then announced confidently, "I have a cure for his problem."

"Oh, sir, if you can help me with that, I'll be grateful to you forever!"

"Well, here's what you do: The next time he comes home late at night, drunk . . ." He interrupted himself.

"Have you a large oven?"

The man glared suspiciously. "Say," he demanded, "what have you got in mind?"

"No, no, just wait." Yogananda spoke reassuringly. "I'm offering you a solution to your problem."

Hesitantly the man replied, "Yes, I have such an oven."

"Has it a large door?"

Suddenly again apprehensive, the man cried, "Just a minute! Where is all this heading?"

The Master spoke soothingly. "Just be calm. I'm going to solve everything for you."

The other sat back, relaxing slightly.

"Now then, here's what you do: The next time your son comes home drunk. . . . well, first, have the oven good and hot . . ."

The man sat up again, horrified.

Yogananda was now speaking hurriedly: "Grab him; tie him up with a strong rope, and shove him into the oven!"

Furiously indignant, the man shouted, "Blasphemer! Evildoer! Whoever heard of a father throwing his own son into an oven! Get out of my house this minute!"

Yogananda then spoke appeasingly. "Don't you understand what I've just said to you? You said God wants to throw us all into hell. But He is our true Father! You, a mere human being, were horrified at the thought of throwing your own son into an oven despite all the trouble he's given you. Can you seriously believe that God, who is Perfection Itself, has less love for you than you have for your own son?"

From panting fury the man grew gradually calm. "I see now," he said. He reflected a moment. "Yes, you are right." He looked at his visitor with a grateful smile. "Oh, thank you! You've cured me of a serious error. God is love. He *can't* wish our destruction! Thank you! Thank you!"

Paramhansa Yogananda welcoming Chief Yowlache and his wife
to Mt. Washington, 1925.

CHAPTER ELEVEN

He Goes Across the Country

*L*ouise Royston, an elderly disciple, described Yogananda to me as a lecturer. "He would come running out onto the lecture platform, his long hair streaming out behind him. His first words then were, 'How is everybody?' They joined him in shouting, 'Awake and ready!'

"'How *feels* everybody?' he next shouted.

"'Awake and ready!'"

He was only willing to lecture to people who met him at least partway in their level of energy and enthusiasm.

In 1925, he crossed the country by car. "My heart calls me," he said, "to Los Angeles—the 'Benares' of America." Two men went with him: Ralph (I've never known his last name) and Arthur Cometer. Ralph was, I think, more of a hired driver than a devotee. There weren't the freeways crossing the country that we have today. Mostly it was country roads. Ralph took great delight in running down rabbits, and killing them.

"Please don't kill those rabbits!" the Master pleaded. "You aren't even going to eat them. You run them over for the sheer delight of squashing the poor things."

"Ha! What does it matter? I'm having fun."

"If you go on that way, you will attract something you won't like at all."

"Come off it! All that karma stuff you talk about. No one's ever proved it to me."

They drove on a bit further. Suddenly the Master cried, "Stop the car this instant! Stop!" There was an urgency in his voice that caused Ralph to apply the brake. Just as they came to a stop, one of the front wheels came off the car and rolled down the road. Had they not stopped just then, they'd have had a serious accident.

From then on, Ralph (without admitting a thing!) drove much more circumspectly.

In Los Angeles, a diet fad group served what they called "unfired foods." Because Yogananda was a vegetarian—an uncommon thing for Americans in those days—and because he was famous, this group invited him to a "sort of" banquet, at which they hoped he would also speak.

"They took me proudly through their kitchen," he said later. "Everything I saw there seemed designed to awaken distaste!

"Later, they led me to their dining room and served me the 'feast' they'd prepared. Carrots, carrots, and more carrots! I was able to get some of it down!

"After this ordeal, they asked me to speak to them and their guests. I demurred.

"'Oh, please say just a few words.'

"'I really don't think you'd like what I have to say,' I replied.

"'Oh, come now! You must have enjoyed what we fed you. You *must* say something.'

"'Very well,' I said. 'Forgive me, but I must be truthful. To begin with, the meal I have just eaten is the most tasteless I have ever had in my life.'

"'Oh, for shame! It was wonderfully healthful.'

"'Food, to be healthful, should also please the palate. But that is my next point: You all consider it healthful, but it was seriously lacking in important dietary ingredients.'

"'You're wrong!' they shouted. 'It was completely scientific!'

"'No. It's as though you took pride in punishing yourselves. But I warn you, unless you change your ways, in fifteen days one of you will die of malnutrition.'

"Well, they were outraged, and refused even to listen to me further. Fifteen days later, one of their members did die of malnutrition. The police came in, and closed their entire establishment."

So many wrongs have been committed in the name of "scientific" dieting! A woman follower of the Master developed cancer. She decided to enter a sort of hospital that promised cancer cures through a special diet. She entered there, but steadily worsened. "I investigated," Yogananda said, "and found that all they were giving their patients was water, not even specially treated. When my friend died there, I prayed to God, 'Lord, *destroy* that place!' Within a very short time the police came; the place was closed down. And those who'd been running it were sent to prison."

Years later, during the Depression years, the Master gave a lecture in New York. Certain rich people were taking advantage of poor ones who lacked the means even to protect themselves. In his lecture, Yogananda spoke out very strongly on the subject. He actually named a few names, accusing those he named of causing great suffering to others.

After the lecture, several people warned him, "Don't go back to the station alone. Let a few of us, at least, accompany you."

"I'm not afraid," he said. "God is with me."

He was in a dark alley, approaching Grand Central Station, when he felt a gun in his back. A menacing voice said, "Why did you say such things against those people?"

Yogananda turned around and confronted his assailant face to face. "God," he said, "is as much in His poor children as in His rich ones. And He is not pleased when the rich ones take advantage of the poor." Imagine speaking like that to someone who is pointing a gun at you!

Yogananda then gazed at the man with the spiritual power of Bliss. Suddenly, the other began to tremble violently. His pistol fell to the ground.

"What are you doing to me?" he cried. "I was sent to shoot you!"

"You can never win," Yogananda told him. "Pick up your gun."

"I can't go back to my old ways!" cried the other. Then, terrified of what had happened, he ran away into the night.

The above events were attempts to hurt or kill him. In this same category would be attempts to discredit him, of which there were many. One such event I'll tell here, though it didn't occur until, I believe, 1932. It concerned a man who had come to visit Mt. Washington. Either this man was distressed, because his sister had accepted Yogananda as her guru, or he had become fiercely jealous of the Master. Whatever the case, he decided to give the Master a good thrashing, and then to spread the news of how he had bested this "charlatan." Delusion takes many turns! How he imagined that beating up this man of God would redound to his credit is completely beyond me. Nevertheless, he was coming up the stairs one day toward Yogananda's apartment, as the Master was meditating with crossed legs on his bed. In his meditation, the Master saw him coming. When the man reached his door, the Master opened his eyes and said calmly, "I know why you have come. And I want you to know that I could beat you up easily. I am very strong. But I won't resort to physical measures. Nevertheless, I warn you: Don't cross that threshold!"

"Go on, prophet!" the other sneered. "What could you do?"

"Remember, I warned you."

"Yeah, what do I care for your bluffing?"

He stepped over the threshold. An instant later he fell to the floor crying, "I'm on fire! I'm on fire!"

He leapt to his feet, then ran down the stairs and out the front door. The Master got up and followed him. When he came outdoors he found the man rolling about on the front lawn, still shouting, "I'm on fire! I'm on fire!"

Yogananda went up to him, reached out, and touched him on the head. The pain left.

"Don't you touch me! Don't touch me!" the man cried. He wouldn't even reenter the building. He had his sister fetch his things, and fled the grounds immediately.

Paramhansa Yogananda meditating in lotus pose.

CHAPTER TWELVE

Mt. Washington

"Los Angeles," Yogananda used to say, "is the Benares of the West, even as the city of Benares, in India, is the holy city of the Hindus."

One might cavil, "But Los Angeles is the hub of every sort of 'mystical goofiness' in America! If any group were to come forward with the claim that they are in intimate telepathic contact with a high civilization beneath the surface of Mars, that group would have its center in Los Angeles!"

The Theosophists claimed to know a prophecy that the next "race of man" (whatever that means) will begin in Southern California. There is also a tradition that a very high civilization once existed here, many thousands of years ago. If I'm inclined to believe that tradition, you may account for what, to you, may seem my own "goofiness" by the fact that I myself lived in Los Angeles for ten years! I have to say, however, that I *am* sensitive to the vibrations of places, and every time I go to Los Angeles I feel, beneath all the traffic and the hubbub, exceptionally high vibrations.

In India there is a tradition that Arjuna lived here, in *Patal Desh*—the lower, or opposite, side of the earth. Yogananda told us he *was* Arjuna in a former life. Could he also feel a special, personal affinity with this part of the globe?

Well, enough of speculating. Suffice it to say that when he was traveling across the country, the Master said, "My heart calls me to Los Angeles." He had had a repeated vision, during his boyhood, of a building on top of a mountain. I assume the vision showed him that this building was situated in Los Angeles, but in any case when he reached this city he determined to establish his headquarters here.

His reception in this city was more enthusiastic than ever, even for one who was accustomed to drawing thousands. From his room in the Biltmore Hotel, he could see thousands of people lined up around the block to get into the auditorium where, in a matter of minutes, he would be giving his lecture.

When he announced that he would be making Los Angeles his national headquarters, enthusiasm ran high. Almost immediately he began looking for land. Ralph and Arthur Cometer, who had accompanied him by car across the country, also went with him on his search for land. Naturally, given his vision, he searched primarily among the hilly spots in the city.

One day he spotted Mt. Washington, and asked Ralph to drive him up there. As they passed the front gate of one large property, the Master cried, "Stop the car!" Ralph parked, and the Master got out. He was about to go onto the land when Ralph expostulated, "You can't go in *there*! It's private property!"

Saying nothing, the Master entered, and walked down the long driveway to the large building at the end of it. When he reached that building, he said quietly, "This place feels like home!" He had *recognized* it.

The property, a once-fashionable hotel that had long since fallen on hard times, was for sale. So certain was he that it was destined to be his that he invited all his students in Southern California to a dedication of the property—though he had yet to complete the formality of actually purchasing it. "This place," he announced during a short speech that day, "is yours."

The asking price for the property was $65,000—a lot of money in those days. Even so, the Master was on the very point of signing the purchase agreement when his hand froze into immobility. God wanted him to have the property at a lower price. A few days later, another real estate agent agreed to negotiate terms. The seller consented to come down to $45,000, provided that the full amount was paid at the time of purchase, and that it was paid no later than three months from the day Yogananda signed the agreement.

The money would have to come from his students. One of them exclaimed in dismay, "Why, it would take twenty years to come up with that much money!"

Yogananda replied, "Twenty years, for those who *think* twenty years. Twenty months for those who think twenty months. And *three* months, for those who think three months!"

He did, in fact, acquire the money in three months. The story of how he did so illustrates wonderfully the power of faith.

The husband of a student of Yogananda's, a Mrs. Ross Clark, had contracted double pneumonia a few months earlier, and the man's doctors had said he couldn't live. Mrs. Clark had turned to the Master for help. "He *will* live!" was Master's reassurance. Going to her husband, he had sat at the sufferer's bedside and prayed deeply. The man was cured. Now, when Mrs. Clark learned of the Master's dilemma, she told him, "You saved my husband's life. I want to help you. Would you accept a loan of $25,000 without interest for three years?" *Would* he ever!

"Other money," he told me, "began pouring in from our centers around the country. Soon we had another $15,000, making

$40,000 in all. But the final purchase date was approaching, and we still lacked $5,000 of the total price. I wrote Mrs. Clark again to see if she could help us with this amount. Regretfully she answered, 'I've done all I can.' I thanked her once again for the enormous help she'd given already. But where would that final bit of help come from?

"And then, suddenly, only one day remained! The situation had become desperate. If we didn't get those five thousand dollars by noon the next day, we would forfeit our option."

The Master chuckled as he told me the story. "I think Divine Mother likes to keep my life interesting!

"I happened to be staying in the home of a rich but insincere businessman, who could have helped us easily had he been so inclined, but he made no move to do so. I was battling with God, 'How do You plan to give me that money by noon tomorrow?'

"'Everything will be all right,' my host said soothingly.

"'Why do you say that?' I demanded. I knew the money would come, but God needs human instruments, and this man had shown no interest in being such an instrument. He calmly left the room.

"Just then a gust of wind turned my face toward the telephone." (The gust of wind was a manifestation of *AUM*, the Cosmic Vibration. Saint Bernadette Soubirous felt it also, just before her first vision of the Virgin Mary. I will discuss the Cosmic Vibration at length a little later on; the philosophy behind it is important for an understanding of the deep teachings Yogananda brought to the West, and of the deep teachings he revealed in the message of Jesus Christ, in the Bible.) The Master continued: "There I saw the face of Miss Trask, a lady who had come to me twice for interviews. A voice said, 'Call her.' I did so at once, and explained my predicament to her.

"After a pause she said, 'Somebody just the other day returned a loan I made to him years ago. I never expected to get it back. It was for $5,000! Yes, you may have it.'

"Silently I offered a prayer of thanks. 'Please,' I urged her, 'be at Mt. Washington Estates tomorrow before noon.'

"She promised to come. By noon the next day, however, she hadn't yet arrived! Other prospective buyers were waiting there like wolves! One of them was telling everybody that he had plans to create a movie school there. The seller announced, however, 'I'm willing to wait the rest of this day.'

"Only minutes later, Miss Trask arrived. The drama was over. We paid the full purchase price, and Mt. Washington was ours!"

Thus was founded the international headquarters of Self-Realization Fellowship, the institution through which Paramhansa Yogananda disseminated his yoga teachings throughout the world.

I mentioned that "wind" earlier, which turned his face toward the telephone, where he saw Miss Trask. This wind, I said, was a manifestation of *AUM*. My reference was to the Cosmic Vibration, which is an important aspect of the eternal Trinity: in Hinduism, *AUM TAT SAT*; in Christian theology, God the Father, the Son, and the Holy Ghost.

AUM is the Holy Ghost. Let me begin at the top of the scale, move down it, then move back up again.

"In the beginning"—that is to say, before Cosmic Creation—there was in existence only the ever-calm Spirit, vibrationless, fathomless. Its nature is ever-existing, ever-conscious, ever-new Bliss, or *Satchidananda*. (It was Paramhansa Yogananda who added "ever-new" to the translation.) Why would perfect Bliss, complete in Itself, feel any need to create at all? In India it has been suggested that "God wanted to enjoy Himself through many." Swami Sri Yukteswar answered the inevitable question of why God created the universe by saying, "Leave a few mysteries to be solved after you reach the Divine." Yogananda's expression, however, "ever-new," in addition to the concept of Bliss suggests a more fully satisfying explanation (satisfying, that is, to human reason). What it hints at is that the very nature of Bliss is to want to express Itself. The ever-new aspect of Cosmic Bliss causes It periodically to express Itself creatively, expanding Self-awareness into outward manifestation.

In Its Self-absorbed condition, as the Supreme Spirit, the Absolute Truth is Brahman. When It manifests Cosmic Creation, It *is* that Creation: It *is* the created universe. A portion of Its Infinite Self moves, becoming vibration.

Wherever there is vibration, there is movement in opposite directions from a state of equilibrium at the center. The Cosmic Vibration has to be self-canceling, for in fact nothing really exists except Absolute Consciousness: the Infinite Spirit. Everything else is a dream of God's (God being the Supreme Consciousness in Its aspect of Creator).

The Cosmic Vibration, *AUM*, has three aspects: Brahma (the Creative Vibration), Vishnu (the vibration which keeps everything in a state of manifestation), and Shiva (the vibration which dissolves everything back into the Vibrationless Spirit again). These three vibrations are distinct and different from one another even in tone. Brahma has the highest vibration, and produces the highest tone; Vishnu's tone is in the middle range; Shiva's in the lowest. We might compare these three, humorously but not inaccurately, with an automobile or a motorcycle. When the motor starts, it emits a high sound as it "revs" up. Once the vehicle reaches a cruising speed, its tone settles down to a softer, continuous purr. When the vehicle stops, and the motor is turned off, the sound dies away in a low-pitched, descending growl.

In India, people often chant what they call "the threefold *AUM*," beginning with three high notes; then two more, somewhat lower; and finally two notes again, the lowest and slowest of them all. The first three are, properly, chanted loudly; the next two notes, somewhat more softly; and the third two, very softly.

AUM itself, when properly pronounced, has three sounds. In English the word is often written OM for the simple reason that the *O* sound in our language consists really of *two* sounds. (Few vowels in English are pure.) The *A* sound, incidentally, should be a *short A* as in our word, *was*, and not long as in our word, *happy*, nor (again) still longer as in the word, *car*. (Well, let's face it, beautiful though English is, it is an embarrassment even to those for whom it is their native tongue! Its spelling, particularly, is atrocious. Yet in some ways English is perhaps the best language in the world, the easiest to learn—at least to speak badly!—and certainly the richest in vocabulary, having several times more words than any other language!)

AUM is the Divine Mother aspect of Creation. When it is heard in meditation, its vibration takes one inward to his source in Bliss. In its outward aspect, however, it draws everything away from that source. Conscious Creation is center everywhere, circumference nowhere. But the creative impulse, being an outward manifestation of *Satchidananda*, seeks to expand itself constantly. We may say that conscious Cosmic Creation, having once been set in motion, seeks ever to keep on moving outward from its essential, central reality.

Thus, Creation Itself has two basic impulses: the one, moving outward, and the other, inwardly withdrawing. This is the ultimate expression of Duality. Within the realm of Duality, everything possesses its corresponding opposite. Modern physics has actually found that every electron possesses its own dual: wherever that dual exists in space, if either aspect of it moves, the other aspect moves in sympathy with it.

This fact may account for the expression, "twin souls," a concept which Yogananda, to the best of my knowledge, addressed only once in his life: in a magazine article which appeared in the 1930s. Obviously, he didn't want people seeking their soulmates on every street corner! What he wrote in that article was that, before the soul can reach final liberation, it may have to achieve spiritual union with its twin, which may be living on another planet, and reachable only in vision. In any case, the union must be spiritual: it can never be sexual. And it need not be between two people of opposite sexes.

Oh, yes, there is life on other planets—countless numbers of planets! I once asked my guru, "Will the same people who are now on earth return here when the earth enters Satya Yuga (the highest age)?"

"Oh, no," he replied. "I've already told you, there are countless planets on which to live. If one always came back to the same planet, he would find out too soon! God's will is that man 'find out' by exercising his own discrimination."

I mentioned the outward pull of delusion (*Maya*), or Nature (*Prakriti*). The inward pull is called *Paraprakriti* (the Divine Mother aspect of *AUM*). The self-manifesting aspect is known as *Aparaprakriti*. It is also Cosmic Delusion itself: Satan.

And what is evil? Everything in the realm of delusion is relative. Evil is that aspect of delusion which tries to draw everyone outward (that it is to say, also, downward) from whatever level of evolution one has attained so far. Thus, if one has attained the stage of wanting to feel himself expansively in others, and of seeking to share with them whatever happiness he has found, it will be a step in the wrong direction for him to try to keep all that goodness for himself. If he is basically lazy and dull-minded, however, for him to make any effort to achieve happiness—even happiness for himself alone—this, for him, will be a good thing. To be even more specific, if a Mahatma Gandhi were to decide one morning, "I'm tired of serving humanity. I'm going to work now, make money, and become a millionaire," even worldly people would say, "This man has fallen." But if a lazy fellow, indifferent to doing anything positive with his life, were to wake one fine morning to the resolution, "I'm going to work, earn money, and become a millionaire," even saints would declare, "This man is behaving rightly."

Satan, however, like everything else in existence, is a part of God. There can be no duality in the Absolute.

I have written that the Spirit, when creating, is "center everywhere, circumference nowhere." That center is the still, unmoving center at the heart of each Cosmic Vibration. It is the Christ consciousness, the motionless reflection of Spirit beyond Creation, existent in every atom. Thus, we have the Holy Trinity— in Christian teachings: Father, Son, and Holy Ghost; stated in the reverse in the Hindu teachings: *AUM, TAT, SAT*.

SAT represents the Father aspect, beyond all vibration. *AUM* represents Creation itself. And *TAT* represents the Son aspect, the *Kutastha Chaitanya*. In Christian teachings, Christ is "The Only-Begotten of the Father"—not as the man, Jesus Christ, but as the infinite consciousness with which Jesus had become identified.

In meditation, one hears the *AUM* vibration in the inner right ear. There is a corresponding portion of the brain, just above the right ear, which can, when stimulated, give spiritual experiences. Listening to that sound, the devotee should try gradually to bring the sound over to his left ear as well; then feel it vibrating throughout his body; then expand with it to blissful oneness with

AUM all through Creation. At that point he finds himself able to perceive the Christ consciousness in his body at the point between the eyebrows; then, gradually, to perceive it throughout the body; then outward into oneness with the Christ consciousness throughout space.

Therefore the Christian mystics have said that one must go through Mary (the Divine Mother; *AUM*) to reach the Christ, and through Jesus Christ to reach oneness with the Supreme Spirit.

I asked my guru once, "To what level must one have attained, to be called a master?" He replied, "One must have reached Christ consciousness."

To reach that state, however, one must first be tried in the fire: tested to the limit of his strength, purged of all impurities. As Jesus Christ put it, "Blessed are the pure in heart, for they shall see God." Purity of heart means to have no other motive than the desire for union with Him. A master has attained that purity, but his role is to set the highest example for others. Paramhansa Yogananda needed to do more than set that example: he needed to burn off the impeding karma in America that militated against an inwardly, more spiritually, directed energy in man. The satanic force did its best to obstruct his heroic efforts—even to destroy them. This obstruction is, in the lives of saints, perfectly usual.

To commune with *AUM*, one closes the ears with the thumbs. I found it inconvenient and uncomfortable to practice this position.

"Is it all right, Master," I once asked him, "provided one can find a really quiet place, to listen without closing the ears?"

"When the ears are closed," he replied, "one is in the 'motor room' of the body. It is best to close the ears. That is what that little flap is for, in front of the ears."

However, the Master himself had tried to address the question of *how* best to close the ears, by creating what he called a "temple of silence"—a gadget that came over the head and down over the ears, with a little rubber ball at each end. Another solution is earplugs, but the disadvantage of these is that they press against the ears from inside, and subject one excessively to the noise of blood pumping through the veins.

Another solution has presented itself to me. Because I am hard of hearing, I have worn a succession of ever-more sophisticated hearing aids. For one "incarnation" of these, molds were made of the insides of my ears. I had another set made that were the molds only, with no perforation for hearing. These greatly improved earplugs (I have called them, "Doors of Silence," because they transform the head into a Cavern of Silence) fit snugly, without excessive pressure from within, and create no distraction of pumping heart sounds. People can get such forms made at Ananda, and I think they will enjoy them as much as I do.

Well, back to our story:

The Master succeeded in buying Mt. Washington, but only against the heaviest of odds. At first, there were lawsuits. One Emma Mitchell, a former owner of part of the land at Mt. Washington, filed a suit against him in the Los Angeles Superior Court on October 13, 1925 to regain her property. This case was settled out of court. His old friend Rashid sued him, alleging that he himself was entitled to 25% of the "net proceeds of all the lectures, fees, contributions or other monies received by Yogananda." If there was money to buy a hotel, Rashid figured, there was money also to pay him. The news worsened five days later, when Rashid obtained a writ of attachment and levied on two of Yogananda's bank accounts.

Both of these lawsuits were settled to everyone's satisfaction. But Yogananda still had debts that needed to be paid off. He went on lecture tours to meet these obligations. Finally one day, desperate in the face of all these difficulties, and with a large sum that needed to be paid off "immediately," he went out into the desert, determined to turn the whole problem over to God.

"Divine Mother," he prayed, "I didn't ask for all these financial problems. I've never wanted money. I would much rather have spent my life in some Himalayan cave, meditating on Thy presence. Why dost Thou burden me with such heavy trials? I am ready to leave everything: to walk into the desert and never look back!"

The Divine Mother of the universe answered him: "I am Thy stocks and bonds. What more dost thou need than that thou hast Me? Dance of life, and dance of death: know that these come from Me and, as such, rejoice!"

Help came in time, and Mt. Washington was saved. But that occurred only in the early 1930s. The tests continued—all because of his love for souls whose need for his teachings was desperate, even if they knew it not. By the end of his life, he had cause to look forward to his next incarnation which, he told us, would be spent mostly in seclusion.

Nonetheless, it was a heroic life he lived this time. And it was a life destined to have a major impact on civilization itself.

Paramhansa Yogananda in Mysore, India.

CHAPTER THIRTEEN

Attacks: Racial, Religious, Journalistic

Coming from India to America in the 1920s presented its difficulties. Racial prejudice was still strong, and although many people in India do have fair skins, Yogananda was not one of them. His features were not Negroid, for the body types of Indians and Europeans are the same, but even so, his dark-brown skin was sometimes mistaken for "diluted" African.

It is a marvel, truly, how many people seem actually to *desire* that there be others on whom they can look with disdain. As Sri Yukteswar put it, people like to cut off other people's heads in order to appear taller themselves. Thus, the Germans convinced themselves that the Jews were inferior to themselves—although Jews have, in fact, been outstanding in almost every field of endeavor. The English convinced themselves that the Indian people were inferior to themselves. The whites in America persuaded themselves that "Negroes" were of inferior stock. And the Germans were, according to themselves, the "true Aryans." (Blue-eyed, blond—a few such specimens are actually to be found in Germany, though not so many as one might expect, from all the self-promotion. Hitler himself was hardly an example!)

Yogananda said, "If a person smokes but doesn't drink, he will say, 'Well, it's true I smoke a little, but at least I don't *drink!*' And if he drinks but doesn't smoke, he will say, 'Well, yes, I do drink a little, from time to time, but at least (said disdainfully) I don't *smoke!*'"

Yogananda taught us that the true races of man depend not on skin coloring, but on a person's *consciousness*. An accountant in San Francisco may feel more affinity with another accountant in Nairobi than with the artist living next door to him. And that same artist may in fact be closer, spiritually, to another artist in Vietnam than to, let us say, a farmer in his own state.

Originally, Yogananda explained, the caste system defined the true races of man. The upward evolution of man was discerned as existing in four distinct stages, with subcastes to indicate transitions between one stage and the next.

The four basic castes were *sudra, vaishya, kshatriya,* and *brahmin. Sudras* (those belonging to the lowest caste) were classically defined as peasants; *vaishyas* (the next higher caste), as merchants; *kshatriyas* (the third) as warriors; and *brahmins* (the fourth and highest) as priests. Of course, society even in those days was not so simply stratified. There were artists, scholars, teachers, artisans— indeed, the whole gamut of categories that we know today. And though presumably they had no computer technicians, they had people of much higher ability, unequalled in our own day.

For instance, at least two literary works seem to have originated in descending Treta Yuga (an age when, tradition states, man can demolish the delusion of time, as he will be able, in our this present age, to demolish that of space). Those works were written by two sages, Bhrigu and Agastya. The works contain detailed prophecies regarding the lives of people still unborn, some of whom would not be born for thousands of years. I myself have had some experience with these works, and have found them to contain proof of ancient India's extraordinary greatness.

(Agastya is mentioned in Yogananda's autobiography, in the chapter on Babaji. There, the Master wrote, "A considerable poetic literature in Tamil has grown up around Agastya, a South Indian avatar. He worked many miracles during the centuries preceding and following the Christian era, and is credited with retaining his physical form even to this day." Bhrigu is mentioned in the Bhagavad Gita, where Krishna states, "Among saints, I am Bhrigu.")

The caste designations—to return to our theme—were intended to symbolize certain basic traits in human consciousness as it evolves toward perfection in God. When man first ascends from the animal state, he is accustomed to using his body, rather than his mind, to achieve happiness, which is the conscious goal of all life on its return journey to the eternal state of divine bliss. *Sudras* were called peasants only because farmers, in any social system, are the most likely to work only with the strength of their bodies.

As the soul continues to experience the relatively higher human state, it comes naturally to realize that this human intelligence it has been given is a priceless boon. One can accomplish much more for himself with keen intelligence than with bulging muscles. Thus, he reaches the *vaishya* level of awareness, symbolized by the merchant—not because merchants are never refined, sensitive, or altruistic, or, for that matter, never body-bound—but because their typical calling is to make money and become rich: to be clever, in other words, in the achievement of these ends.

As the *vaishya* becomes further refined in his development, he finds that the happiness he seeks is more truly his when he can expand his self-awareness sharing with others whatever happiness he achieves. Therefore did Jesus Christ say, "It is more blessed (blissful) to give than to receive." Thus, the person of *vaishya* temperament gradually evolves to the next, *kshatriya*, level of consciousness.

A *kshatriya* is classically identified as a warrior, or a nobleman. Needless to say, there are many aristocrats who are anything but noble in nature, and there are many warriors who display only a cruel nature. Still, an ideal nobleman considers his role in society to be one of helping others, and uplifting them in every way possible. And an ideal warrior is one who is willing to sacrifice his life for the defense and well-being of his fellow countrymen. Thus, a *kshatriya* is one, ideally, who seeks happiness also for others, in the understanding that happiness expands with the inclusion of others in one's own happiness.

As the ego evolves still further, one comes to realize that material gifts can be enjoyed only temporarily; that intellectual knowledge is superficial, and never fully satisfying; and that spiritual wisdom is the only knowledge truly worth having. Thus, one tries to include wisdom along with whatever gifts he bestows on others. Thus it is that one becomes a *brahmin*.

The *brahmin*, or priest, only symbolizes this spiritually sharing type of person. There are, of course, plenty of priests for whom priesthood is merely a profession. Equally, there are many non-priests whose temperament is, in this sense, priestly. Still, a priest should, ideally speaking, be one at least who administers to people's spiritual needs.

These, then, are the four castes, and the four races of men—defined not by heredity, but by people's own natural inclinations. To become enlightened is to go beyond the four castes altogether: to be defined no longer by one's ego-type, but by one's degree of freedom from every ego-association.

This ancient system has merit also in the fact that it indicates, universally, the right direction of development for every human being. Again I want to emphasize that the caste system, originally, was not hereditary. People can evolve in one lifetime, moreover, above their own natural caste level. (For that matter, they can also sink below it.) As the Bhagavad Gita states, "Even the worst of sinners can, by steadfast meditation, attain Me."

Sin, alas, is always there to pull one downward again, if he is so inclined. The caste system was originally intended to encourage people to keep moving upward. Their old animal inclinations, however, can also exert a downward pull, and continue that effort until one has risen above ego-consciousness altogether.

Thus, too, society itself, and also other individuals, may go to great lengths to pull the virtuous person downward, the justification for doing so being, "It is presumptuous of him to pretend to be better than myself! If I can't climb up to that level, then that level cannot even exist."

Yogananda came to America's shores with a message of divine promise and hope. To many people he was a disturbance and a menace. Religionists were not happy with him, for he showed the inadequacy of their own dogmas. White supremacists were not happy with him: he showed himself infinitely superior to themselves. Newspapers, on the other hand, were delighted with him: They could say about him what they liked, and if they went too far they could always insert a small retraction on one of the back pages of a future issue, where it would be unnoticed—but no one could say they hadn't apologized.

Yogananda hadn't a very high opinion of the press. He saw it as cheerfully destroying lives and reputations for the sake of a little notoriety. After all, notoriety was what sold papers. Not a very honorable profession.

His problem also was that he was what is called in Sanskrit *triguna rahitam*: a person who is beyond all the qualities of ego, and free also from any personal motive—indeed, free from *any* motive at all, except the upliftment of others. Ego-bound man is unable to understand such a rare human being. One who is in delusion reasons, "Everyone has a motive of some kind. If anyone won't state openly what his own motives are, it can only mean that those motives are dark." This explains why William the Conqueror has been so much misunderstood by historians. It also explains why many people couldn't "figure out" Yogananda, and felt threatened by him.

Yogananda reached what might be called his nadir in Miami. The police chief there was a classic villain. Someone told me that this man actually used black people for target practice. In fact, he ended up being tried for murder (I've no idea what the outcome of that trial was). Among white supremacists in the Deep South of America, the murder of blacks was, believe it or not, considered even laudable by some people. I once actually heard a white man in Charleston, South Carolina, say, "The only good nigger I ever saw was a dead one." (Of course, such a person would inevitably reincarnate, the next time, in a black body!—from which position, again "of course," he'd hate whites.) With such ego-enclosing attitudes as these, is it any wonder that souls sometimes regress back to the animal level, and even lower?

That police chief's name was H. Leslie Quigg. Yogananda had come to Miami to give lectures at the Scottish Rite Temple, followed by yoga classes at the Anglers' Club. Posters were placed all about town. His plans were cut short when police chief Quigg abruptly ordered Yogananda to leave town. The local press reported that Swami Yogananda, "East Indian love cult leader," had "his life threatened by a group of indignant citizens" during a class. Many prominent people across the country came to his defense. Finally Yogananda simply left. Two months later, Chief Quigg stood trial for murder. Who knows whether he might not have even tried to murder Yogananda?

Churches, also, (like Queen Victoria) were "not amused" by what they considered Yogananda's "attack" on them with the sword of crystal clear logic. In fact, of course, he never really attacked anybody: he simply stated the Christian truth as he'd been sent to do, by—as he told people—Jesus Christ himself. But he did draw a clear line between Christianity and "Churchianity." And, as he said, he had been sent to teach "original Christianity."

One time, two gunmen came to kill him (this was years later) at Mt. Washington. The Master knew they were standing by the elevator, waiting for him, so he simply remained upstairs. The person who told me this story said they'd been sent by churchmen, but I've no way of verifying any of this account.

Several times people over the years sued him for various reasons. The most painful of these betrayals was Swami Dhirananda's. (I'll discuss this case in a later chapter.)

Paramhansa Yogananda with the famous opera singer,
Amelita Galli-Curci, Washington, D.C., 1927.

CHAPTER FOURTEEN

❧ Famous People

*P*aramhansa Yogananda also met many famous people during the course of his career. I must admit that to me, personally, he himself was the only famous person in whom I had any interest. But it may interest the reader to learn of a few, at least, of those whose paths crossed his.

First in national importance was President Calvin Coolidge, who spoke well of him afterward. The Master became so well known in Washington D.C. that a prominent photographer placed a life-size photograph of him on the sidewalk outside his shop.

The Master also got to meet President Portes Gil of Mexico. He went to that country, I believe, in 1929, seeking temporary escape from one of his many "crucifixions." To Dr. Lewis he wrote that he didn't know when, or even whether, he would ever come back. I grieve to think how many persecutions he had to endure—and in a country to which he had come with nothing but the wish to uplift people.

The persecution that resulted in his flight to Mexico concerned betrayal by his close childhood friend, Dhirananda.

It was in Washington that he met the famous Italian opera

diva, Amelita Galli-Curci. Louise Royston, an elderly nun at Mt. Washington, told me of one evening at which she herself was present. It was a concert given by Mme. Galli-Curci in Washington. "At one point," Mrs. Royston said, "Mme. Galli-Curci saw Yogananda in an upstairs balcony. She interrupted her concert to pull out a handkerchief and wave it enthusiastically in Master's direction. Master then stood up and bowed to her, smiling. The audience, when it saw to whom she was waving, broke into enthusiastic applause. It was a very moving moment!"

Mme. Galli-Curci was very small, but she had strong will power. Her first marriage had been an arranged affair. Her husband was, unfortunately, an alcoholic. One day, drunk again, he lifted a chair, intending to strike her with it. She stood before him, tall in her dignity and said, calmly, "Put that chair down." Surprised by her firmness, he did so. She thereupon left the house, and, as far as I know, never saw him again.

Homer Samuels was her second husband; Yogananda described their marriage as a "real soul-union." Mr. Samuels, whom the Master also knew, was a distinguished pianist.

George Eastman, the founder of Kodak, was another famous person Yogananda got to meet. At that meeting, the president of the famous film company said to him, "I'm disgustingly healthy, and I'm disgustingly wealthy."

"But you aren't disgustingly happy!" interjected Yogananda.

"No, I'm not." Eastman became a student of Yogananda's.

Another student was Alvin Hunsicker, President of Standard Textile Company, who had first thought that yoga had something to do with crystal ball gazing.

"Listen," Yogananda said to him, "crystals were imported into India from France. Crystal gazing had nothing to do with India's teachings. True 'crystal gazing' means to look into the hidden dimensions of space and time. This feat can be accomplished only by gazing into the spiritual eye in the forehead."

"That's when he became a student of mine," Master said.

Warner Oland, the Hollywood actor who played Fu Manchu in that series of movies, and also Charlie Chan in seventeen other movies, was a rather dour man, but he was famous. Yogananda found himself seated opposite to him on a train journey. The actor gave the Master a look of disgust, then turned away.

"Excuse me," the Master said, "why are you wearing that expression?"

"None of your business!" replied the other, rudely.

"Forgive me, but it *is* my business," Yogananda answered. "I have to sit here and look at you! It would be much pleasanter if the expression you wore were not so sour."

"You seem to be a very audacious sort of person," Oland commented with a laugh. "Who are you?"

"That's just the thing!" Yogananda replied. "We have a great opportunity before us today. You know, everyone in the world is a little bit crazy, but no one gets to find out about his own craziness because he mixes only with people whose craziness is of the same kind as his own. I know about your kind of craziness, because I've seen you on the screen, but you don't know about mine. If you can convince me that your way of life is better, then I will become a movie actor. But if I can convince you that my way is better, you ought to follow me."

"Well, he agreed to my terms, and we talked everything out. And—I never became a movie actor, but he did become my student!"

Greta Garbo visited him at the ashram he obtained later on, in Encinitas, California. Daya Mata remembered her especially for the fact that Garbo envied St. Lynn his long eyelashes!

The most spiritual of the famous people Yogananda met in America was Luther Burbank, to whom he dedicated his *Autobiography of a Yogi*. Since the Master devoted a whole chapter of his book to that friendship, I will say nothing more about it here.

Others he met were the following, whom I'll present for my convenience (and yours) rather like a shopping list, making brief comments here and there where they seem appropriate. Many of these persons, I may as well admit, I don't know from Adam (or Eve). But my readers might do so.

Herb Jeffries. I was with my guru every time Herb came to visit him. He was a partially black man, who had sung with Duke Ellington's orchestra and was also known as the "Bronze Buckaroo," the first black actor to play in Westerns.

Dick Haymes. I was also present in the room every time Dick came to see the Master. And the two of us together attended the banquet on March 7, 1952, when Yogananda left his body. Dick thought Master had fainted, but I knew he wouldn't faint: I knew he had left us. Dick was the vocalist for Harry James' orchestra, and also with Benny Goodman. He went on to become a Hollywood actor, and married the famous actress, Rita Hayworth. His mother, Marguerite Haymes, became a friend of mine.

Oscar Saenger was another well-known singer, whose funeral Yogananda conducted in 1929. Mr. Saenger was also one of the first to capitalize on Edison's invention of the gramophone, presumably by recording his own singing onto the clay discs they had then.

Vladimir Rosing was an eminent tenor who also directed the American Opera Company. I was with my guru when Mr. Rosing conducted Johann Strauss's "Die Fledermaus" in the Hollywood Bowl. Afterward, Margaret Lancaster, a nun at Mt. Washington who had been sitting in a separate section from ours, commented to our guru, "That wasn't exactly a spiritual show, was it!" (It certainly hadn't been the ideal fare for monastics!)

"It was a *good* show!" the Guru commented. I was deeply touched to see his firm loyalty to an old friend.

Walter Y. Evans-Wentz was an anthropologist and writer. He authored the excellent book, *Tibet's Great Yogi, Milarepa*. He also wrote the preface to *Autobiography of a Yogi*.

Grant Duff Douglas Ainslie, Scottish poet and author.

George Liebling, pianist-composer.

Leopold Stokowski, very famous (because flamboyant; I myself didn't care much for his style) orchestra conductor.

Luigi von Kunits, founding conductor of the New Symphony Orchestra of Toronto, Canada.

Maria Carreras, famous pianist.

R.J. Cromie, owner-publisher of the "Vancouver Sun," who was a great supporter of Swami Yogananda's.

Jan Paderewski, pianist. He had also been the second prime minister of Poland. Paderewski was a signatory for the Treaty of Versailles, and an ambassador for his country, before he returned to his musical career.

Ruth St. Denis, modern dance pioneer. I saw her dance when she was in her seventies. She was as limber as a woman fifty years younger: a good recommendation to take up dancing as a career!

Clara Clemens Gabrilowitsch (later, Samossoud) daughter of Mark Twain.

Harry Lauder, Scottish poet and singer.

And many others, including a number of prominent figures in India, some of whom are mentioned in his autobiography.

Yogananda in India.

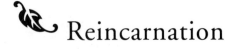 Reincarnation

Living with Paramhansa Yogananda, one became quite accustomed to hearing about reincarnation. He referred to it frequently—not as a concept, merely, but as a simple fact.

Yogananda once went to a performance with several women disciples. One of them, Vera Brown (later Meera Mata), kept looking intently at a little girl, about three years old, in the row before them. Later the Master said to her, "I noticed you looking at that little girl."

"Yes, Master! I couldn't take my eyes off her. Somehow she looked so sad, and at the same time so wise."

"In her last life," he said, "she died in a German concentration camp. Her experiences there were very sad, but they have also made her a saint."

On another occasion, someone gave the Master a newborn baby to hold and bless. "I nearly dropped it," he commented later. "I could see that the person in that little body had been a murderer in his last life."

To Jan Savage—a little boy of nine—I heard him say once, "Jan isn't a little child. He's an old man!" Indeed, one could see the old man in that small, thin form. I remember Jan's lying on his stomach once on the grass.

"What are you doing, Jan?" I asked.

"I'm trying to influence the ants here to go in the direction I tell them." This seemed to me a fairly sophisticated interest for a nine-year-old child. One day Jan was meditating with an older disciple; suddenly he exclaimed, "I see Jesus Christ!" They decided to ask the Master whether the vision had been true, so they stood in line to greet him after church the next Sunday.

"So!" Yogananda cried the moment they came to him. "Little Jan had a vision of Jesus Christ! That's good! That was a true vision." He tousled the child's hair affectionately.

Jan later left Mt. Washington; it was his mother's decision not to stay. However, I've often hoped that Jan remained faithful to God and Guru. Yogananda once said to me, "Several of those who leave here will end up with centers of their own," and in this connection he mentioned Jan. I've often wondered: could he have said that simply to encourage me? For my superiors ended up throwing me out of SRF in no gentle way. (I had shown myself more creative than was comfortable for them.) For myself, I simply could not imagine even living without serving my guru. "Just take any job that comes along," they told me after stranding me in New York City with only the money in my wallet. For myself, however, I could not but continue my service to him. However, I didn't want to rival them in any way. His words, therefore, "Many who leave here will end up with centers of their own," were my encouragement to remain actively his disciple, even though I could no longer serve him within his organization.

Jan's attempt to direct the movements of those ants brings to mind something I heard that I simply can't resist telling here, even though my justification for doing so is not even slim. A very psychic woman I met in Sedona, Arizona, once told me, "One day I baked a chocolate cake, and placed it on the window ledge to cool off. I came back later to find it covered with ants. So I leaned down and said, softly, 'I want to talk to your leader!'

"For a moment there was frantic activity. Then all of them became still, as if prepared to listen to me. I then said to them, 'This cake is in my home. I baked it for my family. I don't want to hurt you, but if you stay here I shall have to. Now then, at the bottom of my garden there is a tall tree. I want you to go there. When I come back here in a few minutes, I want to see this cake cleared. I'll know that you've obeyed me if I see you on that tree.'

"I came back fifteen minutes later. The cake was free of ants. I then went to that tree, and saw a long line of ants going up and down it."

Well, all right, I *can* offer one tiny justification for my telling this story here—apart from the fact that I don't know where else to tell it!: I have not wanted to portray my guru as unique. Though I've talked about him because his mission was indeed unique, what I've really been trying to talk about is universal principles.

Norman, a brother disciple, once had a vision of being with our guru on Lemuria, 80,000 years ago. I didn't know whether this was a true vision, but I was horrified at the mere possibility that it could take so long to find God.

"Sir," I said to Master soon afterward, "have I been your disciple for thousands of years?" (I didn't dare ask him how many thousands!)

"It has been a long time; that's all I will say."

Norman once said to Master, "I don't think I have very good karma, Sir."

"Remember this," replied the Master. "It takes very, *very*, *VERY* good karma even to want to know God!"

How long does each soul wander in delusion? I was not prepared for this truth, but in fact it may take even more than a day of Brahma! How many more? I'd rather not contemplate the question! In the Bhagavad Gita, Krishna says, "With the beginning of a new Day of Brahma, I throw all these souls out again into delusion." And in *The Rubaiyat of Omar Khayyam* (a true scripture, and not at all the mere love poem so commonly believed) Yogananda explains a particular quatrain as meaning, "Many of those who enter into creation at the beginning of a Day of Brahma are still wandering in delusion at the end of it."

It takes five to eight million lives for a soul to evolve to the human level. From then on, the gift of free will can make the journey very long indeed. Not to discourage anyone, it *always* makes the journey very long. I asked Master, concerning my own case, "Does it always take so long?"

"Oh, yes," he replied quite casually. "Desires for name, fame, etc., take one away again and again." My assumption was that he'd named my own particular, paramount delusions, though in this life I've always had almost an abhorrence for those "sticky sweets."

Thus, Master told us that Hitler had been Alexander the Great. Interestingly, both men, Hitler and Alexander, developed a tactic which Hitler named "*Blitzkrieg*": a sudden and very rapid attack.

"Hitler was bad," our guru said to us, "but compared to Joseph Stalin he was a boy scout." Master told us, I think (though he may have said only that he had read this account in the memoirs of Stalin's one-time chauffeur), "Stalin, which in Russian means 'steel' [Stalin's actual birth name was Joseph Besarionis dze Jughashvilli], would sit in the back seat of his car repeating over and over, 'I am *stalin*, I am steel!' When his wife died, Stalin was heard to remark: 'When millions die, it is a statistic; when one dies, it is a tragedy!'

"Stalin was Genghis Khan in a former life. Stalin's karma is such that it will take him another hundred thousand years to find freedom!"

"Only a hundred thousand years?" marveled Debi Mukerjee, a young disciple from Calcutta.

"And how long do you want one person to suffer?" asked the Master. (Well, as we all know, many pious Christians are almost fiercely happy at the thought of some of their brethren suffering "forever" in hell!)

"Winston Churchill was Napoleon," Yogananda added. "Napoleon wanted to conquer England. As Winston Churchill, he succeeded in that ambition. Napoleon wanted to destroy England. As Churchill, he had to preside over the dissolution of the British Empire. Napoleon was sent into exile on the island of Elba; came back to power; then was defeated at Waterloo and banished to the island of St. Helena. So Churchill fell from power, then came back. He was never actually defeated, except as politicians so often get voted out of power, but he did have to suffer the defeat of witnessing that dissolution of the empire.

"Mussolini was Mark Antony—a lesser figure."

He wouldn't tell me who Franklin Delano Roosevelt was. ("I've never told anybody. I was afraid I'd get into trouble!") Bill Brown, however, the brother of Mrinalini (SRF's fourth president), told me he had some reason for believing that Roosevelt was Benedict Arnold. Arnold had injuries to his legs in three battles, including the shattering of one leg, and found it extremely difficult, thereafter, to walk. Roosevelt was confined by polio to a wheelchair for the last twenty-five years of his life. Yogananda, in fact, felt that Roosevelt had betrayed America by bringing in big government with his

"New Deal," and also because he was soft on communists. He was very fond, for example, of Joseph Stalin, to whom he referred in a friendly manner as "Uncle Joe."

Charles Lindbergh, the Master said, had been Abraham Lincoln. Lincoln's amazing achievement in preserving the unity of the nation was undervalued during his lifetime. He received the compensation of extraordinary fame, as Lindbergh, for an achievement remarkable in itself, surely, but his fame was just as surely unanticipated by him. The eulogy at his funeral stated, "This was no ordinary man. He was like a president." An excellent book on this subject has been written by Richard Salva, a member of Ananda.

Yogananda said that his student and disciple, Amelita Galli-Curci, had been Jenny Lind, the famous Swedish singer of the preceding century. One time Mme. Galli-Curci said to him, "I have lost all my desires!" He waited a few moments while their conversation continued. Then he got her speaking about the astral world.

"When I'm in the astral world," she enthused, "I shall sing and sing!"

"Remember what you said," he reminded her: "You have no desires!"

"You are right. Oh, well, I have very *few* desires!" she responded, smiling.

Karma is not only individual. It affects groups of people, whether families, communities, nations, or even whole planets. We are now, as I stated earlier, at a turning point in history: entering a new age. Many changes will come about. "Europe," Yogananda said, "will be devastated; Russia, annihilated. Japan, for its cruel invasion of China in the 1930s, will be conquered by China. America will survive all difficulties, for its karma is basically good.

"England is finished."

"What do you mean, Sir?" I asked.

"Finished. Finished!" he replied. England was too grasping in its efforts to dominate other countries. Still, it also helped those countries. Its karma, therefore, must also be mitigated. How, then, will it be finished? Perhaps the Gulf Stream will shift its course, and England will become like Greenland. But then—what about Ireland? I must confess these matters are beyond my ken. It is only interesting to contemplate them. Edgar Cayce said that England "and the north of Europe" will sink into the sea in the blink of an eye. Is that what Yogananda meant? Well, time will tell.

The United States and India, he said, are destined to work together for the balanced development of the whole world: India, in her role of guru to the world, and America in her greater attunement to the rays of this new age, and in her material efficiency. "Many Indian souls," he said, "are being born in America, and many American souls are being born in India," so as to bring about this eventual balance.

One can intuit the karma of people from many things about them: their posture, for example. People with low karma have visibly lower-chakra energy. They walk heavily, sit heavily, move about heavily. People, on the other hand, with lighter karma are almost visibly centered higher in their bodies, and seem lighter on their feet.

A person's vocabulary also says much about him. If his karma is heavy, he will continually use words and concepts that refer to lower-chakra activities—words that I myself don't care even to think about. If the karma is light, a person's language will reflect a centeredness in the upper chakras. People in whose presence one feels a spiritual upliftment have either very light karma or no karma at all. Being in the presence of Yogananda, and of other great saints, brings a feeling of great love and bliss. Also, the lighter-colored or more refined a person's aura (whether it is actually seen or only felt), the closer he is to liberation. Often one can tell the color of an aura from a person's favorite colors.

Indeed, you might try the following little experiment on yourself to see whether your own karma is heavy or light. (Of course, I expect that anyone reading this book will have light karma. Were it heavy, he wouldn't even be drawn to reading it.) Lie on your back, and gaze up at the ceiling. Find some spot there—a light fixture, perhaps, or some other smallish point—and gaze either at or just next to it for some minutes. Soon, I think, that spot will seem to move as your eyes drift away from it. If the spot moves downward, that will be an indication that your gaze is slowly moving up, toward the spiritual eye. And if the spot moves upward? Well, anyway, I think whatever direction your eyes move will have some significance for you.

One can feel such influences also in different nations. When I went to Cambodia in 1958, for example, I felt a heavy, dark cloud over that country. And most people know what suffering that country had to endure, later on. I have also felt a dark cloud over Germany, though not so dark as the one over Cambodia. Time will tell what Germany has to endure, but certainly the whole country will have to pay for the atrocities of Hitler and his Nazis.

Consciousness is everywhere, for Creation itself is a dream projected by the Divine Consciousness. Even the rocks are conscious, though of course very dimly so. I was looking at a slow-moving worm moving imperceptibly over the floor of my bathroom a few minutes ago, and I thought, "Now there, definitely, is no lightning thinker!" Still, when I hear that scientists claim that computers will be complex enough, someday, to start demanding "computer rights," I think of that worm and its ancestors. Simple though the worm is, it has two things that no computer will ever possess: self-consciousness, and feeling. Prick the worm with a pin, and it will wriggle away. As I said earlier, these are the two things that science will never be able to create: feeling, and self-awareness. We don't get our self-awareness from comparing ourselves with others. It is an intuitive certainty, innate in every living creature.

But what a long, long journey the soul must make once it enters into outward manifestation! Yogananda said he could remember back to when he was a diamond!

He told us that Therese Neumann, the German stigmatist, whom he visited in 1935 at Konnersreuth, had been Mary Magdalene. When, in her youth, young swains would come acourtin', she'd drive them off the land—sometimes with a pitchfork. I imagine that, after that earlier incarnation, she'd had it with men!

In the Bible, Jesus asked his disciples, "Who do men say that I am?" And they answered, "Some say you were Jeremiah or one of the other prophets." That answer makes it clear that many, at least, of the Jews of those times believed in reincarnation.

Jesus also had a vision of Elias during his transfiguration on the mountain. The disciples asked him afterward, "Why do the scriptures say that Elias must come first?" And Jesus replied, "Elias is come already, and they knew him not." The Bible goes on to say, "And they understood that he spoke to them of John the Baptist."

I myself had been with Yogananda hardly a month when he dictated a passage in my presence that declared, "The three wise men who came to the cradle of baby Jesus were Babaji, Lahiri Mahasaya, and Sri Yukteswar." Who, then, was Yogananda? All I can say is, That's a very interesting question.

Yogananda also remembered having been the great warrior-prince Arjuna—the hero of the war of Kurukshetra thousands of years ago in India. His guru then was Krishna, and Krishna became Babaji, the deathless saint still living in the Himalayas. And so the cosmic play goes on.

Yogananda's true guru was Babaji. So then, what, truly, was Sri Yukteswar's role? I remember Yogananda quoting Sri Yukteswar (but I cannot now find that quote) as saying something to him about "until our twin souls merge in the Infinite." Could it be that those two are soulmates? Master did state once, as I mentioned earlier, that it may be necessary to meet one's soulmate before merging, in final liberation, into the Infinite.

It is interesting that Arjuna, in the Bhagavad Gita, presents himself as only a humble seeker. That is the attitude Yogananda assumes in *Autobiography of a Yogi*. The reader of both works may not easily guess that both men were actually great masters already. Arjuna and Krishna were reputed also to have been two great sages of historic times relative to their own already ancient times, as Nara and Narayan. And Yogananda often said to us, "I killed Yogananda long ago. No one dwells in this temple now but God."

He told us—and this one was difficult for me to swallow— that he, as I mentioned earlier, had been William the Conqueror. This news posed a problem for me. I'd been raised in the English system, and had always thought of William as one of history's great villains! Now I learned that he was my own guru! Needless to say, I did a lot of research to find out what William was *really* like.

I learned that he was a truly great man. His only close friends were saints, and people of saintly nature. He was always true to his word. He resorted very rarely indeed to the practice so common among kings and rulers in those days: execution of their captives. And in an age of great sexual license, he was completely faithful to his wife.

Both Arjuna and William were said to possess bows which only they could string.

William has been blamed especially for three things: his harrying of the north; his sequestering of a large part of the countryside as a hunting preserve for himself; and his so-called "Domesday (or "Doomsday") Book." Catherine Kairavi, in her excellent book, *Two Souls: Four Lives*, shows that the harrying of the north was forced upon William by unrelenting and unreasonable opposition to him, which involved repeated treachery on the part of those who had earnestly pledged him their loyalty. The Domesday Book was a necessary investigation into the true state of prosperity and the further needs of England during his day. And the New Forest was a farsighted project, setting aside a portion of the countryside as a "green" area. Modern ecologists would have heartily approved. As for hunting in it, I doubt that William ever had much time for hunting. The story, told in Yogananda's autobiography, of the deer he had loved at Ranchi, and of its death, raises doubt as to whether, during his life as William, he even *enjoyed* hunting deer.

William's body was exhumed 430 years after his death, and was found to be incorrupt.

Catherine Kairavi's book gives so much evidence of William's greatness that I feel there would be no point in examining it here in greater detail. Suffice it to point out, as she has done, that William's influence on history has been very great—much greater, indeed, than most people realize. I think that it was because of the vast extent of William's influence that Yogananda told us about that incarnation. He wanted us to realize the history-making importance of his own present incarnation, so that we might set our own sights accordingly.

Instead, many of my fellow disciples claim it was his mission only to start a monastery! His mission, I myself deeply feel, was to help usher the whole world, with greater understanding and spiritual insight, into Dwapara Yuga. Indeed, to me he is the *avatar* of Dwapara Yuga.

There is an amusing detail from Yogananda's own visit to the Tower of London, which was constructed by William I. Yogananda said later, "I asked a guard, 'Wasn't there a toilet here once?' Almost rudely the guard replied, 'No'—as if the question itself was ridiculous.

"I then asked the curator. He answered, 'Yes, there was a toilet there. It was used by the kings of old.'"

Yogananda's political roles in past lives gave him, in this life, an interest in the destiny of nations. During World War II he said it was he who placed the thought in Hitler's mind to invade Russia, thereby dividing his fronts and making it possible for his "invincible" army to be destroyed. When North Korea invaded South Korea, the Master told us it was he himself who put the thought in President Truman's mind to go to South Korea's defense. "Otherwise," he said, "the North Koreans, with China's help, would have gone on to conquer Japan, then the Aleutian Islands, putting themselves in a position to attack America through Alaska. Communism is a God-denying evil; it must be stamped out for the continued progress of mankind."

Many of the Master's disciples, he told us, were with him during his incarnation as William. To Norman, a brother disciple of mine, he said once, "You were my giant." Norman was very strong in this life also. To Jerry Torgerson he said, "You were good. You used to fight for me."

Interestingly, though all the other men disciples asked him if they'd been with him in that life, it never occurred to me to ask him that question—even though I may have asked him more questions than anyone else ever did. It is my opinion that he prevented that thought from entering my mind. Masters have that power, and it was more convenient at that time for me *not* to think of myself as having been, as I now believe, his youngest son Henry. Catherine Kairavi, in her book, makes a strong case for my having been he.

In the same way, Henry too was told only hintingly by his father that he would someday inherit everything. In that life, William left Henry a large sum of money. Land, in those days, was the true wealth. Henry then asked him, "What shall I do with this money, if I have no land to spend it on?" William could easily have made him an earl. If Henry had had his own land, however, he'd have concentrated on that, and would not have become as aware as he was, when the time came for him to assume the throne of England, of the problems that existed in both Normandy and England.

What happened was that William whispered to him on his deathbed (few could hear the words), "Be at peace, my son. In time you will have all that both your brothers now own." In my case, Yogananda said that I had a great work to do, but he never said it in the presence of others.

Of other prominent figures, Yogananda said that Sri Yukteswar had been Archbishop Lanfranc, as I stated earlier.

Of Dhirananda, who betrayed Yogananda and nearly destroyed his work in America, he said he had been Robert Curthose, William's oldest son, who at the very time that William lay dying was fomenting a rebellion against his father. (And even of him, Yogananda once said, "He'll be liberated in another three lives.") Another notorious traitor, Judas, who betrayed Jesus Christ and aided his crucifixion, has been thought of as Satan incarnate. Yogananda said of him, however, "I knew him in this incarnation, in India. He was a disciple of Sri Ramakrishna. After only two thousand years, he was liberated in my lifetime."

William's second son, William Rufus—his successor as king of England—in this lifetime was Warren Vickerman, a rug merchant in New York. I met Vickerman there in 1955. At that time he said to me, "I feel as though you were my brother." In fact, as I said, I do believe I was his brother Henry when he was King William Rufus. Vickerman himself had very much the same personality as Rufus, this time only slightly softer.

Vickerman told me that he had already been a meditator as a young man, and had reached the point where he could almost go breathless—almost, but not quite. He'd gone to several spiritual teachers, but none had been able to help him over this hurdle.

When Vickerman heard that Swami Yogananda was to give a public lecture—I think he said it was in Philadelphia—he told me, "I didn't want to waste time listening to yet another talk. If this man could help me with my problem, I'd follow him. Otherwise, why even listen to him? So I waited for him at his hotel. When he returned, I went and knocked on his door. He opened it, and asked, 'What may I do for you?'

"'Can you help me to go breathless?' I asked. After all, why waste time?

"'Yes,' he said. 'Come inside.'

"So I entered his room. He, too, evidently not wanting to waste time, just struck me, as I stood, on the chest. Suddenly I entered a state of breathless ecstasy. I've been his follower ever since." (William Rufus, too, for all his rough edges, was always loyal to his father.)

Vickerman also was loyal, yes, but still rough-hewn. He never lived at Mt. Washington, though he donated money regularly.

Daya, so Master told her, was his daughter Agatha, whom he sent to Spain to marry the successor to the throne of Castile-León. She herself had other ideas, however, and prayed to be spared the "terrible fate" of marriage. God answered her prayer: on arrival in port, she was found on her knees in her ship's cabin, dead. In this life also, she had her own ideas as to what Master's mission was, or should have been. It was she who could see it as having been only to found a monastery.

He told St. Lynn (Rajarshi Janakananda) that he had been Arjuna's younger brother Nakula. And he told Durga Ma that she had been Nakula's mother, Madri.

He said also that, after his life as William, he had been a king in Spain, whose job it had been to drive the Moors out of that country. A friend of mine researched the kings of Spain to find the one most likely to have been William the Conqueror before. It was Fernando III, *el Santo* (the Saint), whose body remains incorrupt to this day. I myself visited that tomb a year ago, in Seville. I found the vibrations at that tomb very powerful. Fernando's son was Alfonso X, el Sabio (the Sage), who I believe, again for several good reasons, to have been myself.* Alfonso's son, Sancho, was friendly to the Moors, and stopped trying to rid Spain of their last foothold in the country. Thus, the final liberation of Spain didn't take place until the year 1492.

These are only a few, fascinating facts. But I think they may help the reader to achieve deeper insights into the vast drama we all live on this earth. No one who has ever found God, and who has (inevitably) in the process remembered all his countless past incarnations, has ever cried in disillusionment, "What a scam!"

* He wrote over four hundred pieces of music. I, too, have written over four hundred pieces of music. He was an astronomer; my first interest in this life was in astronomy. There are many other similarities.

CHAPTER SIXTEEN

🦢 Dhirananda's Betrayal

S everal times, and for various reasons, people sued the Master over the years. Dhirananda (Basu Bagchi) had been a boyhood friend. Yogananda had called him to America to help with his mission to the West. While Yogananda toured the country, lecturing, Dhirananda remained at the international headquarters on Mt. Washington, "keeping the home fires burning." In 1929, Dhirananda showed up unannounced at Yogananda's apartment in New York, and talked him into signing an $8,000 IOU. He returned forthwith to Mt. Washington, where he packed his bags and, within a few days, left Mt. Washington forever. With his departure, Mt. Washington became stripped of most of its residents. One of those who left and returned later was Margaret Windberg. Miss Windberg once asked the Master, "Why did I ever leave?"

"Karma," he replied. It had been the karma of the work in America, decided partly by the karma of America itself, partly by the work, and partly by those who were coming to the work. Margaret Windberg's karma, added to that of many others, resulted in the sum total of near-disaster that followed upon Dhirananda's departure.

You may have noted that I didn't add to this total Yogananda's own karma. He *had* no karma. What karma he suffered was to help lift the karmic burden of others.

One may ask, "Didn't he *know* what he would suffer through Dhirananda?" On this point, we don't need to speculate. Sometime during the early fifties, Margaret Lancaster, another disciple, went on a pilgrimage to India. In Calcutta she stayed at the home of Tulsi Bose, another boyhood friend of Yogananda's. There Tulsi told her, "One day, when we were boys together, Yogananda told me almost casually, 'Someday Bagchi will betray me, and will marry a white woman.'"

How then, knowing that such would be the outcome of their relationship, did he pursue it so confidently? I think a master's life is, in many ways, only a movie swirling around him: interesting storms, heartrending betrayals, triumphs which he knows will only be temporary, transitions from one dream image to another. When one sees a movie for the second or third time, he knows very well what will be coming, but he holds that knowledge at a distance in order to enjoy yet again the scenes as they unfold before his eyes.

Masters do not try to escape pain and suffering as most people do. They know this world is, as Krishna described it, God's "ocean of suffering and misery." On the human plane they participate in the show, but inwardly they remain completely unaffected.

How else to account for the Master's signing that IOU for $8,000 for Dhirananda? I can vouch for his perfect knowledge of the psychology of his disciples. He once said to me, "I know every thought you think!" And he proved that statement again and again. Once at Hollywood Church I told an insincere member that I would be giving next Wednesday's class. "In that case," the member said, "I will be sure to come." Well, I knew he would have come anyway; therefore it irritated me slightly that he would pretend to be coming only because I would be giving the class. Wanting to deflect his insincere flattery from myself, I answered him (not very elegantly, I'm afraid), "In that case, would you please stand outside and check people's pockets for vegetables as they come in?"

A few days later I was with my guru while he entertained guests for lunch. After they'd left, as I sat at the table alone with him, he remarked to me casually, "By the way, when you are talking with a congregation member, don't talk about vegetables! It isn't dignified."

He showed the same insight with all his disciples. One evening another disciple, James Coller, came by car from Phoenix, Arizona, to see him in Encinitas. James grew very hungry during the drive. All the restaurants along the highway were closed. At last he came to one that was open, went inside, and found, alas, that all they could serve him at that late hour was hamburgers. James hesitated. After all, we were supposed to be vegetarians. But James was very hungry! At last he told himself, "Oh, well, he won't know!" He ate two hamburgers.

When he reached the Encinitas hermitage, he telephoned the Master. At the end of their conversation, and just before they hung up, the Master said to him, "Oh, by the way James, when you are out on the highway late at night, and come to a place that sells only hamburgers, better not eat anything."

So then, I cannot but ask, Is it possible that Master *didn't* know what Dhirananda was up to, in asking him to sign that IOU for $8,000? I have to reply, Of course he knew! It was a part of the show. He had no desires in the matter at all.

Dhirananda began teaching classes. But just as had been his lack centuries earlier when he was Robert Curthose, so now, too, he could not hew a straight line. Soon he left Los Angeles for the University of Iowa. There he obtained a Ph.D., and went on to become a professor of electroencephalography at the University of Michigan. Like Robert Curthose, he always preferred show over substance. Robert was an inept leader. Dhirananda was inept as a spiritual leader. But the same indwelling ego continued to harbor resentment over Yogananda's continued success. For many years, though how many I've no idea, my guru sent him each year a box of mangoes from Florida. Dhirananda always returned them, unopened.

One might wonder at the Master's persistence in continuing to send those mangoes. Wouldn't it have been better (I can imagine the question arising in some people's minds) to discipline him by *not* sending them? Wouldn't it have been more dignified? Didn't it show rather a weak, somewhat pleading spirit, as if Yogananda were *begging* for Dhirananda's friendship? Wouldn't it at least seem as though Yogananda were confessing weakness, perhaps out of shame? And shame over what? Perhaps for having been in the wrong?

Moreover, wouldn't it seem, in Dhirananda's eyes, to be a confession that he himself had been in the right, and Yogananda in the wrong? In fact, wouldn't Yogananda's persistence in sending those mangoes only strengthen Bagchi's delusion of unrelenting rivalry?

A master doesn't think in terms of one life only, but of the soul's progress through even thousands of years. In the eleventh century, Bagchi was well on his track of rivalry and practical ineptitude. Probably that trait was already present in him long before that. But the Master also saw that three lifetimes from now his soul would be freed. Evidently he realized that love alone would save this soul. He had no personal interest in the matter. If Bagchi's soul could remember this outstanding example of unconditional love, perhaps it was the only way he could be rescued from his outstanding delusions.

Bagchi's resentment never abated. On May 3, 1935, he filed a lawsuit against Yogananda in the Los Angeles Superior Court, to collect on his promissory note. "The press," wrote Jon Parsons in his book, *Fighting for Religious Freedom*, ". . . had a field day in reporting how the process servers were on the prowl for one of the country's most famous lecturers. Yogananda did not get away in time." He was to return to India, but was served just weeks before leaving town.

He had known the suit was coming, and on March 29, 1935, had filed papers incorporating the Self-Realization Fellowship Church as a nonprofit California corporation. A couple of weeks after being served, Yogananda signed a general assignment giving the new corporation (quoting Parsons) "all of his personal property located at Mt. Washington. . . . No one could touch the assets now."

Bagchi, from what I can understand, was a pompous and somewhat woolly-headed intellectual. As Robert Curthose, he had invaded England to seize it back from his youngest brother, Henry. Robert's army was notably larger than Henry's, because many of Henry's nobles had gone over to Robert's side, thinking that under his *laissez-faire* leadership they'd have more freedom to do as they pleased. The two armies met. The brothers convened on the field of battle. Robert then turned around and went back to Normandy—without striking a blow! When I say he seems to have been somewhat woolly headed, I mean that, like so many intellectuals, he was vacillating in purpose.

When Yogananda went to Japan, years before he came to America, he wrote the outline for a book, *The Science of Religion*. He had gone to Japan, presumably, because it was the most Western-like nation in the Orient. I imagine he wanted to get a taste of what it would be like in America. But he did not like Japan; he found the people there too sensual.

When he returned to Calcutta, he asked Bagchi to turn his notes into a book. This Bagchi did. Laurie Pratt, Yogananda's chief editor, described his book to me, however, as "pompous, much too stuffy, and intellectual." She told me, "Master never liked it." With this thought in mind, I studied it in depth to see if I could save its important message by rewriting the book. I found that Laurie had been right indeed. I therefore rewrote it completely, bringing out the salient points and leaving out all the intellectual huffing and puffing. Daya Mata, SRF's president, objected strongly to my keeping the same title ("Master *loved* that book!" she cried). I therefore renamed it, *God Is for Everyone*.

Well, Bagchi remains an important figure in the Master's life, albeit a disturbing one. He was one of the reasons the Master wouldn't listen to, and toward the end of his life could no longer enjoy, the recording of a Bengali song, "Come to Me as Sorrow."

Paramhansa Yogananda sitting for sculptor Ulric Dunbar.

CHAPTER SEVENTEEN

Yogananda's Salient Characteristics

It may be interesting to learn about some of the salient characteristics I observed in Paramhansa Yogananda during the years I lived with him. I will number them here, for convenience.

1. The outstanding trait I observed was his complete absence of ego. When I looked into his eyes, it was like looking into infinity. One time, Debi Mukerjee, a disciple from Calcutta, said something to Master about his humility. The Guru replied, "How can there be humility, when there is no consciousness of ego?"

A perfect example of his freedom from ego is a story I'll tell in the next chapter about a certain judge. My point here is that the Master could accept any insult and never be affected by it. As you'll see, he accepted that judge's withering contempt with utter good will. I never saw him affected to even the slightest degree by anything that anyone ever said about him.

2. Another trait that always amazed me in him was the deep, impersonal respect he gave everyone. His unwillingness to

let Debi criticize a man for being in a state of "feeling no pain"; his perfect willingness to have people with whom he didn't agree have the last word: these are examples, merely, of a characteristic that is marvelous to contemplate in one as great in the eyes of the world as Yogananda was.

3. He had an impish, and utterly delightful, sense of humor. This trait may be seen in some of the jokes he told, many of which he'd heard from others.

One was a somewhat left-handed compliment, which he told with a childlike smile: "Your teeth are like stars: they come out at night!"

Another was of three men, an Irishman, an Englishman, and a Scotsman. All three were drinking whiskey when a fly landed in each of their glasses. The Irishman simply sloshed his glass sideways, losing a fair amount of whiskey along with the fly. The Englishman carefully flicked the fly out of the glass. But the Scotsman *squeezed* the fly! I still remember vividly the little touch of glee with which Master uttered that word, *squeezed*.

In still another joke, three Scotsmen attended church. As the collection plate was approaching them, one of them fainted, and the other two carried him out.

I'm sure he would have greatly enjoyed this one too, though I confess I'm not sure he heard it: An Irishwoman was coming through U.S. customs carrying a suspicious-looking bottle. "What's this?" cried the customs inspector.

"Oh, Sir, it's only holy water." The official opened the bottle and sniffed its contents.

"Aha!" he cried, "As I suspected: Irrrish whiskey!"

"Glory be to God!" she cried. "A miracle!"

In dictating his Bhagavad Gita commentaries, the Master

gave the advice to eat only a little bit, but frequently: "*Sto-kam, stokam, anekoda.*" (Sanskrit scholars, please forgive me if I have that wrong. This is how I remember the foreign-sounding words he pronounced.) Dorothy Taylor, his secretary, mistyped the phrase to read: "*Stone 'em, stone 'em,* a little bit but frequently." This was too delicious for Master not to quote to me later with a hearty chuckle.

Finally (because I could go on indefinitely in this vein), I recall how he once came into the monks' dining room between meals, and found it an embarrassingly utter mess! All he did was say with a smile, "Well, it might be worse!" (So much for certain disciples' description of him as a stern, even scowling, disciplinarian!)

4. He understood others *from within themselves*, and not as other people do, from the outside.

There was a young disciple, Abie George, whose talk was rather "salty," and who didn't show the usual respect for his guru. In fact, he was inwardly extremely respectful, but such had been his upbringing. He would actually sit in a chair with one leg over the armrest as he talked with the Master. But Master saw behind that façade. After some particularly unusual display of what, in other disciples, would have been blatant disrespect, Master embraced Abie with a loving laugh.

5. Yogananda was completely centered in the Infinite Self. As he wrote in his poem "*Samadhi*": "I, the Cosmic Sea, watch the little ego floating in me." Even a master requires enough ego to keep his body moving and active in this world, but such a person's true center lies by no means in his little body. I remember once walking with him at his desert retreat. He was deep in the Spirit. Two or three times I had actually to support his body in order to keep it from falling. He re-

marked to me one day, "I am in all bodies. It is difficult for me to remember to keep this one body, especially, moving."

In Los Angeles, I was told, he sometimes walked up and down Main Street in a locale that contained many bars. He didn't say a word, but to me it is clear that he was centered in those people inside the bars, perhaps protecting them from those low astral entities which are always eager to possess people who are on the brink of unconsciousness.

6. Desirelessness was another strong trait in the Master. One time, James J. Lynn, a wealthy disciple, wanted to buy him an overcoat and took him for that purpose into a men's clothing store. Yogananda saw one coat that appealed to him, but when he read the price tag he hastily looked elsewhere: the coat was very expensive. Mr. Lynn said to him, "I saw you looking at that one. Let me get it for you." Yogananda had to agree. To the coat, Mr. Lynn added a matching hat.

The Master always felt awkward wearing this expensive coat. After some time he prayed, "Divine Mother, it is too good for me! Please take it away." Some days later he entered a restaurant. (He continued the story:) "The Divine Mother told me She would be taking it away that evening, so I carefully emptied the pockets. When the meal was finished, I returned to the rack where the coat had been hanging. To my great relief, the coat was missing. But then I noticed an omission. 'Divine Mother!' I prayed. 'You forgot to take the hat!'"

One day at Mt. Washington he came downstairs, and saw a small group of us standing there, waiting for him. "Isn't it a warm day?" he asked.

We, knowing that he had it in mind to give us money for a little ice cream, answered, "Oh, it's not *so* warm, Sir."

"Are you *sure* it isn't a little warm?"

"Well, it is if you say so, Sir."

Finally, with decision, he concluded, "I can't keep money, and I won't! Here's a little money for ice cream. Go out and buy yourselves some."

It was only a little money. In any case, it wasn't the money, but his statement, "I can't keep money, and I won't!" that touched me especially. I spent some of my own money for the ice cream that day, in order to keep the bills he'd actually handed me. Those bills now rest in the little shrine-museum on the hill above my house.

7. Complete nonattachment was another characteristic of his. Toward the end of his life he made plans to go to India. I was one of the people he wanted to take with him. Twice he had to cancel his plans. The last year, those plans were canceled permanently by his final exit from the body. The last year but one I asked him, "Sir, shall we be going to India this year?"

"I am not curious about these things," he replied. "What Divine Mother wants, I do."

Not curious about a trip to India?! I was amazed.

8. He treated all people equally, and was as respectful toward any garage mechanic as toward someone prominent in the world of politics, business, or the arts.

He used to walk with a cane—not, as a rule, because he needed one, but because to him a cane was like the *danda*, or wooden staff which many swamis carry in India as a reminder to keep their spines straight and to live more at their own center. A few days before he left his body, he went to a dilapidated shop to buy a new cane. It was a small item, but he wanted to be a conscientious custodian of the organization's money, so he bargained carefully. Once he'd got the price he thought right, however, he looked about him. Seeing what a very poor shop it was, he gave the owner much more money than he'd saved by bargaining.

"You are a gentleman, Sir!" said the owner, and thereupon gave him a particularly fine antique umbrella.

Back at Mt. Washington, hours later, the Master said, "That man was so poor! He had a linoleum floor! I think I'll buy him a carpet."

9. He had the ability to enjoy everything *with the joy of God.* In this he made a strong contrast with a sadhu I once met in Puri, India, who said to me, "You shouldn't enjoy anything."

"Not even a beautiful sunset?" I asked.

"No, nothing!"

I thought, What a dry outlook. My guru, by contrast, enjoyed almost *everything*! In his enjoyment, however, he was attached to nothing. His enjoyment was the joy of God. Complete nonattachment was evident even in his eyes, the gaze of which was always, in a sense, remote from this world.

10. He was surprisingly innovative. He built, as far as I know, the first motor home. He called it a housecar, and used it to travel about the country, lecturing.

He told me he'd invented the toilet lid. He was also the first to suggest placing the gearshift of a car on the driving shaft rather than in the floor. "We drove in to Detroit with our invention," he told me. "People were very impressed."

11. Another fact I noticed about him was that he was completely positive. One time I mentioned something humorous, but not complimentary, about someone. He scolded me for being negative.

"*Am* I negative, Master?" I asked.

"Sometimes," he replied. "But there is a great deal of positive in your nature also."

"Why look at the drains," he said to us on another occasion, "when there is so much beauty all around?"

12. As you will see in the next chapter, he was concerned for the upliftment of all mankind. That was his mission on earth: quantitative, not only qualitative. Qualitative also, of course, for he brought techniques for transforming human consciousness through people's awareness and use of energy.

Some of his disciples were concerned only with their own salvation. That was fine by him, but he was grateful when he found anyone who wanted to bring his message to the whole world.

"New hope for all men!" was his motto.

13. Nothing ever excited him. Always, he was deeply calm. He could laugh. He could also move quickly, when he had to. But he was always calm.

Once, late for a lecture, he set out at a run. "Don't be nervous," a student cautioned.

"One can run nervously, or one can run calmly," was the Master's reply, "but not to run when you need to is to be lazy!"

14. One thing I noted about him was his always-blissful outlook on life. I would notice this fact not only in his calm, inward expression, but also from the deep bliss I often felt in his presence.

15. He was deeply loving to all, and concerned for their well-being. My mother once visited me at Mt. Washington, and was scheduled to have an interview with him. I asked him beforehand, "Sir, will you please pray that she be brought onto this path?"

"Yes," he said, so almost abruptly that I wasn't sure he'd even heard me correctly.

At the end of his interview with her, and as she was leaving the room, he followed her to the doorway. There they shook hands in farewell. He continued to hold her hand, however. Speaking out loud, he prayed to God and to our line of gurus, and said, "May you be brought onto this path." This, for me personally, was a deeply moving moment. With tears of gratitude, I touched his feet. In fact, toward the end of her life she did begin meditating.

16. Always, he was very much the leader. Wherever he went, something about him commanded respect. This fact was clearly evident, of course, in the demeanor of the thugs who menaced him during his early years. But he always emanated a quiet aura of authority.

One woman in the Hollywood Church congregation told me that when she first saw the Master, it was through a restaurant window. Suddenly, then, she tugged at her husband's sleeve.

"Look, Dear, through that window! That has to be the most spiritual man I've ever seen."

He was always, and quite naturally, in control of every situation. Wherever he went, people deferred to him. Speaking for myself, though I loved him deeply, I always held him in deep awe.

17. He had a strong, deep voice, filled with power. There was no self-abasement in his humility. There was a suggestion, rather, of his attunement to the power of the universe. Yet there was lightness also.

One night at the monks' retreat at Twentynine Palms, in California, I was suddenly awakened by a feeling of a great divine presence in the room. I was sleeping, along with several other men, on the floor of the living room. At once I sat up to meditate. Then I looked out the front window, and saw the Master walking slowly outside. Instantly I got up, went out, and touched his feet.

Later he commented with a smile, "I thought I was seeing a ghost!"

18. He had great divine power, as we saw in the story of that thug who menaced him in Lakeside Park, Chicago.

19. Yet he was respectful toward, even appreciative of, others' opinions, even when these differed widely from his own. One time a disciple, Dan Boone, wrote him a scathing letter, which reflected the delusions Boone himself was going through at the time. When the Master next saw him, he said to Boone, "You should take up writing. That was the best letter Satan ever wrote me." There was no sarcasm in his voice: only admiration and respect.

20. He wanted nothing from others except their own highest happiness. Once, after he'd scolded a disciple, the disciple said, "But you will forgive me, won't you?"

His question surprised the Master. Pausing briefly, he then said, "Well, what else can I do?"

21. He had keen insight into human nature. For even though a master no longer has any delusions—to the point even of wondering how anyone could be so blinded by them—he well remembers all the incarnations he himself suffered as he went through those same delusions himself.

Yogananda offered the above explanation, indeed, for the reason why Jesus would have had, first, to transcend delusion in a former life to be able to help others in this one. No human being, even a master, is ever directly a Son of God. I have read that claim on the part of disciples of other paths besides the Christian. Yogananda's answer to that was, "What would be the point? It is the destiny of every soul to merge back into oneness with God. But if a miraculously produced, direct incarnation of God were to descend on earth, what encouragement would that give to human beings to 'Go and do likewise'?"

22. The Master was a flawless mirror* to the world. Thus alone could he bring out the best in people. To everyone he met—whether a disciple or chance acquaintance—he reflected back his or her own higher Self. In fact, he actually appeared physically different depending on the consciousness of the person he was reflecting.

There are two photographs that dramatically demonstrate this phenomenon. The first is one of Master with a famous opera singer and disciple, Amelita Galli-Curci. Yogananda's face is transformed with a gentle, feminine quality, and his physique seems delicate and frail like Mme. Galli-Curci's.

In the second, Master stands next to Senor Portes Gil, who was then President of Mexico. By contrast, Master face appears like a mirror of Portes Gil's hearty, masculine, jovial visage, and his body looks stocky, sturdy, and full of energy.

These two photos of Master seem hardly to be that of the same man, the change in facial expression, comportment, and energy is so dramatic.

These photographs and this subtle, unannounced, and serviceful activity of Master's demonstrate two things: First, Yogananda's complete lack of ego, to allow him to reflect back to each individual his own inner, divine Self—unmarred, on Master's part, by any egoic identification with or attachment

* As Kamala Silva described him, in her book by the same title.

to his own body. Second, Yogananda's unflagging commitment to spiritually help and act as a divine instrument for everyone he encountered.

As Master said, "Everyone whose path has crossed mine in this lifetime has been for a specific purpose."

23. He was inwardly childlike. I myself had always thought that a sage must be solemn, smiling only in concession to the weaknesses of ordinary human beings. To correct this impression in me, he once bought a few toys. (This episode occurred at his Twentynine Palms retreat.) We were seated in the kitchen at the time. He asked that something be brought to him. Whatever it was came enclosed in a paper bag.

The Master asked someone to turn out the light. We heard a few chuckles from him, along with a little crinkling of paper. Suddenly, sparks began flying out the barrel of a toy revolver. The light came back on. Then the Master looked at me.

"How do you like that, Walter?" he asked. (Walter was the name by which he always called me.)

"It's—fine, Sir!" I replied, still trying to get over my astonishment.

Then, gazing at me penetratingly, he spoke, quoting the words of Jesus: "Suffer little children to come unto me, for of such is the kingdom of God."

He finished that charming lesson by firing, from another toy pistol, an object which rose in the air, then opened into a tiny parachute. We all watched solemnly as the parachute descended to the ground. I never saw him play with those toys again. I suspect he'd bought them only for my sake.

24. He laughed readily, but when he chose to be serious, no one could make him even smile. His control in such ways was remarkable. I never saw him succumb to hilarity.

25. His generosity extended far beyond mere money or material gifts. It included also, for example, allowing others to have the last word; deferring to their opinions; applauding whatever good they did.

26. He never judged anyone. Judgment he left to God. He was, truly, a friend to all.

27. I've indicated this before, but he had a strong will power. I remember a public function when he wanted to blow a conch shell. It seemed he had all but lost the knack for doing so. Instead of giving up with a self-deprecating smile, however, he continued determinedly through several tries until some sort of sound emerged. I can't say the sound was pure or beautiful, but it was, unmistakably, the sound of a conch shell!

One afternoon, after I'd served lunch for him and a few guests, he had me sit at the table with him for a time. He then tried to flip a fork into his empty glass. Again and again he failed. When finally he succeeded, the fork broke the glass.

"But I got it in!" he announced with an impish smile. I think he was teaching me a lesson in perseverance, whenever I set my will to anything.

28. His nature was enthusiastic, but never "bouncy." He never reacted emotionally to anything. His enthusiasm was always an expression of his bliss in God.

29. He always knew how to act appropriately.

One time, a newspaper sent two young women to interview him at a hotel. They wanted to enter his room, but he said, "Let's talk out here in the corridor." Both women wore provocatively low-cut blouses. The Master, throughout the interview, gazed fixedly into their eyes. As they left, they seemed disappointed. Yogananda went to the newspaper and asked the editor why he'd sent them, really.

"If you'd invited them into your room, or allowed your gaze to shift down for even a second," the editor responded, "I'd have plastered that story all over the front page."

"That's a terrible thing to do!" exclaimed Yogananda. "So in that way you ruin the reputations, and maybe the lives, of perfectly innocent people. I call that contemptible! A newspaper should *report* the news, not create it. And even if it does create it for editorial purposes, it should not be scurrilous."

30. Yogananda had an amazing ability to speak insightfully on any subject. When doctors were present, he could speak with them, using even their own specialized terminology. No matter what the subject, in fact, his ability to tune in to the consciousness of others made it possible for him to know everything they knew.

This gift was particularly evident in his ability to know every trend in religious history without having studied that era. He was no scholar, but somehow he knew all about the history of Christianity; the special missions of Buddha, of Shankaracharya, of Ramanuja, of Chaitanya. And he made clear his own place in that progression. Equally, without having studied it, he understood the whole history of Christian schisms, sects, movements, and countermovements. I myself had studied Christian history, and was amazed at his insight into all of it.

31. Physically speaking, I was impressed by his posture. It was always firmly upright. Somehow it was evident to me that his consciousness was always centered both in the spine and at the point between the eyebrows.

32. Although the Master was very accepting of others as they were, when it came to their aspiration for perfection he was uncompromising. In my own efforts to develop devotion, I

had finally reached the point where I felt I had some cause for self-satisfaction. Master, however, was not satisfied. Soon afterward, he said to me, "If you love yourself, how can you love God?"

Bishnu Ghosh (Yogananda's brother), Motilal Mukherji (disciple
of Sri Yukteswar), Yogananda's father, Richard Wright, Paramhansa
Yogananda, Tulsi Bose, and Swami Satyananda (Ranchi school).

CHAPTER EIGHTEEN

🍃 He Returns to India

In 1935 Paramhansa Yogananda was telepathically summoned back to India by his guru, Swami Sri Yukteswar, speaking to him in his inner ear. His guru said, "I will soon be leaving my earthly body."

Embarking at New York in June, Yogananda went first to England, then Scotland, and to the European continent on his way back to his own homeland. In Scotland he visited Sir Harry Lauder, to whose melody for the song, "Roamin' in the Gloamin'," Yogananda wrote the words of a chant of his, "Sitting in the Silence." And in England he visited Stonehenge, where he told Richard Wright, his secretary, "I myself lived here thirty-five hundred years ago." In Germany, he visited the famous Catholic stigmatist, Therese Neumann, whose brothers years later paid a return visit to Mt. Washington. In Italy he visited the home town of St. Francis, Assisi, where he felt the presence of Christ everywhere. He used often to call St. Francis his "patron saint."

Interestingly, the prayer for which St. Francis is best known, "Lord, make me an instrument of Thy peace," has been discovered in recent years, in the archives of a monastery in Belgium, actually to have been written by William the Great (also called "the

Conqueror"), who Yogananda himself said he had been.*

When he arrived in Calcutta, a truly impressive homecoming awaited him: a parade through the city streets, organized by his former aid and secretary, Rashid.

My guru told me many years later, "In that way he fully compensated for the trouble he had caused me in America." Many more years later I learned that this "trouble" had consisted in Rashid's trying to block the acquisition of Mt. Washington, the Master's international headquarters, by suing him for the free help he had given Master during his early lectures in America. Fortunately, good sense and kindness prevailed, for Rashid had withdrawn his lawsuit.

His father; his earthly family; his guru: all were thrilled to have him back. Now he had lectures to give in Bengali. Yogananda *was* Bengali, of course, but he had never before lectured in that language, except in the classroom. He also gave lectures in English. Wherever he went, he created a great sensation.

On his way to Calcutta from Bombay, he had stopped in Wardha to visit Mahatma Gandhi. The two of them had interesting discussions on *ahimsa*, or harmlessness. Gandhi's attitude was absolute. It was, indeed, his absoluteness that enabled him to prevail against India's British rulers. But my guru commented to me, "Had he tried using *ahimsa* against the Russians, it would not have worked. His method was successful in the present instance because the English are gentlemen. If one tried practicing *ahimsa* on a tiger, unless one had spiritual power, he'd only end up in the carnivore's stomach!

"I asked him, 'What if a madman came to your village and started shooting everyone on sight? How would you handle that predicament?'

---

* I have mentioned before the fascinating account on the subject of this particular past-life memory, presented by Catherine Kairavi in her book, *Two Souls: Four Lives*, Crystal Clarity Publishers, Nevada City, California.

"'I'd let him shoot me, first,' was Gandhi's reply.

"Well, I let him have that last word. But in fact, that sacrifice would have solved nothing, had the madman gone on to shoot everyone else in the village, too. *Ahimsa*, like everything else in this relative world, is only a relative truth. One must practice it mentally, but it isn't always possible to practice it literally. It may be the better part of valor to shoot the tiger if one can, and even to shoot that one madman rather than let him kill hundreds."

Ahimsa, in this case, would be practiced by not hating the animal or the person one was preventing from doing harm. One can discipline or prevent devastation without *wishing* harm.

Yogananda's kind nature, however, prevented him from pursuing this subject to its logical conclusion. He let Gandhi's answer stand.

There was an English lady who lived in Gandhi's ashram, and was quite close to him. He gave her the Indian name, *Mirabehn*, after a medieval woman saint (Mirabai) in India. Mirabehn was very much taken with Yogananda—so much so that Gandhi wouldn't let her take Kriya Yoga initiation, when he himself took it from the Master.

"Gandhi was a great man, but he did have that little bit of jealousy," was Master's comment to me. "Well, nearly everyone on earth possesses at least a few weaknesses."

He went on to say, "I gave a lecture there in Hindi. Of course, I don't know Hindi well, and I was just coming from fifteen years in America. Someone after my lecture, however, made a derogatory remark about my Hindi. Human nature! It must always find reasons to make itself look taller by belittling others. But Gandhi himself was a true saint—not on the same level as masters like Sri Yukteswar, but a man sincerely dedicated to doing God's will and to helping others."

In India, as Master traveled about the country, the English authorities followed him about with the inevitable concern of officialdom. He was stirring people up, and filling them with pride in their own heritage. The English wanted the Indians to go back to sleep, and to accept their English rule in a docile spirit.

At one point they tried to discredit Yogananda in the eyes of the public, even as that critic had done at Gandhi's ashram. They got an English lady to approach the Master after a lecture, throw her arms about him as though they knew each other very well indeed, and give him a big, congratulatory kiss. At that moment photographers, primed in advance, would quickly snap pictures of the scene.

Yogananda knew what was about to happen. As the lady came up to him with outstretched arms, he grabbed her by the waist and held her high above his head. Then he turned to the photographers and cried, "Now, take your photographs!" The English simply didn't know what to do! He was breaking no law.

Gentlemen the English may have been, but that was an over-generous assessment of some of the things they did in India. Yogananda told me, for instance, of how they'd once bought up all the rice in Bengal at a price no one could resist. When people found themselves without rice and tried to buy it back, they could get it only at a price very few could afford. Six million people in Bengal starved to death, entirely in consequence of that sleight of hand. There were other atrocities. Master told me, "I made a study of those things. They were terrible! It was only in the end that England's nobility of character finally won out over its butchers."

A Bengali song appeared at the time of that rice tragedy in Bengal: "*Shyama amar, nirobo kano Ma?*—Mother, why are You silent?"—and, "*Dukhero beshe ashiyo*—Mother, come to me as sorrow, for in grief I will never be able to forget You." The Master loved these songs, and possessed beautiful recordings of both of them. It is painful to recall that, toward the end of his life, he felt he'd suffered enough, especially through betrayal by people whom he'd loved. He would never listen to them, especially to the second of them, again.

Sometime while he was in India—probably during his trip to Mysore—he visited the ashram of Ramana Maharshi, a great saint in southern India.

Because Ramana Maharshi was very much focused on inner enlightenment as the only cure for human woes, he had little interest in mass upliftment. This attitude is common among saints in India. I have often thought it may be due to English suppression, which left only one exit—negative perhaps, but at least rewarding spiritually—escape into the inner Self. That attitude is praiseworthy also, but in its world-negation it rejects the beauties of God's creation. The ancient scriptures were not so wholly rejecting. As Jesus Christ himself said, "Seek ye first the kingdom of God, and all these things shall be added unto you." (Matthew 6:33) The "things," then, are not wholly wrong. They are wrong only in relation to a higher reality.

Yet the role of *avatars* is also to raise humanity, as a whole, to a higher level of consciousness. As Sri Krishna says in the great Indian scripture, the Bhagavad Gita, "Whenever virtue declines, and vice is in the ascendant, I incarnate myself as an *avatar*. Appearing from age to age in visible form, I come to destroy evil and to reestablish virtue" (4:7,8) Qualitative and quantitative good: both are necessary for the spiritual upliftment of mankind. Most saints are not concerned with the needs of humanity as a whole. Their concern is with getting out of the cosmic dream. For them, human woes offer only an added incentive to rise above the human state altogether.

Yogananda's mission was both to sincere seekers and to suffering humanity. His teachings were destined to offer people everywhere a major incentive to improve their lot by pointing them in the direction of ever-greater spirituality.

No doubt to satisfy his curiosity as to Ramana Maharshi's attitude toward mass development, he asked the saint what he thought of mass upliftment.

"There can be no good accomplished except through personal enlightenment," was the reply.

Yogananda once more, as he had graciously done toward Mahatma Gandhi, allowed Ramana Maharshi to have the last word. It was never his way to argue. The ashram annals, reporting this exchange, make it seem as though Ramana Maharshi had had the best of an argument.

Later, however, Ramana's brother, who was no saint and was very ego-centered, tried to get Yogananda into an argument on the point—no doubt to persuade him of the uselessness of the work he was doing in promulgating truth by lectures, books, and the like. Ramana Maharshi, seeing him from inside the satsang room, called to him quietly, "Come away." He knew Yogananda's stature.

There was a great disciple of Ramana Maharshi's living in the ashram. My guru told me, "He was even greater than his guru, for he had attained final liberation. It does sometimes happen that the disciple is greater than the guru. This saint's name was Yogi Ramiah. He and I walked around the ashram grounds hand in hand. If I'd remained in his company another half hour, I could not have persuaded myself to leave India again!"

The Master also told me he sometimes "hid" himself, when visiting saints, so that they would speak with him naturally, as if with a seeker.

My guru once told me, "Of the saints in *Autobiography of a Yogi*, the only ones who had attained final liberation were our own line of gurus (in previous lives), and two disciples of Lahiri Mahasaya: Ram Gopal Muzumdar (the 'Sleepless Saint') and Swami Pranabananda (the 'saint with two bodies') in this life." It was then that he told me about Yogi Ramiah.

At Sri Yukteswar's hermitage, Master wanted to buy a number of conveniences for his guru. The Guru replied, however, "That is your world out there. I am satisfied with my little *asan* (meditation seat) and my bed. You see them both perfectly neat and clean." It was not that he was reproaching his disciple in any way. He himself it was who had sent this disciple out into the world to uplift humanity. Yogananda's own strong tendency had been to go to the Himalayas and meditate. He told us that, in his next life, which he said would be in two hundred years, he would live in the Himalayas—"to compensate for the intense activity of this present lifetime." People sometimes claim to be Yogananda reincarnated. The Master's own prediction on this subject should suffice to lay all those claims to rest.

Sri Yukteswar did balk at the flamboyant way his disciple promoted yoga in the West. Yogananda replied, "You, Sir, are the goldsmith. I am the jeweler. To make jewelry functionally beautiful, a few alloys are necessary." At this explanation, his guru smiled appreciatively.

There is a book available that purports to be a biography of Yogananda. It is by someone who seems to have served as the Master's Indian secretary during the year he spent in that country from 1935 on. The fact that the Master never mentions this man in his autobiography suggests that he didn't think much of him. The man's name was Dasgupta; he is no longer alive. His book expresses a regrettable trait that I have observed occasionally, especially among Bengalis: a tendency to offer praise in such a way as actually to damn the person one is praising.

This man wrote in glowing terms about the Master's warm personality and magnetic manner of public speaking, only to go on to say that Yogananda was highly imaginative, that indeed his so-called visions were false, his devotion to his guru a travesty, and that most of his miracles never really occurred. Of the Master's cure of a lame man, he almost suggested that Yogananda had so frightened the poor man by shouting at him that the fellow was able to walk again.

Dasgupta wrote of one time, during this period of the Master's 1935 sojourn in India, when Yogananda had asked those in the audience to clasp their hands together. Next he announced, "Now, you will not be able to separate your hands!" Most of the people there could in fact not do so. The Master said, "Now, I release your hands." Most people were suddenly able to do so. But then, Dasgupta wrote, one person was unable to separate his hands, and the Master himself was not able to separate them. Only (again, in Dasgupta's account) when another disciple of Sri Yukteswar, Motilal Thakur, took this man outside was he able to help the man to separate his hands and make him normal again.

I heard this same story, from an eyewitness, when I went to India in 1958. What I learned was that, when people's hands were locked together, this same Motilal Thakur went about the audience, blowing on his fingers and then flicking them at the crowd, trying to prove himself spiritually greater than Yogananda. His attempts were ineffectual.

No one who was in tune with the Master could release his hands again. Only when Yogananda gave the command could people again free their hands.

The Master had implied that those who were not in tune would be untouched by his influence. Dasgupta said to him later, "Look, your curse has not affected me! I was able to release my hands immediately."

"That," the Master answered (as Dasgupta himself wrote), "is because you are a critic." The Master was being kind. Behind that word were others he might have used: cynical, doubting, judgmental.

I mention this man's book only because it is being circulated at present in America. I consider it a deliberate attempt to besmirch the name of a great man. One reason I am writing this book on Yogananda's life is to set the record straight on the greatest man I have ever known, and known well (at least outwardly), in my life.

One day, Yogananda was coming from his guru's ashram in Serampore, perhaps to go to the bus or train station. On the way he heard a great hubbub issuing from a house he was passing. He went inside, and learned that the man of the house had just died. He went to the bedside of the deceased, touched him, and after a time the man's body began to vibrate. A few moments later, he opened his eyes. He had returned to life.

Dr. Lewis, when the Master told him this story, asked him, "Sir, would you have gone in there if Divine Mother hadn't told you to?"

"Oh, no," was the reply. "I do only what Divine Mother tells me to."

During Paramhansa Yogananda's return visit to India, he managed to get his school in Ranchi on a sound financial footing. At the time, a large function was held to commemorate the accomplishments to date of this *Brahmacharya Vidyalaya*, as he called the school.

"Whom shall we get to preside at this event?" the Master asked.

There was general agreement. The best possible person would be a judge in that district, one Gurudas Bannerji. Yogananda went there to extend an invitation. He was not at all prepared, however, for the reception he received. The judge, on hearing this swami's request, launched into a tirade against all the swamis in India.

"India is overburdened with these worthless fellows," cried the judge, "of whom I see a prime example before me. I have no time to waste on their useless functions. Why on earth should I attend your absurd event?" He went on for some time in this vein, leaving Yogananda well assured that this visit had been fruitless. Calmly and politely the Master replied, "Thank you for your answer. Nevertheless, we shall be honored to have you preside at our event, should you care to grace us with your presence." He left, and then devoted himself to finding a substitute. Everyone agreed at last on the principal of a local school.

The event began. The principal initiated it, then asked the first speaker to address the large crowd. This man had hardly begun his speech when a car drove up. Judge Bannerji stepped out. Way was made for him as he walked up to the lecture platform. The school principal gladly turned the meeting over to him.

Bannerji sat and listened while the report was concluded.

"Many graduates of this school," the speaker announced, "have gone on to become swamis. Our school's glory is spreading throughout the land." He finally sat down, and Judge Bannerji rose to his feet.

"This day," he announced, "is one of the happiest days of my life. When your Swami Yogananda came and invited me to preside at this function, I felt a thrill of joy go through me. I decided, 'I must test this man, to see if he really is as good as he seems.' I said everything I could think of to insult him and the principles he represents. And I have to tell you, he passed my test better than I would have thought possible. I have something else to tell you: Never mind about the swamis that are being produced by this school. India has many swamis. But if you can produce even one man as great as this one, not only your school, but all of India will be glorified!"

Indeed, the Master's return visit to his motherland, though it was only for a year, had a significant impact on raising the level of Indians' faith in the high spiritual destiny of their own country. That faith had been brutally shaken by the three-hundred-year reign of the English. When the Muslims had invaded India, they conquered by the sword, mercilessly killing any who resisted their religion. Aurangzeb, in Kashmir, had demanded that one maund (about 80 pounds) of brahminical threads be delivered to him every day. This delivery could be accomplished by only slaughter or conversion. Still, India had remained proudly upright.

But when the English came, their conquest, at first, was purely mercantile. They sneered at these "brown heathens," whom they considered utterly beneath them. This demoralizing blow undermined Indians' faith in themselves. Even today, they have not yet regained full confidence in their own high destiny. They are imitating the West, and turning away as if in shame from their own spiritual heritage. (Well, in my opinion this is not an unmixed misfortune. India needs to claim her place among the great nations of the world. And she will not be able to ignore for long her own deep spiritual roots. Meanwhile, she is becoming great in Western, materialistic terms as well as in spirituality.)

In the thirteenth century, Marco Polo passed through India on his return from China to Italy. He described India at that time as "the wealthiest country in the world." A scant century later, India was well on the road to becoming one of the poorest, and England, simultaneously, was becoming one of the richest. One cannot but suspect, here, a see-saw relationship.

Mahatma Gandhi was the primary force which returned India to its own sense of high destiny. To a lesser but still-important degree, Paramhansa Yogananda's visit played a role also in this national upliftment of consciousness.

On one occasion during that visit, someone, while speaking with Swami Sri Yukteswar, compared Yogananda to Swami Vivekananda, the great disciple of Sri Ramakrishna, who also had gone to America decades earlier, and had made an excellent impression there.

"Don't even mention them in the same breath," Sri Yukteswar replied. "Great though Vivekananda was, Yogananda is much greater."

It was during Yogananda's one-year return to India that Sri Yukteswar left his body. That account, and also that of the resurrection of Sri Yukteswar at the Regent Hotel in Bombay, is beautifully covered in *Autobiography of a Yogi*. I will omit both accounts here because they are told there so well. The "Resurrection of Sri Yukteswar" is perhaps the most inspiring chapter in Yogananda's whole book (although Dasgupta dismisses it, typically, as only a fantasy). Several of the things Yogananda wrote in his book had never before been expressed in mystical literature: his poem "*Samadhi,*" and his account of the astral and causal universes in this chapter on resurrection. "The Resurrection of Sri Yukteswar" gives a complete, comprehensible account of the way the very universe was made, and explains Swami Shankara's statement that God's Creation is His dream, showing just how that actually took place. Indeed, only now, in this new age of energy, can such concepts be grasped, at least by thoughtful people.

Interestingly, though Yogananda treats that revelation as totally new to himself, many things that Sri Yukteswar said on that day had actually been written by Yogananda also, years earlier. Yogananda gives us in this account, as he explains in the book itself, telepathically transferred images rather than a long verbal dissertation.

One day, Yogananda was leaving Calcutta by the Howrah station, perhaps to return to Bombay. He was standing on the lowest step of the train, talking to a crowd of people, when the train tried to set out from the station. It wouldn't budge. The conductor descended, looked at the train, looked at the crowd, looked at the Master, then folded his hands in fervent appeal.

"Holy man! Please let the train go."

The Master smiled, blessed the crowd, then ascended into the train, which at once departed.

In this, the Master's one return visit to India, he also met a great woman saint, Ananda Moyi Ma. Again, I won't try to compete with his beautiful account by offering another of that sacred event. But I will say that when I myself got to go to India, in 1958—I remained there for several years—I got to meet and spend considerable time with this saint also. To me, she was like the Divine Mother incarnate. I was forced to disagree with her—not openly, but in my own mind—when she showed a strong disinclination toward outward spiritual work. In this she was like Ramana Maharshi, and like many other saints in India. But my guru, as an avatar, had both a qualitative and a quantitative work to do. Seeing my own zeal for bringing everyone in the world to

God, he had assigned me to this kind of activity also, in addition to my own meditations. "Your duty in this life," he told me, "will be one of intense activity, and meditation." I could not help noting that he had put activity first, even before meditation.

Ananda Moyi Ma, by contrast, would not even look at the magazine her followers put out in her name. "It is *your* magazine," she told them. Her spiritual magnetism was such, however, that in her presence I felt continuous waves of divine love flowing over me.

When Yogananda returned to the West in 1936, there was a subtle shift in his way of reaching people. It was as though his outward service, which had been ordained by God, was now directed more inwardly. He began to concentrate more on training the disciples, and on developing their way of life. I myself, who came to him only in 1948, received from him the task of creating a renunciate order for the monks. No one had had this responsibility before me. The Master himself began increasingly to concentrate on his writings: *Autobiography of a Yogi*, and commentaries on the Bible, the Bhagavad Gita, and *The Rubaiyat of Omar Khayyam* (a true scripture, disguised as a love poem). From him I received the responsibility of helping to edit those scriptures.

His India visit became for him, in a true sense, a sort of fulcrum in his mission on earth. For these reasons, it was a very important period in his life.

Yogananda meditating on the beach at Encinitas, 1951.

 Encinitas

*B*efore leaving for India in 1935, the Master mentioned that he was interested in a property on the Pacific coast, in the town of Encinitas. On his return he was taken to that property, without being told what awaited him. And there in the southern part of town, right on the coast, a new ashram had been built for him on a high bluff overlooking the water. It was just what he had wanted. After years of campaigning around the country, followed by another year of lecturing about India under the ever-watchful gaze of the British police, and after the deep reflection that must have been inspired by the death of his guru, he was ready for a period of rest. This was to be his at the new hermitage in Encinitas.

The new construction included a beautiful structure which he called the Golden Lotus Temple. Overlooking the ocean, its beauty and tranquillity seemed to call to him, "Settle here for a time. Give all your lectures and services here. Let people come to *you* for a change, instead of forever going out to them."

And come people did. It was an unforgettable experience for everyone, to be with him in that perfect setting.

In Encinitas, also, the Master began a project he had long envisioned: a self-sustaining "world brotherhood colony," wherein not only renunciates, but married couples with children could live too; a place where schooling could be in keeping with the ideals he had inculcated at his school in Ranchi; a place where "home, job, church, school, and farm could all be in one place."

And now, married people with children did begin to arrive. The children went, for the time being, to the local public school, until he could develop a school on the colony property that would be in keeping with his ideals. Meanwhile the children, accustomed to daily energization exercises and meditation, excelled at their studies in the public school and drew unstinting praise from its headmaster. The farm thrived. The colony project seemed well on its way to success.

Alas, Americans themselves were not ready for the altruistic spirit demanded by such a place. They had only recently emerged from a devastating depression, during which most of them, perhaps, had developed an attitude described by Yogananda as, "Us four and no more." When he scolded even slightly those who were married, their partners sided with the one being scolded. It was impossible for him to discipline them as disciples.

Gradually his ideal had to be "put on ice"—not labeled as a failure, but rather as premature for the consciousness then prevailing in this country. Many years later, I was able to develop his community ideal, and also the schools he'd envisioned, as he had dreamed they would be. Ananda communities are at present eight in number, with altogether about a thousand people living in them. The Ananda communities thrive on three continents, and most of them can boast highly successful schools, also.

Yogananda's Encinitas community had not only a farm, but also businesses to sustain it financially: a papaya grove; a flower business; a hotel; a restaurant; a processing plant where carrot juice was made for the restaurant.

The Master's vision was too broad to be incorporated completely during his lifetime. It takes time for people to adjust to new ideas. Some of his disciples simply dug in their heels and, operating on the principle of passive resistance, wouldn't cooperate to bring all his ideas to fruition. The papaya grove was sold; the restaurant was closed; the hotel was sold. There was nothing Yogananda could do about it. The couples left also. The renunciates had their victory: their way of life triumphed. "We are here for God, not for worldly things" was the attitude that finally prevailed. Fortunately, here too I have been able, in my lifetime, to rescue his original concepts.

Dr. and Mrs. Lewis moved west and took up residence in an apartment over the garage at the entrance to the hermitage property. They too were a couple, but they managed well there. St. Lynn, as the Master called his most advanced disciple, lived in the main building when he was able to get away from his home in Kansas City, something he managed to do with increasing regularity.

The Master later gave St. Lynn the Indian name, *Rajarshi Janakananda*. St. Lynn, as he was still known until near the end of Yogananda's life, would often be seen lying on the grass in *samadhi* (superconscious ecstasy). At other times he would go down to the beach and out into the water, where he floated on his back and thought of himself as floating in the Spirit. The Master always appointed someone on those occasions to be down on the beach with him, lest the ocean currents sweep this foremost disciple of his out to sea.

In Encinitas, Yogananda had the leisure to work without stress on his writings. One book he wrote was commentaries on *The Rubaiyat of Omar Khayyam*. This book of poetry, widely considered to be purely a work extolling human love, is in fact a deeply mystical work. Yogananda, holding Edward FitzGerald's famous translation in his hand, suddenly had a vision in which he saw in sweeping panorama the deeper meaning of every stanza, carefully concealed behind flowery images of human passion with a view toward "passing muster" in a culture that was unfriendly to mysticism. Master didn't rely on FitzGerald, however. Somehow he was able to tune in to the original Persian, a language he didn't know.

In Australia one year, a man in the audience at a lecture of mine challenged Yogananda's interpretation of a particular passage, which he said didn't at all follow the FitzGerald translation. At this point a lady in the audience raised her hand and said, "I am from Persia, and I'm familiar with the quatrain to which this gentleman has referred. I grant that it isn't true to FitzGerald's translation, but it is completely true to the original Persian of Omar Khayyam."

This uncanny ability to communicate with, or in, languages that he didn't know appeared once more in my association with him. In 1954, I was speaking with Señora Cuaron, the wife of our center leader in Mexico City. She told me in Spanish, "I once had a one-hour interview with Master. He didn't know any Spanish, and as you can see, I don't know any English. And yet, somehow, we understood each other perfectly! I still don't know how it happened."

It was in Encinitas that Paramhansa Yogananda wrote *Autobiography of a Yogi*. It was probably here also that he wrote most, if not all, of his commentaries on the New Testament and the early part of his commentaries on the Bhagavad Gita.

Meanwhile, the ground beneath the Golden Lotus Temple was gradually being eroded by water seepage. The city could have stopped the leakage from the street, but the officials kept putting the matter off. One night, the residents in the hermitage were wakened by a horrendous crash. The temple had fallen down the steep slope toward the ocean!

Much of what would otherwise have been lost was rescued before the temple slipped even further. The swimming pool became unusable. A large portion of the charming little garden disappeared. This was a major tragedy in the Master's life, and though he took it as Divine Mother's will, it forced him once more to become outwardly active.

He now built two new churches, one in San Diego, the other in Hollywood. Of the great test of losing his Golden Lotus Temple, he wrote an anguished prayer which he later inserted in the next edition of his book, *Whispers from Eternity*:

> In disease or in health, in success or in failure,
> in poverty or in prosperity, in joy or in sorrow,
> in disaster or in safety, in life or in death,
> I stand immutably, unalterably, unshakably loyal,
> devoted, and firmly loving Thee,
> My heavenly Father, forever, forever, and forever!

I was with him years later in his third-floor interview room at Mt. Washington when a guest said to him, "What a pity you lost your Golden Lotus Temple in Encinitas!"

The Master, ever positive, declared firmly, "It was the best thing that ever happened to me!"

Paramhansa Yogananda in New York, 1926.

CHAPTER TWENTY

🪶 Church Properties

*W*hat made the loss of that temple "the best thing that ever happened" to him? It was the fact that it forced him back into the public eye. His idyll of rest and retirement had ended. He used to say that the loss of Golden Lotus Temple had resulted in the gain of two new churches.

The purchase of the San Diego temple went, as far as I know, without a hitch. The Hollywood church, however, was another story. The only property he found available was a vacant lot on Sunset Blvd. World War II was approaching its height, and restrictions were in effect which prohibited new construction. Yogananda, however, was ever highly creative. He looked on obstacles as fresh opportunities, not as permanent blocks.

"Very well," he decided, "if I can't have a new building there, I'll buy an old building, move it, and renovate it." There were no city restrictions on remodeling. Some distance away he found what can only be described as a derelict ruin, and moved it onto the property. The neighbors, understandably, were outraged, but they were powerless to stop the project. It was, to be sure, an eyesore. Gradually, however, this "ruin" was strengthened, plastered, made beautiful. Windows were still lacking, and its inventive remodeler (the Master) said, "We must have stained glass windows in this beautiful church."

People assured him that official restrictions extended to the construction of stained glass windows also.

"Never mind, we'll do as we did with the church building: We'll get *used* stained glass windows." Well, the finding of an old ruin hadn't seemed an impossibility, but the finding of used stained glass during those war years seemed far beyond anything possible.

Then, one night, the Master had a vision. He saw the stained glass windows of his dreams sitting in a nearby junkyard!

The next day he went there.

"We have no such thing here," the proprietor insisted.

"Would you let me take a look?"

"I told you, we haven't anything like that! I ought to know my own property!" The man stalked off, feeling insulted.

Yogananda then approached a black worker there. "Would you please take me to where I want to go?"

The man looked at him dourly. "Boss say no. Muss be no."

Yogananda tendered a five dollar bill.

Dubiously the man started, "Boss say . . . ," then saw what was being offered, and agreed to help. Moaning and mumbling softly to himself—an infallible sign of laziness, the Master used to say— he went where he was being led.

Yogananda took him out into the open back yard. The man, looking about him, said, "Ya see? Boss say . . ."

"Please, just take me to that pile of boards leaning against the back wall."

They went over to the spot indicated, and the man began again, "Nothing! Ya see, Boss say. . ."

"Please, just pull those things away from there." The man, moaning and muttering to himself, pulled the pile, board by board, away from the wall. Finally, beneath all the boards they found several stained glass windows. They were hanging loose, but the windows were still intact.

The "boss" could say nothing. He sold them to Yogananda for practically nothing, since they looked, in their condition and filthy with dust, like something rather to be thrown away than prized.

"We brought them in triumph to the church. Once they'd been cleaned, everyone could see that there was definitely hope for them. Then Durga fitted the glass panes in place with lead and gold leaf. Suddenly, they'd become jewels! Any church would have been proud to display them."

The Master built two pulpits, one on either side of the raised stage. The pulpit on the left, from the point of view of the congregation, was for our own ministers. The one on the right was for any visiting minister. As far as I know, no visiting minister ever spoke there, but Master called this church a "Church of All Religions."

There are several things he could have meant by this description. I myself have had to speak at congresses of all faiths, and I have found them invariably to be more or less nonproductive. If unity is ever to be achieved among the many religions in the world, then religion has to be lifted out of the category of separate and separating dogmas. Witness the many sects in Christianity alone—I might even describe them, in their long history, as warring sects, though nowadays one gets more the clicking tongue than the persecuting sword. But there is an aspect of religion that goes, or should go, far beyond mere belief.

For many centuries, people believed that the earth was flat. Belief didn't make it so: *Discovery* demonstrated at last that the world is round. The same is true of religion. *Experience* alone is what can truly unite the world's religions.

For religion deals with universal truths. The history of religion shows great masters correcting imbalances in people's understanding of those truths, but it never shows true masters disagreeing with one another.

Buddha came to get people to go beyond *karmakand*—the performance of sacred rites to please the gods and win their favor. He tried to get people to realize that salvation depends also on personal effort. He didn't, therefore, speak of God—not because he didn't believe in Him, but because he wanted people to take greater responsibility for their own spiritual development. He was saying, "Don't wallow there passively in the mud, waiting to be lifted out by divine grace: Climb out of it, yourself!" His followers, however (human nature seems not to like subtlety), concluded that he was an atheist.

Shankaracharya then came to show that there *is* a God, and that while the many gods in Hinduism are rather ideals than idols, the Supreme Spirit definitely exists; It is *Satchidananda* (Bliss). This seeming abstraction induced his followers to take a very dry approach to God. *Advaita* (non-duality) became their fundamental belief. Shankara's definition of the universe, and of man's life in it, as being only a dream caused them to look down upon devotion. Yet Shankara himself was the author of a book of devotional poems to the Divine Mother. Mankind, alas, seems capable of absorbing only one concept at a time. People denied even that man has a separate soul. Yet this was not Shankara's teaching at all.

Ramanuja then came to preach that the soul is, in fact, unique and eternal. Chaitanya came still later to preach that only individual devotion to God can bring anyone salvation. His saying was, "*Harer nam, Harer nam, Harer nam kevalam*—God's name, God's name, God's name is the *only* way!" He didn't say, however—because few were ready to hear it—that God's name is not Krishna: it is *AUM*. Indeed, it is only through union with the Cosmic Vibration that man can achieve oneness with the *Kutastha Chaitanya* (Christ consciousness) and with Brahman (the Spirit beyond creation).

Ramakrishna, in the nineteenth century, taught that God can be found in all religions. It wasn't yet time, however, for him to say, "in the *essence* of all religions, not in their formal dogmas."

Yogananda and our line of gurus, finally, came to show that all these teachings are true. Yes, man must make a supreme effort, himself, to find God. Yes, nothing here is real except as a dream, but Bliss is indeed the highest definition of God, and of what every soul, as God's manifestation, is seeking. Again, the individual soul is eternal, for in Omniscience there remains forever the memory of having once been an individual entity, and that memory will endure always. Yes, it is through devotion alone that one can, as Sri Yukteswar expressed it, set one foot before the other on the path to God. Yes, only through God's name (*AUM*) can He be found, but Yogananda also said, "Chanting is half the battle." Yes, one must respect all beliefs, and judge no one for his particular level of understanding. And, yes, sincere devotion to God is the essence of all religious teaching. One may follow any religion, but if one rises above dogmas and simply loves his Maker, one will find Him. God has no prejudices.

The truth in all religions is that we must return to our own center in Him. If people are taught to find that center outwardly, and to make a decision to reach the equator (as the outer center on a world map), those who live to the north of that central line will be told to go south, while those living to the south of it will be told to go north. Human nature being what it is, once people reach the equator they will keep on moving in their own particular directions. Those moving southward will, on crossing the equator, encounter people coming north who will tell them, "No! NO! You're supposed to go north!" And those coming southward will shout back, "No, we were told to go *south*!" And so the followers of different religions argue, and often come to blows.

Yogananda said that the future religion of the world will be Self-realization. He didn't mean "Self-Realization Fellowship, Inc." He hadn't come to establish a new Roman Catholic Church. Self-realization is a principle, not an organization. This principle, if it is true, cannot but be the underlying religion of the whole universe. Principles, and not specific applications of those principles, are universal.

This is what Yogananda meant by calling his church "a church of all religions." Few people could understand that truth then. Few, even today, have any clear idea what the phrase means.

He never invited ministers from other churches to speak at his Hollywood church, for they would have come without an understanding of what they could contribute, apart from their own dogmas.

CHAPTER TWENTY-ONE

Twentynine Palms

One of Yogananda's last acquisitions was the purchase of a place where he could be completely undisturbed by telephone calls, requests for interviews, and all the demands people make of a public figure. This place was his desert retreat at Twentynine Palms. There was his own retreat, and the monks' retreat located five miles down the same road. Here it was, at his retreat, that I got to spend the most time with him.

The monks' retreat was without electricity. I found, there, a very special aura of peace. I attributed it to the absence of electricity. For electricity generates a magnetic field. People living near high-tension lines have a greater struggle with ill health. In some ways, modern progress has complicated all our lives.

It was at his desert retreat that the Master completed several of his most important works, including his commentaries on the Bhagavad Gita. I got to work with him on these. Many years later I published his commentaries myself, under the title, *The Essence of the Bhagavad Gita*.

He was sitting one day on a little swing in the back yard of the monks' retreat, when he remarked to me, "This swing should never be sold or got rid of. It was here that I was sitting when God told me to purchase this property."

He had some of us construct a swimming pool behind his own retreat. "It will enhance the value of this property," he said, giving this as his reason for wanting the pool. In fact, however, he never used the pool (there was nowhere to drain it when it needed cleaning!), and if he didn't want that swing sold, surely he'd have felt even more strongly about ever selling his own retreat, where God would give him so many timeless scriptures! I believe he had us build that pool just to give us a chance to be near him, and to hear his dictations in the evenings. Certainly it was, for us, a priceless boon.

At the monks' retreat, I received from him a valuable teaching on *ahimsa* (harmlessness). He had said that it is better to keep forms of life under control that threaten human life. "Human beings are more highly evolved than the lower animals," he said. "Their lives are more precious. Therefore, when you see a rattlesnake, for example, near where you live, it is better to kill it than to endanger human lives."

"Sir," I asked him, "what about flies? They aren't a threat to human life. They're just a nuisance."

"Nevertheless," he replied, "in those countries where flies are allowed to proliferate, many people die from illnesses that are incurred because of the existence of those flies."

One day I found a snake just outside the back door of our monks' retreat. I felt very badly in doing so, but, remembering Master's words, I killed it with a spade, and told him what I'd done the next time he visited me there.

He said nothing. After a few minutes, however, he remarked casually, "Do you know, the women disciples are so ignorant in these matters that they actually killed a *garter* snake the other day, thinking it was a rattlesnake!"

I was horrified. Suddenly I realized that what I had killed had not been a rattlesnake, but a harmless garter snake also! I confessed my blunder to him.

"That's all right," he reassured me. Obviously, he'd known what I had done. "Don't feel badly about it." Evidently, he thought it would be worse for me to blame myself than simply to drop the matter. Then, to underscore the fact that God wouldn't hold my little sin against me, he had me bring a pot of water to the boil, and led me out into the "garden" (if one can call that sandy waste a garden!) and had me pour the hot water into an ants' nest, killing I don't know how many of the poor little creatures. This he did to erase from my heart any feeling of self-blame. Indeed, guilt over sins NOT committed is, for the impressions it leaves on the mind, almost as bad as sin itself.

For he used to tell us that the greatest of sins is to call oneself a sinner. One time—not at the desert—he described God as "eating" people. As he made that remark, he made the appropriate gesture with his right hand, as if placing food in his mouth. Death, in other words, is no great thing. It happens to every living being, and is simply a part of life. What's wrong is the *wish* to destroy life.

After finishing his commentaries on the Bhagavad Gita, he had me come over every day and work with him on the editing. We spent many hours together, during which he told me endless stories, shared innumerable teachings, and spoke so engagingly on countless matters that these memories form perhaps the most shining memories of my life.

Of his commentaries on the "Gita" he said, "Millions will find God through this book! Not just thousands—millions. I have seen it. I know.

"This isn't *my* book," he continued. "I tuned in to Beda Byasa, the author of the Gita, and asked him to write these commentaries through me."

One day I was sitting at his feet as he, seated in a chair, worked on editing the manuscript. I was thinking, "What a blessing it is, to be with him, absorbing his teachings and vibrations like this!"

After perhaps half an hour, he asked me to help him to his feet. As he stood there, and while I was still holding his hands, he looked deeply into my eyes.

"Just a bulge of the ocean!" he said quietly, reminding me to think of him as the manifestation of a divine principle, and not only as a human being. The human being would die, but the principle would live on forever.

The other monks would come out occasionally to be with him. It was wonderful to see him so equally gracious and loving to all. Never did he project himself as more important than any of us. He was our divine friend, wanting always to help us over our karmic bumps, whether large or small, which we ourselves had created in the past.

One day, Jerry Torgerson said to him, "I'm sorry I'm so stubborn, Sir."

"Well, that's all right," the Master responded, "I attract stubborn people."

One time, when a giant of a man named Norman and I were digging out the gaping pit that would become the swimming pool, our guru came out and worked beside us silently. Seeing him panting very slightly from the exertion, I said sympathetically: "It's hot work, isn't it?"

A little sternly he looked at me and replied, "It is *good* work!"

In the evenings, when I was with him alone, he would walk around the enclosure with me, holding onto my arm for balance.

Sometimes he would stand still for a moment, swaying a little. Once or twice he almost fell, and I had to catch him. On one occasion when he had almost fallen, he said to me, "I am in all bodies. It is difficult for me, sometimes, to remember which body I am supposed to keep moving!" Certainly he had demonstrated to me many times that he'd expressed the simple truth when he told me, "I know every thought you think!"

One day, a fellow disciple with the unlikely name of Daniel Boone accompanied Master and me on this daily walk. Boone was going through certain delusions at the time—mostly, sexual desire. Master was holding onto his arm as we walked. At a certain point Master said, "Hot!" He then moved his hand from Boone's arm to mine.

Boone asked him, "Sir, who was that saint you saw in vision in Encinitas?"

"Well, I don't know whom you mean," the Master answered.

"It was on the bluff overlooking the ocean."

"Well, so many come to me there, it is difficult to remember which saint, specifically, you are referring to."

I showed some surprise that he should have seen so many saints. Master then said, "Why be surprised? Wherever God is, there His saints come."

Some years later, Laurie Pratt, his chief editor, editorially changed that sentence. I had submitted this account for a book of Yogananda's sayings called, *The Master Said.* In her revised version his answer appeared as follows: "Wherever a *devotee of God* is, there His saints come."

He had distinctly, however, said "God," not, "a devotee of God." Moreover, I myself am a devotee, but I cannot claim ever in my life to have been so pestered!

In his last years, the Master no longer presented himself to others as a humble devotee. One day he said to me, "When you are one with God, you *are* God!"

This is a difficult concept for people to follow. Yet, in all the universe, only one reality exists: God. The waves of the ocean are all part of that infinite body of water. They can never separate themselves from it, for it is the ocean alone which gave them their reality.

Many of the Jewish people were unable to accept Jesus, because he uttered statements like, "My Father and I are one." It was the darkened understanding created by Kali Yuga that made it difficult for them to understand their own claim, "Hear O Israel, the Lord our God, the Lord is one." They took these words to mean that any other expression of that one God was a false god, and that no human being could ever be worthy of human devotion. They were right in claiming that God was the only Reality. They didn't realize, however, that that claim meant that the only "false god" could be something which took their awareness away from the thought of union with the Infinite Spirit: money, sex, power, fame, and the like. They didn't realize that they themselves were only dreams of that same highest Reality.

Thus Jesus on the Mount of Olives, looking down over Jerusalem, wept for his people in speaking of how they had persecuted the prophets before him, who had come in God's name. Never again would they be sent such a prophet, he said, until they had learned to say, "Blessed is he who cometh in the name of the Lord."

Idol worship, too, (as I said) is wrong only if it means worshiping things that take the mind away from God. Otherwise, to see outer images of aspects of God—of His love, for instance, or kindness, or power—as reminders of Him is an aid to devotion.

The Muslims insist on banishing all such images, but, as Guru Nanak pointed out to them, they bow to that black stone at

Mecca. Man simply finds it too difficult to worship God as a pure abstraction. The wave on the ocean, too, is only a manifestation of the ocean.

There is, generally speaking, deeper and more loving devotion to God expressed in India, where people bow to images of God, than in other countries where people try sternly to separate their own narrow definitions of Him from all others. (As if God cared about how they defined Him! It is enough for Him if they love Him, just as He loves them.)

I went through a period of doubt out at the desert. My guru had written, in his commentary on *The Rubaiyat of Omar Khayyam*, "This passage means such and such." Then, a few sentences later, he wrote, "On the other hand, it also means thus and so." It was my task to edit this true scripture (as I now consider his commentary to be). I thought at the time, "Can't he make up his mind?" Our Western training conditions us to think, as Aristotle taught, that a thing must be *either* this or that, and that it can't be both. What helped me through that test was the love I felt for my guru, not my powers of reasoning. When I went to India years later, however, I found that the people there consider it a sign of philosophical sophistication to be able to find many different, and valid, meanings in a single passage of scripture.

The great saint Chaitanya, of medieval times, was once approached by a scholar, Sarvabhauma, who thought, "This sweet young devotee does nothing but sing God's name. He needs to be more deeply schooled in philosophy." He offered to teach Chaitanya, who humbly expressed himself as more than willing to learn. Sarvabhauma then took a single passage of scripture and interpreted it in twenty-five different ways. This was a phenomenal feat, and showed great sophistication. Indeed, deep truths can be applied variously to many different situations, but it takes great wisdom to ferret out so many meanings.

Chaitanya complimented Sarvabhauma, as that scholar certainly deserved, for his depth of understanding. He then said, "Let me see if I can find any more meanings in this passage." He went on to discover some eighty others! At that point, Sarvabhauma fell at his feet and asked this much younger man to teach *him*.

Western intellectuals tend to think in absolute terms. Here again, the thinking in India is much subtler, and much deeper. When modern Western philosophers claim, with Einstein, that everything is relative, they add, "Therefore, there is no meaning in anything." This shows shallowness in their thinking. Relativity means that everything is relative to *something*! It doesn't mean nonexistence. There are relatively great truths, and relatively minor ones. A toy gun in the hands of a child raises nobody's eyebrows, but if an adult were to point even a toy gun at you and say, "Bang! You're dead!" you might worry a little, don't you think?

And if a cynic learns one of life's lessons and decides to speak and behave more kindly, wouldn't everyone applaud him even though he hadn't yet reached the level of universal, selfless kindness demonstrated by great masters like Jesus Christ, who was willing even to be crucified for the sake of others? (People speak of how greatly he suffered on the cross. He didn't really suffer at all! He was not identified with his body. The suffering he felt was for the ignorance of those who had condemned him to death. "Father," he cried, "forgive them, for they know not what they do.")

It was at Twentynine Palms that I learned the deepest teachings I was to imbibe from my guru. He used to say to me in those days, "Write that down! I don't often speak from this level of wisdom."

In fact, I found that in his later years he spoke of truth in all its vastness and subtlety, and much more impersonally than had been his wont earlier. Those disciples who had come to him many years before were not prepared for this new, and more impersonally wise, divine master.

The fact is, his early years were spent in trying to reach a large audience, and to uplift them with general spiritual teachings. In his last years, he turned from mass upliftment to training individual disciples in the higher teachings of the spiritual path. In his earlier years, he had presented himself in such a way as to give people the impression that what he had accomplished, they could accomplish easily. He belittled himself, in order to make it easier for others to identify with him. During his last years, however, he challenged his disciples to meet him on his own actual, exalted level in infinity. Disciples who had been with him for many years tended to treat "youngsters" like me with a certain condescension, saying, "You weren't close to him for many years, as we were." What they didn't realize was that physical closeness to the guru could also draw a bandage over the eyes, blinding a person to his inner greatness. Therefore the great master Sri Ramakrishna said, "One who is enlightened is like an oil lamp which casts its rays at a distance, but creates a shadow directly underneath it."

Since the true guru is not that which appears outwardly, but his inner overarching spirit, it can easily, and often does, happen that those who come to him early in his life actually develop less of an awareness of who he truly is than those who come nearer the end. Ramakrishna's closest disciples were those who came toward the end of his life.

A master often has his own mission to fulfill before he can assume the role of training disciples. Therefore, again (as I said), those who came to him early may see him more naturally in terms of that outer role. In our guru's case, he did train certain disciples from the beginning, but he showed himself to them much more from a level of his human personality.

One difference I noted in him between when he was with us and when he was with the public was that, when he was with the disciples, he spoke more about the importance of attunement with the guru than even about personal spiritual practices like Kriya Yoga. In the first chapter of the Gospel of St. John it is stated, "As many as received him, to them gave he power to become the sons of God." By "received him" much more was meant than mere belief in Jesus Christ. "Received him" meant deep inner attunement with the Savior's consciousness.

It is not possible for the ego to rise out of ego-consciousness by self-effort alone. Every struggle to do so only twists around to affirm that lesser consciousness yet again. Only by attunement with a true guru, who has himself transcended ego altogether, can one understand what it means to see things no longer with a personal bias. Without a guru, it is impossible for techniques by themselves to raise one out of this final, and most fundamental, delusion: that we are each a separate reality, distinct and separate from all others.

Indeed, yoga techniques alone cannot ensure that anyone finds God. As the Master said of Jean Haupt, a male disciple who had practiced endless kriyas, but then had left the path, "He was like a merchant: 'I've done so many kriyas. Now, Lord, You must give me so much realization.' The spiritual path is not like that. One cannot *buy* God!"

I understand, now, that every kriya should be an act of devotional self-offering. For everything comes, in the end, by God's grace. Grace is like sunlight on the side of a building. If the curtains of one room are kept closed, grace will not be able to enter there. Human effort is necessary, but that effort must be in cooperation with God's will. Such effort is indeed necessary, as a means of removing any and every ego-created obstacle to the sunlight of God's grace. Beyond that point, however, self-effort will only strengthen the ego. This is where yoga comes in, but it must be performed with an attitude of aligning one's egoic will with God's will; it must not strengthen the ego. Grace flows most powerfully in the inner presence of, and even more importantly through inner attunement with, one's guru. As the scriptures of India state, "One moment in the company of a (true) saint will be your raft over the ocean of delusion."

The Master told us the story of Draupadi, wife of Arjuna. Krishna once said to her, "Why don't you practice the yoga techniques?"

"I would like to, Master," she replied, "but how can I, when I am unable to take my mind away from you long enough to practice them?"

"Krishna then," Yogananda told us, "only smiled."

Yogananda, in his last years, used the pronoun "I" as Jesus did: not so much in reference to himself, as a human being, as in reference to the divine consciousness which dwelt within him. People like Laurie Pratt, who had come to him during the early years of his mission, were not prepared to accept, or even to understand, the impersonal aspect of his nature he presented outwardly toward the end of his life.

She actually laughed at some of his idiosyncrasies, as though perceiving him only as a human being. Once she said to me, "Every time I think I've understood him, I discover that he's beyond that." I marveled that she could even *want* to understand him—as though trying to figure him out, as one does when trying to analyze a person's motives. I know Laurie did think like that, for she tried it with me. "In everything," she said to Daya Mata, "we must try to understand, 'What are his motives?'" Our guru, at least, had no "motive," beyond a desire to help everybody. Is such freedom from motive something to be *analyzed*? Is an ocean something to be *understood*? Even I had had no motive but the desire to serve his work.

Laurie also scoffed at Master's impracticality in urging people to get together to form spiritual communities. Yet this was a basic aspect of his world mission! He said it would become a pattern of living in the future. The year I put up the first buildings at Ananda, and began to hold retreats there, Laurie Pratt (Tara, as she was then known) suffered a massive stroke, which ended two years later in her premature death. It doesn't seem unreasonable to impute that stroke to her outrage at my "presumption" in daring to think I could create a community in defiance of her edict against it.

Now, however, after more than forty years of Ananda's existence, I can say safely that Master's dream has shown itself to be a very practical reality, indeed. Most Ananda residents wouldn't live anywhere else.

Laurie Pratt's case may prove helpful to many people. Therefore let me present it as I myself have come to perceive it. I should add that, at the same time, I have always considered her a great soul.

During the Christmas meditation in 1949, our guru made several predictions for some of his closest disciples. To Laurie Pratt he said, "Laurie, for your work on *Autobiography of a Yogi*, your reward is God-realization."

I used often to wonder about that prediction, for Laurie certainly showed herself, to me, as being overweeningly egotistical and opinionated. She was my nemesis, in fact, for it was she, primarily, who engineered my ouster from SRF. I knew for a certainty that much of what she was saying in her condemnation of me went contrary to the facts, but when I said to her, "These things you've been saying just aren't true," she replied dismissively, but with great energy, "I don't want your *opinions*!"

I have some reason to believe that she had attained a very high state, spiritually. There are, however, two stages of *samadhi*, or oneness with God, as my guru explained these matters to me. The first stage is called *sabikalpa samadhi*. From this state it is still possible to fall spiritually, for one has not yet overcome ego-consciousness completely.

Laurie's example makes me think she had reached that state: the first stage of God-realization. But I see now that this state can also become the last great temptation on the spiritual path. For as the soul returns to ego-awareness from its state of oneness with God, it can either bring with it a consciousness of infinity, or use that vast consciousness as a memory to reinforce the power of the ego. Supreme, then, among these temptations would be the thought, "I know everything! I know as much, even, as my own guru!"

Therefore Yogananda once said to his chief disciple, Saint Lynn, "Never forget where your power comes from."

With a sweet smile, Saint Lynn answered, "I won't, Master. It comes from you."

The fact that Laurie took issue with her guru on what seemed to me a surprisingly large number of issues makes me think that this was exactly the temptation she was facing. Indeed, I used often to wonder why she had removed from publication several extremely important lines of his poem, "*Samadhi*." She explained to me that the difficulty had something to do with the expense of repagination, but to me it seemed that the omission of even a single line was an unwarranted "solution," considering the importance of the entire poem. The portion she removed contained, moreover, the words, "By deeper, longer, thirsty, guru-given meditation comes this celestial *samadhi*."

Having cosmic consciousness itself as a support for her ego must also have had a disequilibrating influence on her mind. This influence she certainly revealed in her reaction to something that happened once: When Disneyland first opened, she declared (from her interpretation of astrology) that it couldn't possibly succeed: It had opened on the dying moon. Years after it had become one of the outstanding financial success stories in history, I said to her, "I understand you told someone that Disneyland was bound to fail."

"Oh, *yes*! What a pity! After all the money they've poured into that place!" Her edict that it must fail contradicted the widely known facts. Does it not also suggest a hint of at least incipient madness?

One time, a committee of fifteen, of which I was a member, reached a particular decision. The decision did not, as nearly as I can recall, concern anything very important. Tara, who always spoke in exclamation marks, disagreed peremptorily.

The nun who reported our decision to her said, "But there are fifteen of us who agree on this matter."

"My dear," replied Tara, "that just makes you fifteen times as wrong!"

The story of Laurie Pratt as an individual is not my concern here. Her story as an example, however, of what looks to be a very real danger on the spiritual path must surely be worth the telling.

Years after my own ouster, Daya Mata said to me, "Master told Laurie not to practice astrology. She didn't obey him. That's why she fell." So, then, one supposes that her spiritual fall was known generally. Astrology, too, can separate its practitioners from objective reality—those, anyway, who permit the symbol to replace objective reality.

Yogananda once said to me, "Remember, you will not be safe until you have attained *nirbikalpa samadhi.*" He also told me about certain other saints who had fallen after they'd attained the lower *samadhi.*

The other, and positive, side of *sabikalpa samadhi* is that meditators normally return from it, not tempted to strengthen their egos, but eager to reject ego-consciousness altogether after the absolute bliss they experienced in cosmic consciousness. For those who have attained this high level of soul-refinement, the temptation to return to their egos no longer exists. The only thing that "tempts" them is their memory of the paradise to which they have not yet been granted full admittance.

Back to those other disciples from those early years: Some of them seemed never to have quite understood the Master's divine greatness. To them, he had a more human dimension than he revealed to me and others who came later in his life. Dr. Lewis, for example, told me that he and the Master had sometimes, as young men, wrestled together. "Did he beat you?" I asked. "Well," Doctor replied with a slight air of superiority, but quite seriously, "I let him win." I smiled, but said nothing. One who, like Krishna, could have lifted a whole mountain with his little finger would surely have found no difficulty in winning a wrestling match, had he cared to do so!

It is better, in the presence of a true man of God, to assume supreme greatness in him than to presume fallibility.

Yogananda standing with Sri Yukteswar and Richard Wright,
in Calcutta, India, mid-1930s.

 Miracles

A boatload of fishermen in Encinitas came back to shore early one afternoon. Yogananda was walking on the beach, and saw them. He didn't know the men.

"You are back early, aren't you?" he asked.

"Yeah," they replied despondently. "No fish."

"Why don't you go out one more time?"

Something in the way he'd spoken those words induced them to make one more effort. They returned from that final outing with a boat full of fish.

And so grew the legends around this strange swami who had so recently settled in their midst.

Miracles were a part of Yogananda's service to others. He seldom spoke of them, but among those whose lives were associated with his, miracles were common. Rarely did he himself even refer to them.

One day a disciple, Debi Mukerjee, was traveling by car with the Master. Suddenly the Guru said, "Stop here a moment!" The car stopped at the curb, and Yogananda, getting out, walked back a little distance to a small variety shop, which he entered. Inside he wandered about, selecting a few seemingly useless items, then took these to the front counter. When the proprietor, who was a stranger to him, had totaled the sale, she became quite excited. Then, when he paid her, she burst into tears.

"I very badly had to have just this sum of money today. Closing time was approaching, and I'd almost despaired of ever getting the amount I needed. *Thank you*, Sir! I was praying so deeply to God. It's clear to me that you are His answer to my prayer."

The Master returned to the car, got in, and left. He said nothing about the incident. "As far as I know," Debi told us later, "he never used any of the items he'd bought there."

There was another, mostly amusing miracle he performed at Twentynine Palms. This one he did tell us about, chuckling as he related the story, though this was something that happened *to* him, rather than being done *by* him.

Jerry Torgerson, about whom I wrote earlier (the one who said, "I'm sorry I'm so stubborn, Sir"), had decided to make sure the roof *never* leaked. His solution was to cover it with concrete! He had just nailed tarpaper to the top, driving many nails into the roof, when a rare storm blew over Twentynine Palms, bringing with it heavy rains. In the house, buckets, pots, bowls, cups, and every possible other container were placed around frantically to catch the water that dripped in every room. Even so, nothing was really safe.

"Water fell everywhere," Master told us later, laughing, "except in my sitting room where I dictate, and in my bedroom. As the storm ended, Divine Mother played a little joke on me: One drop fell into a waiting bucket in the living room, and another drop in my bedroom, where I was lying on my bed with a bare upper body. In that room, the drop fell onto my stomach!"

He usually attributed to the Divine Mother any miracle he performed. During his visit to India in 1935–36, he went on a steamship with a few friends to "Ganga Sagar," where the river Ganges enters the sea. There, to everyone's horror, the ship began to sink. The passengers were panic-stricken. Suddenly, the ship began to rise again in the water, and everyone was saved. The passengers, seeing this swami on board the vessel in his orange robes, expressed to him their heartfelt gratitude.

"You all did it," Yogananda replied, "by your prayers to Divine Mother."

The captain then approached him.

"Sir," he said, "can you help me? My duty as captain of this ship is to shout loudly when the need arises, but as you can see, I have a constriction in my throat that makes shouting impossible."

"Well, let's see what Divine Mother will do," replied the swami.

Later, friends who had come with the Master heard the captain bellowing his instructions loudly to the sailors.

Encinitas was the scene of other great miracles. One time a local real estate agent came to the Master and asked for help.

"My wife is very ill," he said, "and the doctors are beginning to despair of her life. Would you please come see her, and pray for her?"

"I will pray for her," the Master answered, "but God doesn't tell me to visit her at this time."

Several days later, a secretary came to the Guru and said, "I just got a phone call. The real estate agent's wife died a few minutes ago. His heart is broken."

Only at this point did Yogananda feel the inner guidance to go there. As he entered the house, he found it filled with grieving relatives and friends. When he asked to be shown to the bedroom, they made way for him. There, he asked to be left alone. He touched the woman on the forehead and over the heart. After some time, she opened her eyes, then finally smiled up at him. She was completely healed.

One evening, the Master and Durga had just returned to Mt. Washington when an unbelievably fierce wind arose. He later said, "It was a karmic build-up from World War II." He told Durga to take off one shoe, strike it on the porch, and recite a mantra (which he taught her). In a few seconds, the storm ceased altogether. So unusual was this freak wind that it was reported next day in the *Los Angeles Times*. "For some reason," the paper said, "the storm ceased unaccountably—as suddenly as it had begun."

In Encinitas, the Master was entertaining about ten guests in the living room one day when he decided to serve them carrot juice, newly produced in SRF's processing plant. He called Michael Krull (later, Brother Bhaktananda), and asked him to bring a large pitcherful of it. Michael returned to say, "I'm sorry, Sir, but the supply has become exhausted."

"Isn't there at least a little bit of it left?" the Guru inquired.

"Well, enough for perhaps a third of a teacup."

"Bring that," the Master told him, casually.

Michael brought that small amount, and poured it into a pitcher. "Perhaps," he thought, "there's enough for everyone here to have just a drop!"

He took the pitcher around. Somehow it seemed fuller after each serving. There turned out to be quite enough in it to fill a glass for everyone. None of the guests realized what had happened. Only Michael was aware that it had been a miracle.

The Master told me that really great miracles are reserved for highly advanced disciples. He told us once that Oliver Black, in Detroit, was his second most advanced disciple, after St. Lynn. Mr. Black himself told me the following story.

"I was visiting Master in Encinitas," he said. "It was raining heavily, and I was in my bedroom, glad to be out of the weather. Just then, a young monk knocked on the door, and told me that Master wanted me to go with him for a drive. I looked doubtfully out the window. The rain was falling, if anything, even harder than before.

"'Well,' I said to myself, 'if he says so. But I wonder if we'll even be able to see out the car window.'

"I put on some protective clothing, then went to the front door—only a few feet away, as you know. I went outdoors, then stopped in astonishment. The rain had ceased. The sky was blue. There was no sign even of dampness anywhere. The car and the ground around it were dry. I looked at Master in amazement.

"'For you, Oliver!' he said with a quiet smile."

What amazes me about this miracle is that it required Master somehow to change the very dream of reality for that day. Otherwise, how did every sign of that recent rainfall simply disappear?

Another miracle, far less amazing but still impressive, occurred while Norman and I were plastering the side of a garage. The structure stood near the front gate. The plaster we were using was evidently old, for it kept hardening, and I had constantly to soften it with more water.

A certain point came when I had just mixed a new load of plaster and poured it out onto the board. Just then, the Master's car drove up on its way out the gate. It stopped, and we heard Master call out to us. We came down and spoke with him.

He held us there for about half an hour, talking on a variety of subjects. We were of course delighted to be with him. In the backs of our minds, however, was the thought, "We'll have to take a sledgehammer to that plaster, when we get back to the job!"

Finally he released us about a half hour later. On returning to our work, we found, to our amazement, that the plaster was as soft as though fresh plaster had been newly poured onto the board. We had no more trouble with the plaster for the rest of that day.

Outside Boston, during Master's early years in America, Dr. Lewis and some other people were in his car, driving to participate in a spiritual gathering. It was snowing heavily, so Dr. Lewis drove very carefully. As they came to a narrow bridge, however, another car traveling in the opposite direction skidded suddenly, and stopped in a position that took up the whole road. A collision seemed certain. Just at that moment, as if a giant hand were being placed on the hood of Doctor's car, an unknown force brought the vehicle to a complete stop, only inches away from the other car.

The stopping of a vehicle happened once more that I know of. Norman was driving a large flatbed truck down the steep incline below Mt. Washington.

"At the bottom, as you know," Norman told us later, "there's a sharp corner, below which there is that steep embankment. If I'd gone over that, I'd have been a goner. But when I tried to brake for the turn, the brakes failed! I tried frantically to pump them: They wouldn't work at all! I then looked up briefly and prayed to Master, 'Is this what you want?' Suddenly, it was as though a large hand had been placed on the hood of the truck. I was able to bring the vehicle to a stop, and to curb it by turning the wheels in towards the side. All I can say is, I guess Master still wants me around!"

Jerry Torgerson—the "stubborn one"—hitchhiked one day to town. "I knew Master didn't want us to hitchhike," he said, "and I haven't done so since that day, but at the time it seemed as easy a way as any to get where I wanted to go.

"Well, a car stopped by me. Three men were in it already. No one in the car looked savory. Still, I thought, 'What can they do?' So I got in. And then I found they had no intention of going where I wanted to go. Instead, they drove me well out into the country. There was nothing I could do about it; I just sat there helplessly, praying to Master.

"Finally we came to a farmhouse. Two of the men got out; the third remained in the car to make sure I didn't get out.

"The two men knocked on the front door, waited, then knocked again. No one answered from within. The men, looking a little shaken, went on to knock on all the windows. Still, nobody answered.

"At last, very nervous, they returned to the car, took me back to the highway, pushed me out, and then drove off at high speed.

"The next Sunday I stood in line to tell Master what had happened. When I reached him, his first words to me were, 'Jerry, I *told* you not to hitchhike! Those men wanted to involve you in a crime. I had to stop the ears of everyone in that house so they wouldn't hear their accomplices knocking.'"

Another hitchhiking incident involved James Coller. He was driving a car, with another monk beside him. James stopped to pick up a hitchhiker. They drove some distance further, when he heard a voice in his ear. "Look out! He's got a knife!"

"I looked back," James told us later, "and saw the hitchhiker poised with knife, wearing an expression of unholy glee, just about to drive the knife into my friend, seated beside me.

"'Put down that knife!' I shouted loudly. The man was shaken out of his uncanny trance. I stopped the car, and he got out immediately, offering no argument."

In 1955 I visited Switzerland. A woman came to visit me from Czechoslovakia. She had known the SRF center leader in Prague, a Professor Novicky (pronounced Novitsky). Czechoslovakia was under communist rule at that time, and in people's hearts there was much fear of their government.

One day, a man came to Professor Novicky and asked for guidance in his yoga practices. The professor was in a quandary. He didn't know the man, but he didn't want to refuse help to a sincere seeker. On the other hand, if this man was a spy, Novicky would be sent to prison. The professor asked Yogananda inwardly for guidance.

"Suddenly," my informant told me, "he saw Yogananda standing behind the man. Yogananda slowly shook his head from side to side. Novicky then acted accordingly, telling the man he didn't know what he was talking about.

"Later, he learned that the man had indeed been a spy."

Some of the miracles the Master manifested were not done directly by him, but happened at a distance to disciples who had placed themselves under his guidance and protection.

He decided to construct a new building on the same grounds as the Hollywood Church, after such structures became once more legal. It was to be called India Center. Andy Anderson, the foreman in charge of the construction project, told me one day with a bewildered chuckle, "I don't know why all you yogis don't get killed on this job! Around construction work, one has to be extra careful, but you all act as though you were in your living rooms. Some of you walk about, never looking up to see if anything's falling. Others will drop a two-by-four and never look down to see if anyone is below them. I've seen with my own eyes a two-by-four drop just as another yogi was coming closer. When the board fell, at an angle certain to tip it over onto this man's head, damaging him severely, it rose up—and, so help me God!— fell the *opposite* direction!"

One day, Joe Carbone (who later took the name, Brother Bimalananda) was climbing a steep ladder up the front tower, which contained one of the golden lotuses that had been rescued from the fallen temple in Encinitas. Henry Schaufelberger (Brother Anandamoy) was twenty feet up, plastering the tower. Joe Carbone had on his shoulder another hod of plaster, which he was carrying up to Henry. The ladder, as I said, was steep, and the hod on Joseph's shoulder was very heavy. As Joe reached up to grasp the highest rung, the weight on his shoulder pulled the ladder backward. There was nothing he could do but pray. According to all the rules of logic, he should have continued his fall and crashed onto the cement twenty feet below him. It would probably have been a fatal accident. Joe did the only thing he could think of at the time. Thinking of Master, he chanted "*AUM!*" in one long breath. As he did so, the ladder came slowly upright; he was able to finish his climb. Henry said afterwards, "I saw it happen. There was no chance for him!"

Dr. Lewis once telephoned his guru, who was in Encinitas, to ask help for a friend of his. The man was in the hospital in Chicago, and was on the point of dying. Yogananda prayed. "Suddenly," the Master said, "what seemed like a bolt of lightning went out of me. That very moment a loud thunderclap resounded in the man's room. Immediately he sat up, completely cured.

"A nurse in the room witnessed it all, incredulously. 'There was no hope for the man,' she reported later. 'And suddenly, he was as well as you and I!' She was a very materialistic woman," finished the Master. This story was one he himself told, to show people that, no matter how ill they are, there is always hope of a cure by God's grace.

Some of his miracles were of prescience. I haven't told any of those here, so as not to clog the pages with a plethora of them, but this one is amusing and I thought to share it.

During the Master's early days in America, he had a student, a young man, who asked the Master to make him a monk.

"No," the Master replied. "I see a good wife in your future."

"I'll never marry," said the man.

Some days later, the man announced to him, "I've met a beautiful young woman. She's . . ."

"No," replied the Master. "She's not the one for you."

"What do you mean?" expostulated the other. "She's perfect for me! We are soulmates."

"You're setting yourself up for a disappointment," the Master concluded.

Again, some weeks later, the man returned with a long face.

"You were right!" he announced. "She took my money, then left me for another. I want to become a monk."

"Your bride has still to come," insisted the Master.

"Never! I want to be a monk."

"Let's wait and see," Yogananda replied with a smile.

Again a few weeks later the man came, laughing, "You'll never believe this, Sir. A large, fat, very plain woman has been following me around. She . . ."

"Oh, oh!" exclaimed the Master. "She feels like the right one."

"Oh *no*, Master! No! *Please* don't be right. You were right the first time; please be wrong this time."

"She feels like the right one for you."

Well, the woman turned out to have an angelic heart. The man fell deeply in love with her; they married, and settled down to a very happy marriage together.

After the Master's death, he appeared to several people in physical form. To Swami Atmananda, in India, he came and embraced him with divine love.

To Daya Mata he once appeared in physical form also. Though he didn't speak a word, he conveyed consolation to her, which she'd been needing.

Norman Paulson left the ashram to get married.

"This is the first time in many incarnations that he has fallen," the Master said. "But he is deeply devoted. He will be all right."

One night, Norman was lying in bed when the door burst open and the Master appeared by his bedside, looking very stern.

"Leave sex alone!" he ordered. Alas, Norman, who had often disobeyed him, disobeyed him again.

The Master's influence continues to this day. In the mid nineteen-eighties, a woman came to the Ananda retreat to buy something at the boutique. She saw a small, laminated photograph of someone she didn't even know. It was a picture of Yogananda, but she bought it only because she liked the face. She placed it, face out, on her bookcase. Some weeks later, she returned to Ananda, saying, "I just had to return and tell someone what happened to me.

"I've had a hard life. My first fiancé died of a terminal illness. My second was killed in a car accident. I was so heartbroken that I finally decided to kill myself. I was walking toward the door to get into my car and go drive off a high bridge.

"Suddenly that photograph expanded and became life-sized. It stood in the doorway, and wouldn't let me through. I decided at that point to drop my plan of committing suicide."

Another story (which I'll relate more fully in Chapter Thirty-One): Three weeks after Yogananda's death, his body was found to be incorrupt. This same phenomenon accompanied his incarnations as William the Great in England and Fernando el Santo in Spain. Is Yogananda's body *still* in perfect condition? The world will never know, unless and until someone breaks open the copper seal.

One day, the nuns went to his crypt to pray. Louise Royston, the elderly nun to whom I've referred before, suddenly felt him standing beside her. Distinctly, then, she heard his voice say, "I'm not in *there*!"

Let me end this chapter with a sweet story that occurred in his presence, a miracle that was brought about *for* him, but not *by* him.

He was in his living room in Encinitas with Sister Shraddha. Beside him, in a vase, stood a single rose.

A monk came to the door, and Yogananda went there to speak with him. Sister Shraddha looked casually at the rose, and saw it pointing toward the door. "But," she thought, "I could swear that, a moment ago, I saw it pointing at his chair!"

The Master returned to his armchair. Shraddha looked at the rose again somewhat absentmindedly. Wasn't it pointed at the door a moment ago? Now, it was pointing toward the chair! "Is my memory deceiving me?" she asked herself.

After a while, another monk came to the door. Again the Master went there to confer with him. This time, Shraddha made it a special point to look at the rose. It was now definitely pointing toward the door. Master came back. A few minutes later, she noticed it pointing, again, toward his chair.

"Sir," she said at last. "You have a new devotee!" She explained what she had been observing.

The Master looked at the rose, and smiled lovingly.

Paramhansa Yogananda with Rajarshi Janakananda and Dr. Lewis.

CHAPTER TWENTY-THREE

🦋 A Miscellany

*T*oward the end of October, 1949, Yogananda went north by car, accompanied by the Lewises, Mrs. Clarence Gasque (the president of another spiritual organization, the Mazdaznans), and Norman as the driver, to the city of San Francisco for the final inauguration of the United Nations. Another reason Master went there was to meet India's new prime minister, Jawaharlal Nehru.

I got the impression that he didn't think much of Nehru. In fact, I remember him using the expression *pompous!* (When I got to meet Nehru in person years later, in India, he helped me, but I could see what Master had meant.) The Master had told us also, "He went about with his nose in the air, much too proud of his position to speak warmly to anyone."

Nehru was self-declaredly anti-religion. Social reform was, to him, the only thing that would uplift the world.

I asked Master what he thought the chances were that the United Nations organization would become an effective power in the world. He didn't seem very hopeful. To my mind—and I think he felt the same—bringing in every country that wanted to belong had been a·mistake. They should have allowed only those to enter who expressed a *desire to work together* with others. Instead, Russia was given veto power, and resorted to it later, again and again, blocking any constructive effort on the part of others to work for peace. Essentially, the United Nations organization rendered itself more or less impotent from the start.

Why had they accepted Russia for admission? Russia was outspokenly interested only in itself. The United Nations could have grown strong as a harmonious unit, dedicated to the concept of world peace and harmonious cooperation, had they allowed in only those nations which were dedicated to supporting the concept. In time, they would have become strong enough—especially if they made it a point to favor one another in trading—for the other nations, one by one, to sue for entry into that smoothly working body.

Russia, and the anti-American groups that abounded in later days, would have been rendered increasingly impotent.

What happened further on that trip to San Francisco I will quote more or less verbatim from my book, *The New Path*.

Doctor Lewis returned to Mt. Washington with tales of their journey.

"The Master," Doctor told us, "asked me to join him one morning in practicing the energization exercises on the hotel porch in San Francisco." Doctor chuckled. "I nearly died of embarrassment! But what good reason can there be, after all, to feel embarrassed about doing a good thing? My self-consciousness had no worthier basis than the fact that our exercises aren't known to most people! Master decided to cure me of this false notion.

"As we were exercising, a policeman walked by on his beat. Master, affecting a guilty conscience, stepped hastily behind a pillar, and continued to exercise there. The policeman glanced at us suspiciously. I was praying for a miracle that would dematerialize me on the spot! But Master went right on exercising as though nothing had happened.

"Minutes later, the policeman returned. Again Master ducked behind the pillar. This time the policeman, his suspicions thoroughly aroused, came over to us.

"'What's going on here?' he demanded. He probably suspected us of being two crooks planning a crime.

"'Oh, *nothing*, Officer!' Master assured him with an exaggerated air of innocence. 'Nothing at all. We're just exercising. See?' To demonstrate his utter sincerity, he repeated a few movements, then smiled as if in hope of a reprieve.

"'Well,' muttered the officer, 'see that you don't get into trouble.' With massive dignity he moved on. By this time I was shaking so hard with suppressed laughter that my embarrassment was forgotten completely."

Master and his little group visited a Chinese restaurant in San Francisco. The "vegetarian" meal they'd requested had been served with bits of chicken in it. Mrs. Gasque stormed angrily into the kitchen and denounced the staff for this "outrage."

"Master," Doctor told us, "considered an uncontrolled temper a far worse 'sin' than the relatively minor one of eating chicken. 'It's not important enough to make a fuss over,' he remarked to the rest of us. Pushing the bits of meat to one side, he calmly ate the rest of his meal."

That night Master and the Lewises had adjoining hotel rooms. "Master kept the door open between us," Doctor said, "in case he wanted anything during the night. I knew he didn't really want us to sleep that night. He himself never sleeps, you know. Not, at least, in the way you and I do; he's always in superconsciousness. And he wants to break *us*, too, of too much dependence on the subconscious—'counterfeit *samadhi*,' he calls it. So I guess he saw here an opportunity for us to spend a few hours in spiritual fellowship together. We don't get many chances for that anymore, now that the work has become worldwide.

"The problem was, Mrs. Lewis and I were both tired—she, especially so. We'd been traveling all day. 'We're going to sleep,' she announced in a tone of finality. That, as far as she was concerned, was that.

"Master, however, had other ideas.

"Mrs. Lewis and I went to bed. Master lay down on his bed, apparently submissive. I was just getting relaxed, and Mrs. Lewis was beginning to drift off peacefully to sleep, when all at once Master, as though with deep relevance, made the following statement:

"'Sub gum.'

"Nothing more. Sub gum was the name of one of those Chinese dishes we'd eaten earlier that day. I smiled to myself. But Mrs. Lewis muttered with grim earnestness, 'He's *not* going to make me get up!' A few minutes passed. We were just drifting off again when suddenly, in marveling tones:

"'Sub gum *duff*!' Master pronounced the words carefully, like a child playing with unaccustomed sounds.

"Desperately Mrs. Lewis whispered, 'We're sleeping!' She turned for help to the wall.

"More minutes passed. Then, very slowly:

"'*Super* sub gum duff!' The words this time were spoken earnestly, like a child making some important discovery.

"By this time I was chuckling to myself. But though sleep was beginning to seem rather an 'impossible dream' for both of us, Mrs. Lewis was still hanging on fervently to her resolution.

"More minutes passed. And then the great discovery:

"'*Super SUBMARINE* sub gum duff!'

"Further resistance was impossible! Howling with merriment, we rose from the bed. For the remainder of the night, sleep was forgotten. We talked and laughed with Master. Gradually the conversation shifted to serious topics. We ended up speaking on spiritual subjects, then meditating. With his blessings, we felt no further need for sleep that night.

"I was telling you," Dr. Lewis continued his recollections, "that the Master never sleeps. I've found this to be true even when he snores! One day, many years ago, he was lying in his room, apparently asleep, and snoring quite loudly. I tiptoed stealthily into the room and tied a string to his big toe, doing my best to make sure he felt nothing. I should add that we were both young then. The Master was still snoring peacefully as I crept back to the door. I was about to tie the string onto the doorknob when he stopped snoring long enough to say, 'Aha!'"

It may have been on this journey, though I rather think it happened on another occasion, that the Master was traveling by car with the Lewises.

As Doctor related to us, "He told Mrs. Lewis that she had been Queen Elizabeth I of England. Certainly, in this life, she has had a certain imperious air about her. We were in the car together when Master opened the window beside him for some fresh air.

"Without a word, Mrs. Lewis reached over and closed the window again.

"The Master lowered it. Mrs. Lewis raised it. This happened several times. Master wouldn't give in. Had he done so it would have harmed her spirit of discipleship. Finally she gave in. From then on, she was always more submissive to him."

I have already written of the ego, imprisoned by self-reminding feelings, as the supreme obstacle on the spiritual path. Hence the importance of the devotee's submitting his will to the wisdom-guided will of an enlightened guru. In the above story there was, of course, no wisdom-guidance, but there was just that kind of stubborn resistance to the will of the guru which, as I have often seen, can cause even sincere disciples eventually to fall from the "straight and narrow" and return to a worldly life.

One young man came to Mt. Washington to become a monk. The Master said to me, because he'd placed me in charge of the monks, "Tell him he can find salvation in this life." I of course did so.

But, alas, this young man could not understand why he should have been given work that was far beneath his intellectual abilities. He left, owing to a lack of humility. Yet he was perfectly right in his belief that the work he'd been given was beneath his deserts. He was wrong in thinking that those abilities were important in God's eyes. The true devotee understands instinctively that the only thing that truly matters is the depth of one's love for God. This, partly, is why Jesus said (and Master endorsed his saying) that only those with a childlike spirit can find God. To be childlike, as I said earlier, does not mean to be childish. It means to have no exalted opinion of oneself, based on past accomplishments.

The best solution I know is to tell oneself firmly, "Thou, my Dearest Beloved, art the Doer of everything. I can act only as Thy instrument, and deserve no credit for anything I do."

Even devotion can lead to egotism, if one thinks, "What a great devotee I am! Few there are who love God as I do!"

One day, my guru said to me, "All of those who are with me are saints from before—or most of them."

I hoped that by "with me" he didn't mean "always close to me," since whole days would pass without my seeing him. So I asked him, "How come some of them don't seem so saintly?"

"Well," he replied, "some of them are fallen saints."

"I was thinking of myself, Sir," I said.

He answered, "It is best to have neither a superiority nor an inferiority complex." Of course, I understood fairly soon that he'd been referring to those disciples who were in tune with him. But I also realized that by "complex" he'd meant anything that entangles the ego.

Attitude is everything. It was on this point that Mrs. Lewis had needed correction. When one sees his guru daily, and is physically close to him, it is easy to develop an attitude of being special. From there, it becomes easy to see him primarily as a human being. If he is a true guru, however, he is much more than human: his humanity is only an outer shell, concealing a vast, impersonal consciousness which stretches out to Infinity.

In the Bhagavad Gita, Chapter Eleven, Krishna gives Arjuna a vision of his cosmic nature. Arjuna is overwhelmed. At last, however, he pleads, "Lord, please let me see Thee once again in Thy human form. Thy true infinite nature is more than I can grasp!" (I'm paraphrasing, of course.) Being close to the guru makes it easy for the disciple to think of the guru as fallible, like himself.

Thus, Mrs. Lewis could presume to insist on having her own way concerning that car window. Dr. Lewis was able to say, "I let him win." Tara Mata was able to laugh at what she considered Master's impracticality in wanting communities. And when, in 1958, I asked Daya Mata, our president, "When will we begin founding the communities Master envisioned?" she actually responded, "Frankly, I'm not interested."

Tara (Laurie Pratt) was his chief editor, and a good one. But her ability to handle words expertly made her once say to me, "I can make a person think exactly as I want him to, just by the careful manipulation of words." No person of integrity, surely, could be so hoodwinked. This attitude, and the fact that Master had asked her to edit his words, made her speak slightingly of his own ability with them. "Even when he was William," she told me, "he never mastered the English language." Well *of course* he didn't. English didn't even exist as a language in William's day: William helped to create it! But the Master once told us that, in a former life, he had been a poet. Presumably he was a *good* poet, too—even a famous one.

This tendency to humanize the guru is a very human failing. Yet it isn't easy to keep always in mind that one's guru is really not that personality in his little body: he is infinite.

I was struggling with these thoughts one day. Master was standing hardly two yards away from me. There, in his presence, I tried to tell myself, "He isn't really there: he's everywhere!" At that moment he came over to me and, with a slight smile, presented me with an apple! Obviously, what he *wanted* me to do was relate to him on both levels. This was not a matter to be resolved with an either/or philosophy.

He said to us once, "The spiritual path is like running a race and performing stunts along the way." Different levels of reality must be juggled constantly, and one must conscientiously, meanwhile, maintain his centerpoise!

The safest attitude is always to maintain an inner conversation with the Guru, as God. One may be serving him his meal, but in one's heart one must preserve a certain distance of complete respect.

And this, finally—as one discovers—is the attitude one should hold toward every human being on earth. It is God, God, everywhere! A man may be foolish, deluded, and in many ways even far beneath oneself, but he, too, is a part of God's dream. As the English mystic and poet William Blake said, one must learn to see "a World in a Grain of Sand . . . and Eternity in an hour." Yet one must learn also how to deal in a practical, down-to-earth way with that hour—which is to say, with passing time—and with that grain of sand, which is a symbol for the whole earth of which it is a part.

Yogananda had said to his guru, "You are the goldsmith, who deals with pure gold. I am the jeweler, who must add alloys to shape his jewelry beautifully." Sri Yukteswar had virtually driven students away by his strictness. Yogananda encouraged them with love to emerge from their darkness of egoism and fly upward in the free skies of Spirit. Was *love* that alloy? Certainly not!

But why does jewelry need alloys? The answer is that gold is a soft metal. To form it beautifully into lasting shapes, alloys are needed. Alloys are not at all introduced for the purpose of debasing the gold's value. The case is not like debasing a hard currency with lead or copper. The "alloy" that Yogananda introduced was one of cheerful, positive expectations—hope, in other words, and faith in the possibilities of a new approach to fulfillment, in an endeavor that may still, in fact, require much longer, and much more effort, than one's first expectations. By the time a person realizes how arduous the path really is, however, once one has been tempted to set foot upon it, it is to be hoped that he will have also realized that there is no viable alternative to the spiritual search.

In this country, Yogananda found that it was necessary to "lure" people to the spiritual search. He was competing with "glitzy" advertisers who promised supreme fulfillment with every bar of soap! As he said with regard to advertising, "If Wrigley's can advertise to get people to chew gum, why shouldn't I advertise to get them to chew good ideas?" Such, whether for good or ill, is human consciousness. And such, particularly, is American consciousness.

For one thing, since the typical American is hardly famous for his patience, Yogananda, in order to reach him, presented his teachings as being at least "sure-fire" in their effectiveness. And he was perfectly right. Meditation and yoga practice increase one's happiness and peace of mind within a matter of days. I have observed many visitors to Ananda retreat, for example, and have seen them in a single weekend derive benefits that are really quite striking. Lined faces become smooth. Preoccupied frowns become smiles of peace, happiness, and acceptance.

So, then, at what was Sri Yukteswar caviling? The higher purpose of the spiritual path is infinitely higher than mere peace of mind or happiness. Yogananda's mission, however, was to a whole culture. In India, people are aware of the great personal dedication needed, to find God. In America, where the most people ever hoped to achieve had always been to get to heaven after they died, and to live there still, in limitation, for all eternity, there was a need to awaken them to an understanding that the soul's true destiny is final and complete union with God. They needed to be inspired to take the first serious steps toward that union, by the practice of yoga meditation.

In Minneapolis, the Master once lectured to 5,000 people. Dr. Lewis (who was there), on seeing so many in the audience, commented to him, "Sir, this is marvelous!"

"We'll be lucky if we get five students out of this number," was the Master's calm reply.

"And that," Dr. Lewis told us many years later, "was exactly the number that signed up for his classes."

Americans like the thought of instant success. Yogananda made them think, therefore, that what he had achieved, everyone could achieve with a little sincere effort. A member of my congregation in Hollywood once lamented to me tearfully, "I've been practicing these teachings for six months, and I haven't experienced *samadhi YET*!!!" Yogananda commented favorably on the typical American attitude, which he summed up in these words: "Eventually? Eventually? Why not NOW?" And of course what he'd said was true: The spiritual path *is* easy, compared to every possible alternative. For no other way ever works except momentarily! His purpose, then, was to get people simply to set foot on the spiritual path. As he said, every step of the way brings one more joyful fulfillment. Even the tests, through which everyone must go, lead in time to ever-increasing bliss. How soon? Well, time, in eternity, doesn't really even exist!

Americans like to be independent. Therefore, Yogananda stressed first of all what they could do, themselves, to attain salvation. To those of us disciples who lived close to him, however, he stressed above all the importance of attunement with the guru.

Americans like high energy. Yogananda emphasized the importance of an energetic, positive attitude in every circumstance. The typical Hindu attitude, recommended by many present-day saints in India, is one of world-rejection. The Master, by contrast, recommended world acceptance *in the right spirit*, which leads to rejection also in the right spirit, and is not negative but means only leaving a lesser good for a greater one. Even so, however, he emphasized that the lesser "good" is really only a bubble, and worthless as a thing to be pursued. It should be enjoyed no more than bubbles are enjoyed: fleetingly, with a brief smile, but without attachment.

Americans are not fond of intricate philosophical explanations. They like everything to be simple and practical. This is, in fact, a virtue, for truth itself *is* simple. Yogananda did his best to make the ancient abstractions lucidly clear. He didn't enjoy philosophical conundrums. In Boston, during his early years in America, students at one of his classes complained that what he was giving them was too simple. Boston, of all the cities in America, is probably the most addicted to intellectuality. Yogananda then changed the tone of his lecture to a deep dissertation on Hindu philosophy. "Within fifteen minutes," he remarked later with a smile, "they were all asleep!"

Americans like to laugh. Yogananda emphasized a joyful attitude toward life, and did not concentrate, especially during his early years in America, on the very real difficulties every devotee on the spiritual path must face in the process of transforming his own darkness to light.

Americans are not fond of theories. They simply like things to work. Yogananda emphasized the practical side of religion, showing how, with the yoga techniques, they could obtain definite, demonstrable results.

Truth in this world is, like everything else, relative. For example, to make a thought clear one needs comparisons. Yet comparisons cannot ever be exact. To say that knowledge without wisdom is like a donkey loaded with gold, of which the beast has no notion of its value, is clarifying, but it is not exact. Wisdom is not gold, and man is not a donkey. Knowledge of any kind, certainly, is at least preferable to ignorance.

When Jesus Christ said, "Seek ye first the kingdom of God, and His righteousness, and all these things will be added unto you," he didn't say *how soon* they would be "added unto you"! The search for God is a lifetime job—indeed, one that requires many lifetimes! Yet, those who seek God sincerely find out very soon that, in the search, they are finding all that they ever truly wanted.

Divine protection is theirs, in fact, who live for God above all. When the atom bombs fell on Hiroshima and Nagasaki in Japan in 1945, thereby ending World War II in the Pacific, there were two religious groups, a Jesuit and a Franciscan, only blocks away from the epicenter, who were miraculously saved. Yogananda assured people that those who love God will be protected during the great tribulations he was predicting for the world in the years to come. This was a true promise, not a relative one. It is we, however, and the intensity with which we seek God, which will determine the degree to which we'll benefit from that truth.

The first part of the Master's mission was dedicated primarily to performing "quantitative" good, through public lectures and outward activities of many kinds. The last part of his life saw a gradual shift toward more "qualitative" good. Sincere disciples began coming to him, and he was able to devote himself more and more to their training.

I myself came to him in 1948, at the age of twenty-two. Strange to say, perhaps, when he put me in charge of the monks a year later, and then emphasized this responsibility more clearly in 1950 (making me understand that I must take this duty seriously), it was the first time the monks had ever been organized. I had considered it a presumption at first, especially at my young age, to intrude myself here. There was an exodus of monks during the first part of 1950, however ("Satan is testing the organization," my guru said to me), which strengthened my resolve to do all that I could to make them take our way of life seriously. Master gave me free rein, but guided my efforts from behind the scenes, helping me to understand what I must do.

"I know it is traditional," I told them, "for the monk in charge to expect obedience from those under him. I will not ask your obedience. All I will ask is your cooperation. And I, too, pledge myself to cooperate with anything that any of you asks of me, provided it doesn't go against my conscience or our monastic rule."

Though time alone can show what impact Yogananda's life had

on Western civilization, I cannot but think it will prove to have been very great. To me, Paramhansa Yogananda will appear, in time, as the guru of this Dwapara Yuga, or Age of Energy.

Paramhansa Yogananda blessing Rajarshi Janakananda,
his most highly advanced disciple.

CHAPTER TWENTY-FOUR

Kriya Yoga

*T*he ancient science of Kriya Yoga is explained in a centrally important chapter of *Autobiography of a Yogi*. I have made it a practice in the present book not to duplicate anything my guru wrote there. To leave Kriya Yoga out of this biography, however, would be to deprecate its importance.

Kriya Yoga is like a cut diamond: It has many facets. Perhaps I can present one or two more facets without intruding on what my guru wrote on this important subject. Had he himself written more on it, he would have been intruding unwarrantedly on his own life story.

Kriya Yoga was the science reintroduced into the world by Lahiri Mahasaya, in Benares. There are many kriya yogas, since *kriya* means, simply, "action." When discussing this science with people in India, it helps sometimes to specify one's meaning by saying it is the Kriya Yoga of Lahiri Mahasaya, of Benares.

Why is it called a science? For two reasons: It is universally true, and doesn't depend on any sectarian belief. Second, it produces universal, specific results. As the law of gravity is valid everywhere, so the practice of Kriya Yoga is universal in its benefits: it doesn't depend on anything outside itself. It is not a specifically "Hindu" practice: it can be practiced by anyone, anywhere. Even were some cataclysm to wipe out most of the human race and, along with that devastation, destroy every vestige of knowledge about Kriya Yoga, its basic principles would inevitably be rediscovered in time. They exist eternally in human nature itself.

Indeed, the precepts of science itself are far more fallible. Consider the example I just gave of the law of gravity: It is well known that saints in deep meditation have been observed in a state of levitation. Some of my fellow disciples claim to have seen our guru, also, in that state. I myself was not so fortunate, but I know that levitation has been witnessed so often, by thousands of people over the centuries—when it was neither expected nor wished for—that it seems futile to declare, "I refuse to believe it." Yet this utter refusal even to contemplate facts that pose a threat to one's own belief system is common, and so common among scientists themselves as to suggest that they can be just as dogmatic as any priest.

Hardly ten years pass without science making an about-face on some scientific "certainty." Even Darwinian evolution, long considered a bastion of "absolute scientific certainty," has recently begun to come under fire. I too have wondered: A leopard born without spots may be at an evolutional disadvantage in the jungle, but is a leopard not intelligent enough to know that it can always move to more open country, perhaps to the desert if its hide is tawny? Darwin, in his purely mechanistic explanation of evolution, didn't take into account the role of intelligent awareness, nor the urge for ever-greater self-awareness.

Which affords greater certainty: the reasonableness of a thing, or the actual *experience* of its truth? In this comparison, Kriya Yoga comes out with better grades than any modern scientific discovery.

Kriya is based on certain universally known (because experienced) facts of human nature. Of course, it takes one far

232 • PARAMHANSA YOGANANDA: A Biography

beyond common experience, but its fundamentals can be observed by anybody.

The Kriya science begins with the physical symptoms accompanying emotional reaction. In this reactive process, when one is delighted by, let us say, a sudden and unexpected gift, he tends instinctively to take a quick, sharp breath. When, on the contrary, one meets with a sudden setback, the automatic tendency of people is to blow the breath out. Exultation is accompanied by inhalation, followed perhaps, by a glad cry. Gloom or disappointment is accompanied by a heavy sigh.

If you think about it, you will see that your actual reality lies not in outer things, but in your inner *reaction* to them. It is because watching a beautiful sunset makes you inwardly happy that you continue watching it. If that same sunset makes any impact at all on a turtle, it may be only to waken the idle question in its mind as to whether it is something good to eat. One finds difficulty in even imagining a turtle gazing at a sunset in rapt wonder. To the turtle, the sunset must hardly even exist. What makes that sunset real for human beings is the fact that they feel enough stimulated by it to *react* to it.

So then, back to human beings: Have you ever seen someone who is happy in his outlook on life sitting with a bowed back and leaning heavily on his knees, as one observes in that statue of Rodin's, *The Thinker*? One cannot but think that that man either had a bellyache, or his thoughts were anything but pleasant! When people sit slumped over, with downcast gaze; when their mouths curve downward in a pout; when everything about them looks heavy, then we know they are not happy. We even have *downward-moving* expressions for that mood: "I feel low, heavy-hearted, downcast, depressed." But when people sit up straight, gaze naturally upward, curve their lips up in a smile, even seem somehow lighter in weight, we know they are happy. For such a mood we have *upward-moving* expressions such as, "I feel high, light-hearted, uplifted, 'on top of the world!'"

There are reasons for these universal, and universally observed, realities. The beginning of life in the body, and the place where the sperm and the ovum unite to begin that life, is in the medulla oblongata. From there, the life force moves forward to create the brain, and downward, to create the spine, before it moves outward to create the nervous system and, gradually, the rest of the body.

The spine is the channel between the brain and the body. It is our physical center, our ladder of ascent toward the Spirit. Left and right of the center of the spinal column, the *sushumna*, are two subsidiary channels—observable in fish as those tiny cords that fish-eaters will recognize, along the spine—known in the yoga techniques as the *iḍa* and the *pingala*. The energy rises toward the brain through *iḍa*, and descends from it to the base of the spine through *pingala*. These two currents accompany our emotional reactions to outward stimuli. When our energy is centered primarily in the higher centers of the spine, we are in a state of bliss. When it is centered at the base of the spine, we suffer in mental darkness.

When the energy rises in the spine through *iḍa*, it means there is a positive, accepting reaction in the mind. When the energy descends, it means there is a negative feeling of rejection.

Most people have little or no control over their reactions, for they think these are being imposed on them from without. As they learn that they can control this process, they find that they can react positively even to the most negative of outer conditions: they can speak kindly, for example, when they are slighted, or enjoy a rainy day (which previously they'd have met with a frown of regret) by telling themselves, "At least it will wash away the dust!"

Even so, people are pretty much enslaved by circumstances, until they can control the reactive process in the spine.

"Go within!" is an important maxim in every true spiritual teaching. Few people have any idea, however, of how much is actually involved in this inward-withdrawing process.

The breath in the astral body—which we have with us always, and which becomes our *outer* body after we leave behind these physical sheaths—is not in the lungs, but in the spine. In that world there is no air to breathe: one is kept alive by *energy*. Inhalation, in that body, is the upward movement of energy through *iḍa*. Exhalation is a corresponding downward movement through *pingala*.

In the physical body, the actual *cause* of our emotional reactive process is that flow of energy through *iḍa* and *pingala*. Once we can control this energy-flow, by controlling the breath, we can rise above all reactions. We can also rise above attachment and desire, for it is only our positive and negative *reactions* to the world around us that first cause attachments and desires to arise.

Kriya Yoga helps us to bring our emotional reactive process to a state of inner balance. We can enjoy the world, but our enjoyment, now, is something we give out to the world: it is not determined for us *by* the world.

Duality lies at the heart of all delusion. When we overcome in our consciousness this first "layer" of duality, which it is to say, our emotionally reactive process, not only do we become masters, to that extent, of our own selves, but we can actually *affect* outer conditions and change them for the better. People whose nature is habitually grumpy may behave toward us, now, in a friendly manner. "Coincidences" occur in our lives—we now meet the right people, at the right times. Success comes to us in situations where most people fail. Opportunities open up that would have been closed to us before. Best of all, we find ourselves inwardly at peace, no matter how the storms of emotion howl around us.

There is, in addition, another and deeper bondage to duality remaining to be overcome. It is our soul-separation from Spirit. This separation is due, in every individual, to a duality of consciousness in oneself. We are polarized by a divided energy in the spine—between the "north pole" at the top of the head, and the "south pole" at the base of the spine. Spiritual evolution itself becomes more upwardly directed, once the soul is encased in vertebrate form. Only man has the potential awareness, which develops later, that true happiness lies in higher, not in lower consciousness. A dog, by contrast, finds happiness in the stimulation of its lower awareness: when it is "happy," it wags its tail!

Man, however, has at last the opportunity, and also the divinely appointed duty, to raise his consciousness. His negative pole at the base of the spine must be united with the positive pole at the top of the head. When this union finally occurs—and the process, from our human point of view, is very slow—he becomes united not only personally, but cosmically. Self-union, inwardly, means also objective union with God.

Kriya Yoga begins its effectiveness by neutralizing the dualistic, emotionally reactive process. It then takes one's consciousness into the deep spine, the *sushumna*, and raises it up toward its true home in the *Kutastha Chaitanya* at the point between the eyebrows. From that point it moves up toward the *sahasrara* at the top of the head. When the energy in *ida* and *pingala* is neutralized and, as Yogananda put it, "Breath becomes mind," the downward flow, on reaching the base of the spine, enters the *sushumna*, and begins to flow upward unidirectionally. The duality of *ida* and *pingala* becomes the duality of inward separation of consciousness between one's own lower self and one's higher Self.

It is here, in the *sushumna*, that the innumerable "seeds" of past karma and outward tendencies are lodged, in the form of little vortices of energy and consciousness. Included here are all the karmas and tendencies developed over countless past lives, some of them even millions of years ago. One must wonder how so many memories can be stored in one little spine. But of course, space has nothing to do with it. Moreover, in the overall size of things, man is approximately halfway between the largest and the smallest object in the universe. We are prevented from reaching oneness with God by a vast number of these *vrittis*, or vortices, to which much of our subconscious energy is committed, urging us to seek fulfillment in this or that object of desire. We may, again, have set in motion in the past a tendency, let us say, to hurt others. That tendency represents an energy-flow that must be completed. Action must have its "equal and opposite" reaction. All these tendencies are lodged in the spine, virtually clogging it, and preventing the energy from flowing upward freely to the brain.

Those tendencies lodge, moreover, at their own natural level in the spine. Low desires lodge in the lower chakras; medium desires lodge in the middle-range chakras; exalted desires almost float about in the higher ones.

Kriya Yoga dissolves these vortices, releasing their imprisoned energy and consciousness to flow upward. It is a process of "nudging" them to release their hold to the bank of life's river (the spine), and enter the upward-flowing stream.

Kriya Yoga is scientific because it cooperates with Nature, and uses natural law to accomplish its objective. It is not a magical process, nor is it a ritual of self-purging by flagellation or the propitiation of higher beings.

Yogananda used to give Kriya Yoga initiations to large groups of people. I was at one initiation in which 600 people participated.

Many people in India have condemned his practice of initiating more than one person at a time. *Why?*, I wonder. Is this usage one of the "alloys" he spoke of to Sri Yukteswar? I simply don't see it. The same blessing is there. The giving of the same technique is there.

Yogananda describes in a chapter of his book named, "Two Penniless Boys in Brindaban," how a man came to him, saying that he (Mukunda) was his guru, and offered to help the two youths on that adventure to see the sights of the city. Later, near the Brindaban train station, Yogananda tells us how he initiated this man into Kriya Yoga. While giving the man this technique, Mukunda could not possibly have given it with the long, beautiful ceremony he created for devotees in the West. It had to be a very "bare bones" affair, against a backdrop of arriving and departing trains, passenger and porter activity, and all the noise and bustle commonly associated with any train station. The physical presence of the guru would be enough, one supposes, to compensate for these disadvantages, but, equally surely, a sacred ceremony in a quiet ambience, as well as in the presence of the guru, would compensate for any inconvenience in having others participating in the same ceremony in the same room. And no one, great guru or not, is likely to be willing to conduct an elaborate ceremony day after day for every seeker who comes. In Yogananda's case, certainly, he had very much to do during his lifetime besides initiating people into that sacred technique.

In my eyes, there is nothing wrong with offering the supreme gift of Kriya Yoga to groups of people in the setting of a sacred ceremony.

There are other methods for accomplishing the same ends as the Kriya Yoga of Lahiri Mahasaya. Therefore Yogananda wrote, of certain other great masters, that they "taught Kriya Yoga, or a technique very much like it." Alternate breathing through the left and right nostrils is one such similar technique, although Yogananda said that holding the hands up to the nose with the purpose of alternately closing the left and right nostrils makes it more difficult to internalize one's consciousness.

An ancient Christian technique, about which a scholar in India (Pandit Dina Nath his name was) once told me, came from the Hesychast tradition in Russia. There he had read, "As you inhale, repeating the words, 'Lord Jesus Christ,' you should feel a cool current moving up the left side of the spine; and as you finish the prayer, 'Have mercy on me!' you should feel a warm current flowing back down the right side of the spine."

Other variants are imaginable. The important thing is to centralize one's energy in the spine.

There are progressive stages of Kriya Yoga initiation. The basic initiation, however, is the one most likely to be widely practiced everywhere.

Yogananda wrote in his autobiography that this technique cannot be taught by mail, or in the pages of a book. It should be added that he did indeed offer Kriya that way for those who could not come and take it in person. As we saw in the case of Professor Novicky, in Prague, Yogananda's blessings could be received from afar. Nevertheless, the guru's touch is important for final success in this practice. As Yogananda wrote in his poem "*Samadhi,*" that inner blessing is essential on the path. The lines read: "By deeper, longer, thirsty, *guru-given* meditation comes this celestial *samadhi.*"

Yogananda said, "Jesus Christ knew, practiced, and taught Kriya Yoga, or a technique very much like it."

And finally, in Spain, there is a tradition that the last physical movement Jesus performed on the cross was to move his head left, right, and then down to his chest. Curiously, this is exactly the movement taught in a higher initiation of Kriya Yoga, which helps the yogi to leave his body consciously at death.

Paramhansa Yogananda dining with Mahatma Gandhi,
Wardha, India, 1935.

CHAPTER TWENTY-FIVE

The Eightfold Path of Patanjali

*K*riya Yoga is not purely mechanical in its results. It must be practiced with an attitude of devotional, upward aspiration. Right attitude is essential. As Swami Sri Yukteswar (whom Yogananda called a *gyanavatar*, or incarnation of wisdom) wrote in a passage I mentioned earlier of his book, *The Holy Science*, one cannot put one foot in front of the other on the spiritual path without first developing the heart's natural love.

The journey to God was defined by the ancient sage Patanjali in his *Yoga Sutras*, or aphorisms. Scholars generally have written of his book as Patanjali's "system," as though it were only one of many such systems. Paramhansa Yogananda made it clear, however, that what Patanjali described was the path everyone must follow to God; it is essential for every seeker. When, for example, Patanjali described *asana*, or posture—one of the eight stages to enlightenment—he was not referring to the teachings of Hatha Yoga, the positions of which constitute the physical aspect of India's spiritual science. Hatha Yoga is an admirable system, but it is not universally valid or even useful; for example, it cannot be practiced by the old or the infirm, whose bodies have usually lost their limberness. I myself have invented a system which emphasizes the effect of those physical postures on one's mental attitude. This system includes affirmations. I've called it, "Ananda Yoga." Hatha Yoga, however, including Ananda Yoga, is basically not a devotional practice, and is often ignored by sincere spiritual aspirants.

Asana, then, on Patanjali's eightfold path, refers simply to the ability to hold the body completely without movement, upright, and with a straight spine.

His description of the universal journey is not merely a *recommendation*. Each stage, rather, is a step along the way that every seeker must tread before proceeding any further. *Asana*, which I have named only as an example, is a stage one must attain if he would continue upward to control the inner energy. One has truly reached this stage when he can sit completely motionless for three hours at a time.

The first stages concern right attitude. They are called the *yamas* and the *niyamas: the do's* and the *don'ts* of the spiritual path. Like the commandments of Moses, the *yamas* and *niyamas* are ten in all: five *yamas*, and five *niyamas*. All ten are essential for every spiritual seeker. It is not so much a question of practicing them (though practice may be necessary) as of *attaining* them. One cannot, for example, reach a consciousness of the oneness of all life so long as he retains the slightest desire to hurt anyone. *Ahimsa* (harmlessness) is not fully attained so long as one is merely *practicing* it.

The stages of *yama* (control), then, are as follows:

1. *Ahimsa*—non-violence, or harmlessness. What Patanjali meant here was not to *wish* harm to any creature. The Roman Catholics caution one against "scrupulosity": getting so entangled in a principle that one can hardly do anything else. The Jain sect in India exemplifies scrupulosity. They go

to such lengths in their practice of *ahimsa* that they scruti-nize the ground to avoid stepping on any tiny ant or beetle; they wear masks over their faces to avoid inhaling any germs; they boil their water before drinking it, to make sure they don't (personally) kill any germs or other tiny creatures in swallowing it. It would be easy to make a comedy of some of these practices. (Should they, one might ask, proceed on their bellies, their faces close to the ground, to make sure they aren't killing anything by squashing it? Would it not be better to wear metal hoods over their heads, to make sure that no germs get around those masks? And should they first advertise for people willing to take on the bad karma of kill-ing germs by boiling the water for them? What about boiling their own water: Don't they kill germs in the act of boiling?)

My guru laughed at the practice of some Buddhists, also, who justify their eating of meat by saying, "*We* didn't kill the animal ourselves! We didn't even buy the meat. We sent servants to the marketplace to buy it for us."

To such casuistry is one driven when he seeks to apply the principle of *ahimsa* too exactly in this world. What Pa-tanjali meant, my guru explained (quoting his own guru, Sri Yukteswar), was the removal of any *desire* to harm (and not only to kill) another living being. Sarcasm, for example, may hurt another person deeply. Even the mere *wish* to harm another person, whether physically, mentally, or spiritually, is self-damaging, for it creates disharmonious vibrations in the heart, and undermines a person's inner happiness. In the last analysis, what one must avoid is anything that will damage one's own relationship to the Highest Reality in the universe, God, and to one's own bliss-nature. For the ultimate truth on the spiritual path is that all manifested existence is part of the Bliss-consciousness of God.

When one has developed *ahimsa* to perfection, Patanjali tells us, wild beasts (and, one presumes, their equivalent among human beings) become tame in one's presence.

2. *Satya*—truthfulness. This quality is put among the *yamas*—the attitudes in which restraint should be practiced—because if one restrains oneself from wishing that things were other than they are, one will automatically tell the truth. It is important to remember, though, that truth is that aspect of reality which is most closely in tune with the harmony of the universe. Truth, in other words, is always beneficial.

If I visited a friend in the hospital and told him, "You look *terrible*!" my words might be true, but they might also push him over the edge into death. Far better would it be to say, "Well, well, I've seen you look better, but I do believe you can improve." Don't tell a lie, in other words, but speak whatever truth you can in such a way as to help him to get better, or to be at peace.

There is a substantial difference between truth and fact. The criterion is not a hypocritical desire to be thought of approvingly, but a sincere desire to bring everything into closer attunement with cosmic truth.

Patanjali wrote that when one achieves perfection in this quality, he can achieve the fruits of action without even acting.

3. *Asteya*—non-covetousness. If ever the desire arises in your mind to possess something that belongs to someone else, mentally *give* it to him—as though your desire for it were enough to have made it yours already. Now, bestow it on him again with a free heart.

To covet anything is to form a link with it which can tie you down. It is like the ropes that tie a balloon to the ground. Desires are self-limiting, and self-imprisoning.

When this quality is perfected, one finds that wealth comes to him in any abundance that he needs.

4. *Brahmacharya*—sexual self-restraint, primarily, though literally it means to be schooled in the ways of Brahma. If one aspires to the spiritual heights, sexual desire is like a ball and chain around his ankles. It greatly impedes him in any effort he makes to advance, spiritually or in any other field. Not only does it keep the energy focused in the lower chakras, but, if indulged in, it greatly wastes a person's energy—especially that of the man. To overcome sexual desire is like untying a hawk and letting it soar freely into the sky.

Those, on the other hand, who claim to find inner freedom by indulging their sexual desires find, in time, that it is like the false freedom of a fish which escapes the fisherman's net only to flop out onto the dry deck of his boat.

The benefit of *brahmacharya* is, Patanjali says, the accession of great physical and mental stamina, vigor, and endurance.

5. *Aparigraha*—non-possessiveness. True inner freedom can be experienced only when one has overcome attachment to everything, even to his own body. His so-called possessions are his only on loan: he should be mentally prepared to relinquish them at a moment's notice, as my guru did his motorcycle when he encountered someone else who liked it.

A good practice for everyone would be to give away freely anything that another person covets, or even likes excessively. But if it is something used in the service of God—an expensive computer, for instance—one could always say to someone who wished for something like it, "It isn't mine to give away." My own practice has long been to give away as much as I can, if things are desired by others. And if the other person expresses a desire to pay for something, I reply, "I am not a merchant! I am happy to share it with you freely."

Patanjali taught that perfection in this quality enables one to remember his past incarnations. When one is no longer even slightly attached to his present body, in other words, he becomes aware of the thread of rebirth that follows him from body to body.

Among the five *niyamas*, or "do's" on the spiritual path, the first is:

1. *Saucha*—cleanliness. Cleanliness of the body helps one, when meditating, to rise above body-consciousness. Cleanliness of the mind signifies not dwelling mentally on anything that may pull the mind downward to body-consciousness. Cleanliness of heart signifies having no desire for anything but God.

Jesus Christ said, "Blessed are the pure in heart, for they shall see God."

Perfection in this quality, Patanjali taught, brings inner freedom from the body, and a disinclination for its natural pleasures.

2. *Santosha*—contentment. Yudhisthira, in the *Mahabharata*, calls contentment "the supreme virtue." As Sri Yukteswar said, of money, "Be comfortable within your purse." Contentment means to realize in yourself that nothing in the world can ever *make* you happy: You *are* happiness; you *are* bliss! Everything that you can ever need rests in your own inner Self!

This practice, when perfected, brings the consciousness of divine bliss in everything one does.

3. *Tapasya*—austerity. This means self-restraint, not self-flag-ellation or self-deprivation. In the movie *Sant Dnyaneshwar*, *tapasya* is translated in the subtitle to mean, "devotion"—an inaccurate rendition, but valid in the sense that the word *tapas* means an upwardly directed flow of energy. Everything one does should help to direct one's energy upward, toward God.

Perfection in *tapasya* leads to the development of psychic and spiritual powers.

4. *Swadhyaya*—self-study, or introspection. Most books translate this word to mean "study of the scriptures," but whereas it is true that this study can certainly aid one in un-derstanding his own higher destiny, the word, *swa*, means, literally, the higher Self. One who makes it a practice always to analyze his own motives, to catch any self-justification in the bud, and to accept always with an open mind the possibility that he has been wrong, will direct his footsteps unfailingly toward the ultimate Goal. Such a person will act always without personal motive, to please God.

Perfection in *swadhyaya* bestows on one the power to commune with beings in the higher realms, and to receive help from them.

5. *Ishwarapranidhana*—worship of the Supreme Self. Ish-wara, Lord of the Universe, is the true Self behind everything. Every action one performs should be a conscious act of wor-ship, a divine offering on the altar of that Supreme Perfection.

Patanjali wrote that when one becomes perfect in this *ni-yama*, he enters the ray of upward-moving, divine love which leads to oneness with the Lord Himself.

Asana (the third stage)—posture: the ability, as I said earlier, to sit unmoving with a straight spine for long periods of time. *Asana* makes it possible to rise above body-consciousness.

Pranayama (fourth stage)—control of the energy in the body. Many texts translate this word to signify breath control, but although there is a connection between the breath and the flow of energy, the truer meaning of *prana is* energy, for the control of which the breath is used. The important thing, here, is to have reached a stage where the energy can be withdrawn from what Yogananda called the "sense-telephones." Only in this state of withdrawal is it possible to free oneself completely from outer distractions.

Pratyahara (fifth stage)—interiorization of the mind. One must withdraw not only the energy, but also the thoughts and the attention, from all distractions. Only when one has reached this point can the seeker begin seriously to meditate.

Dharana (sixth stage)—concentration. When one has withdrawn his energy and consciousness from the world around him, he becomes able to focus it one-pointedly. Concentration is only the beginning. One must then be able to direct his concentration one-pointedly toward God in one of His eight fundamental aspects: Peace, Calmness (the positive aspect of Peace), Power, Light, Sound, Love, Wisdom, and Bliss.

Dhyana (seventh stage)—steadfast meditation on God in one of those eight aspects.

Samadhi (eighth stage)—oneness; complete absorption in the Infinite. *Samadhi* comes in two stages: *sabikalpa (sampragyata)* and *nirbikalpa (asampragyata)*. The first stage is conditional and temporary. The ego still remains subconsciously present, and returns to one in full force after one leaves his meditation.

This first stage, then, constitutes not so much a fulfillment as a serious temptation. It is by no means unheard of for devotees to fall back into delusion after reaching this point. For not only can the ego come back with the still-greater force of eager self-affirmation, backed by its memory of oneness with the whole universe, but it can easily imagine itself to need no further help or guidance. "I'm as great as my guru!" the devotee may tell himself. "I am omniscient and infallible. I am supreme!"

Yes, from these thoughts it is certainly possible to fall again. To focus everything on one's little self is to fall from God.

In what way can this teaching be incorporated with the Buddhist teaching of *nirvana*? *Nirvana* is also a yogic teaching. Paramhansa Yogananda explained it as the cessation of all thought, all human feeling—a state, indeed, of utter nothingness. Into that void, when it is attained, rush the great waters of oceanic bliss.

"You will not be safe," my guru told me, "until you've attained *nirbikalpa samadhi*."

Patanjali's "system" is called, in Sanskrit, *Ashtanga*, which literally means, not eightfold, but "eight limbed," *anga* meaning "limbed." His explanation is most easily understood as a series of progressive stages. Understood more deeply, however, to call these stages "limbs" suggests a fuller meaning. For, as we have our own four limbs with us constantly, so the eight "limbs," all the way from *ahimsa* to *samadhi*, are interdependent. As *samadhi* cannot be perfected until one achieves perfection in all the *yamas* and *niyamas*, so these, too, for final perfection demand the state of *samadhi*. *Ahimsa*, for example, cannot be fully achieved until one actually *realizes* his oneness with all life.

Truthfulness, similarly, cannot be fully achieved until one has realized his oneness with Cosmic Truth.

Brahmacharya demands, for its final perfection, that one rise out of body- and ego-consciousness altogether. This state is accomplished only in *nirbikalpa samadhi*.

Again, *santosha* (contentment) becomes a permanent virtue only when one achieves Supreme Bliss. Otherwise, it cannot but be to some extent only a practice, one that will be buffeted constantly by the fierce storms of past karma.

And *swadhyaya* (introspection) will be repeatedly befogged by the heavy clouds of *maya* (delusion), which can make even the most conscientious seeker uncertain, sometimes, as to which is the best course of action.

All the *yamas* and *niyamas*, similarly, demand perfection in the ability to perfect also the limbs of *asana*, *pranayama*, and the rest; *asana* cannot be fully perfected without *pranayama*; *pranayama* cannot be fully perfected without aid from the higher stages.

And none of the eight "limbs" can be perfected without realizing that nothing, finally, can be "achieved": We are all perfect, already, in Infinity. We have only to realize what we have always had, though we have forgotten it: We have always been but *"angas"* of the Omnipresent, Omniscient, Ever-new state of perfect Bliss: Satchidananda. There is no other reality in existence!

Christmas at Mt. Washington, 1949: Rajarshi Janakananda, Mrs. Lewis, the author, Paramhansa Yogananda, and Dr. Lewis.

CHAPTER TWENTY-SIX

His Later Years

Paramhansa Yogananda's *Autobiography of a Yogi* was published in 1946. This occasion was a "benchmark" in his life. A work many years in the writing, it has sold, to date, millions of copies, and has made people all over the world aware of potentials within themselves of which they've never before even dreamed.

During these later years, the Master divided his time between the churches in San Diego and Hollywood, speaking at each on alternate Sundays. He was able, now, to give more personal attention to his followers. More and more they found themselves thrilled and inspired by his wit and wisdom. No longer was he lecturing to the huge crowds of his "campaign" days. Those who came to him now were more eager to *practice* his teachings, and not only to marvel at them.

He devoted much time, also, to giving private interviews. And he began passing responsibilities over to his disciples.

Michael Krull (later, Brother Bhaktananda) had come to him in the late 1930s. Michael was a simple, sincere soul of whom our guru once remarked, "He has no ego." In meditation, Michael used to pray, "I love you, Guru!" The Master saw him walking one day in the garden, and said to him softly, "And I love you, too!"

Michael was able, by his sincerity, to inspire many younger men who came to the Guru for training.

Bernard also came in the late 1930s. He was highly intelligent and capable. The Master gave him many responsibilities, including that of teaching in the churches. Yogananda also had the young man perform demonstrations of yogic feats before audiences: driving a needle through his throat without the throat bleeding—things like that. Bernard wrote articles on Hatha Yoga for the SRF magazine. He himself could do the postures well, but he didn't pose for them, for his own body was twisted: he had double curvature of the spine, and only one lung. Still, with the Master's grace his endurance was phenomenal.

In later years, Bernard became increasingly arrogant. With a falling-off of attunement owing to the pride he displayed in his own abilities, he began to worry about his poor health. The Master supported him in his desire to make his quarters more comfortable and convenient. Master said to us one day, however, "Look at Bernard. As long as he was in tune, he could do *anything*! But he is losing that attunement, and now, though I do everything I can to support his concern for his health, nothing seems to work. His body keeps growing weaker and weaker."

Shortly after Bernard came, a group of his former friends visited Encinitas to capture him and force him once more to join them in their worldly way of life. In their ego-centered view, Bernard was being hypnotized by this "oriental fanatic." Before their arrival, however, the Master sent Bernard on an urgent errand to Mt. Washington, an errand that required him to remain there for two days.

Bernard was important in the work, but his pride led him increasingly to challenge his guru. It was painful to behold: "Well, Master, as I keep pointing out to you, that idea just isn't practical!"

Finally the Master said to him calmly, "For years I have listened to you shouting at me. Now I have only this to say: I am not impressed."

Master's way of doing things did seem, sometimes, to defy common sense. But what he did always worked out just as he'd intended. Bernard's attitude of infallibility and of possessing all the answers was a good lesson to the rest of us, for he was often wrong. This world is not a piece of clockwork: It is a flowing river. It cannot be chopped into clear-cut, logical pieces: it must be understood flowingly, by the heart.

During this period of the Master's life, many good disciples began coming to him. He often quoted the words of Jesus, "The last shall be first, and many that are first shall be last." He saw his disciples in terms of countless incarnations, not of their relationship to him only in this one lifetime. Latecomers were needed, to ensure that his living message be not only continued for as long as possible after his death, but fulfilled.

Bernard did not remain in the work. In his later years, motivated by the egotism he had always shown, he actually turned against the Master. I tried, in the only encounter I had with him years later, to bring him back to the path. He seemed open, and I hope I succeeded, for he died only a few months later.

Yogananda placed Dr. Lewis in charge of Encinitas. Faye Wright he placed in charge of Mt. Washington. Bernard he placed in charge of the Hollywood Church. Dr. Lloyd Kennell he made the alternate minister in San Diego.

Increasingly, the Master turned his mind toward writing as the best means of reaching large numbers of people. During his earlier years in America, he had had editors who considered it their job to correct not only his grammar, but even his teachings! They were people who had already been exposed to metaphysical thought, and who believed they knew the truth in all its subtleties. They were quite unprepared for his much deeper insights, and thought, "He *couldn't* have meant that. He must have meant to say . . ." Really, it is not always easy to separate the wheat from the chaff in some of the writings that appeared in his name in the early magazines. One editor he complained to me about was Virginia Scott.

Miss Scott had been (and still was, as nearly as I could tell) a Rosicrucian; her editing revealed a leaning in that direction. Yogananda had to keep correcting her editorial submissions.

"She would complain at my corrections, and would put things back as she had changed them. When I changed them once again to what I wanted, days of silence followed, then a long letter would come from her, single spaced, pages long, explaining in exhaustive detail how I had misunderstood her!"

Miss Scott was also much taken by the modern fascination with overcoming sexual inhibitions. I think she must have been greatly affected by the writings of D.H. Lawrence.

"I said to her once," the Master told me, "'If I wanted to, I could write a beautiful poem about a bowel movement! But why write about such an unworthy subject? Why don't you leave your erotic—*neurotic*—friends and mix more with devotees?'" Such, alas, was the caliber of editors who came to him, until Laurie Pratt's arrival.

How could Miss Scott have been drawn to such "erotic/neurotic" companions, and to such lower-chakra poetry? It all depends on something Yogananda wrote in his commentaries on the Bhagavad Gita. There we read that the whole universe is an infinitely varied mixture of the three *gunas*, or qualities: *tamas*, *rajas*, and *sattwa*: darkening, activating, and elevating.

The Master stated that entire galaxies manifest primarily one or another of these *gunas*. In our own Milky Way galaxy, for example, the middle quality, *rajoguna*, predominates. Restless activity pervades the entire galaxy. Some galaxies are predominantly sattwic. There, people live together in peace and harmony, in close contact with the astral world, and grouped together in little, happy villages where people's thoughts are all directed toward spiritual progress.

Other galaxies exist where agitation and unrest reign supreme. Carnivores roam about freely in untamed jungles. Fear pervades every heart, and ruthless competition is a reality that no one can imagine doing without.

My guru said that disease epidemics on our own planet are invasions of fallen souls, as germs, drawn here by earth's karma from their tamasic galaxies, in order to receive punishment for their heavy sins by earthly medicines. What a different view his words give of reality from what we have learned in school! Even the thought of those great clouds of germs coming to our planet from distant galaxies simply boggles the mind.

Miss Scott manifested strongly the downward movement of rajoguna in human nature. Rajoguna, the activating quality, is divided in two directions: upward as *rajosattwa*, and downward as *rajotamas*. In fact there is only duality. Rajoguna, the middle quality, represents movement between the two opposites of duality: Tamas and Sattwa.

Yogananda's mission to the West, which was accomplished by his years in America, addressed the rajoguna which he found predominant here, and raised it notably from rajotamas to the level of rajosattwa. There is still plenty of darkness in this country, but he helped to divert much of the downward-moving energy here, and to redirect it upward.

In the last years of his life, however, he concentrated more on those people in whom sattwa guna, or at least rajosattwa, was predominant.

In late July, 1948, Yogananda had an extraordinary *samadhi*. It lasted 48 hours. During this period, the Divine Mother took him all around the universe. A few of the disciples were present. Sometimes he would speak to the Mother out loud; then She would answer, using his voice. When he spoke, the vocal tone was deep, but when She spoke it was in a heavenly, feminine tone of voice.

At one point he exclaimed delightedly, "Oh, *now* I see how You do it!" She was showing him the mysteries of cosmic Creation. Dr. Lewis told me—for I hadn't yet come, then; I came less than two months later—that the Divine Mother had told him his divine experience on this occasion had been unique. Krishna too, in the Bhagavad Gita, said that the divine vision he had just granted his disciple Arjuna was unique. Interesting, isn't it, that the same soul in two bodies had been given such unusual revelations?

Using his voice, but speaking in feminine tones, the Divine Mother said to him, "I sent you many bad ones in the beginning, but now I am sending you angels, and whoever harms them I shall smite!"

From the time of this vision, it may be said that the last phase of his life began. The majority of his long-destined disciples came. He shifted his emphasis on himself as only a channel for God's Infinite Bliss and Wisdom to using the pronoun "I" as Jesus often did, to signify his oneness with the infinity of Christ consciousness.

To the monks Yogananda said once, "It is better to seek God primarily for His Bliss, only secondly for His Love. For in love there can come personal, inward-drawing or egoic thoughts. Sri Yukteswar was a saint of wisdom, but I myself have been an expression primarily of bliss."

Again, only a few years later, at the funeral service of Sister Gyanamata, he said, "Her way was through wisdom. My path has been through bliss."

There is a further story connected with that funeral. He had told us that he himself was the last of the gurus. I understood him to mean, "of our line of gurus." Other disciples have insisted that never again will there be any gurus in this line—that Yogananda will remain the guru in perpetuity.

To me, however, he said once, "There must be at least one physical contact in this lifetime with the guru, for him truly to bring you to God." He also said to me, "One must free at least six others before he can achieve liberation himself." Does this mean, then, that no one who comes to him since he left his body will find God? This, surely, would be a ridiculous interpretation.

"In Bengal during my father's time," my guru told me, "a maharaja was excavating a lake on his property. Deep beneath the mud at the bottom of the lake, the workers came upon three yogis seated in deep meditation. They were apparently still alive. My father was somehow connected to this event, and knew its details personally. Engineers estimated that those yogis had been there for at least three hundred years. The maharaja insisted on bringing them back to outward awareness, and, cruelly, had hot pokers applied to their bodies. At length they opened their eyes.

"'Why did you bring us back?' they asked. 'We were very near liberation. Now we must leave these bodies and take birth again. God will punish you for the sin you've committed!'

"In fact, within a very short time the maharaja and his entire family died. However," my guru explained, "the Divine Mother had not wanted those men to attain liberation without helping others also."

I then asked him, "How many souls must one liberate?"

"Six," was his answer.

Back, then, to Sister Gyanamata: He said, "I watched her sink into that watchful state"—in other words, of complete liberation.

I, mindful of the statement others were making to the effect that there would be no more gurus in his work, thought, "But how could she have reached liberation, since she had no disciples?"

Yogananda, catching my thought, replied, "She *had* disciples." Who would those disciples have been? Undoubtedly, some of them were living in the ashram at present as Master's disciples. Certainly there were persons there to whom she gave special help.

"Once you achieve final liberation," he told us, "seven generations of your family, backward and forward, receive their freedom also."

In 1960, during the four days I spent with Sri Rama Yogi (that fully liberated disciple of Ramana Maharshi's whom I mentioned earlier), I asked him, "If all the family members of a fully liberated master achieve liberation through his efforts, one cannot but ask: Is it quite fair? How can one achieve freedom without any effort at all? And if family members achieve it, will *their* families, too—for example their in-laws—be liberated? I can see this web spinning itself out to infinity!"

Sri Rama Yogi smiled. "No, that isn't what happens. Rather, it's like when one person is made the emperor: it isn't that others, too, become emperor along with him. Rather, his entire family is raised to a higher position in society. Obviously, only one man can be the emperor."

"And how close would that relationship have to be?" I asked.

"Most saints are not married. The relationship, then would include cousins, nieces, nephews, and also more distant relatives who were in tune with him."

Relatives who disapprove of the saint's eccentric-seeming way of life will nevertheless come under an umbrella of extraordinary protection, even if they don't attain full liberation. Therefore it has been a belief in Tibet that at least one member of every family should become a renunciate.

Dr. Lewis, Yogananda's first Kriya Yoga disciple in America, once asked him, "If a master's direct family are granted their spiritual freedom, what about the disciples?"

"Oh, they come first!" was the reply.

Yogananda said, during the Christmas meditation in 1948, "Of those present here this evening, there will be a few *siddhas* (perfected beings), and quite a few *jivan muktas* (those who have achieved oneness with God, but who still have some karma from past lives to expiate)."

Let me tell here the story of one who Master said would be liberated in this life. It was James Coller, of hamburger fame! A simple soul, Master once said of him, "He is like a mouthful of hot molasses: too hot to swallow, but too sticky to spit out!"

James himself told us the story of his first public lecture. The topic had been, "What Yoga Can Do for You."

"I was extremely nervous. Someone had told me that a hot bath would help, so I took a long, hot bath—very hot, and *very* long! By the time I came out of it, I was like a limp rag.

"I then gave my lecture. In five minutes, I had said everything I could think of to say. I next had Horace Gray take up the collection. He's spastic, you know. As he staggered from row to row, leaning on the backs of chairs to keep from falling, I thought, 'And there's my example of what yoga can do for you!'

"The audience left without uttering a word. There was nothing to be said. This was my maiden voyage!"

A few years later, when Yogananda acquired a property about which I have yet to write—the SRF Lake Shrine—a man living there made it a practice of using a BB gun to frighten away the ducks. He didn't try to hit them; only to frighten them. Master told us, "James clicked his tongue disapprovingly. Later, however, he picked up the gun to look at it. Casually he pulled the trigger, in no way meaning to hit anything, but a moment later a duck lay on the water, dead! And just imagine—such is his commotion karma!—the police got word that someone was shooting ducks, and came to investigate James!

"Yet he will find his freedom in this life! I don't know how, but Divine Mother says so, so it must be true."

Señor Cuaron, the center leader in Mexico City, was very close to Master. How close he was to liberation I cannot say, but this story about him shows how a true guru remains ever loyal to his disciples until his "job" is finished, and they find God. And even then, a true disciple remains the guru's loyal supporter throughout eternity.

Yogananda once said to Señor Cuaron: "I lost sight of you for a few lifetimes, but now that I've found you, I will never lose you again."

From time to time, Cuaron would say to him, "Don't forget your promise, Sir!"

"I won't," the Master always replied. "I will never lose you again."

The Master's protection, too, was always with his disciples. One time, Cuaron, who had accepted the job of center leader in Mexico's capital, had no paying job, and felt that he needed more money. When an offer came for a very lucrative job in Matamoros, he wrote the Master "just as a matter of form."

He told me the sequel: "Back came an urgent telegram: 'Absolutely not! Have nothing to do with that offer.' No explanation accompanied his command. I was a bit troubled, but I thought, 'Oh well, he knows I could use a job, but he's my guru, so I'll accept his command.'

"A very few days later, the news came out: The company that had wanted to employ me had been closed down for fraud. The person who held the job I was to have was sent to prison. Master had saved me from a great disaster!"

Swami Shankara, the great exponent of *advaita*, once wrote, "There is no blessing in the three worlds (the physical, astral, and causal universes) to compare with that of having a true guru."

Paramhansa Yogananda with Ananda Moyi Ma (painting by
Yogananda's brother, Sananda Ghosh).

CHAPTER TWENTY-SEVEN

Magnetism

I ended the last chapter with a quote from Swami Shankara.
It would be interesting to begin this chapter with a story my
guru told about that master. So much did Yogananda know about
him, indeed, that I have sometimes wondered whether he wasn't
himself Swami Shankara in a former life.

Babaji, many centuries ago, lived in a house in Benares. He had
a servant. When Swami Shankara came to that city, his renown
preceded him as an astrologer. Babaji's servant went to him for a
reading. When he returned, he was trembling.

"What's the matter?" Babaji asked him.

"Swami Shankara says I will die tonight!"

"Go back to him," said Babaji, "and tell him that it won't
happen."

The servant returned to Shankara with Babaji's message. That
saint replied, "This karma is so strong that, if your master can
prevent its coming to fruition, I will go to him and become his
disciple!"

That night, Babaji extended himself on the body of the quaking
man. A huge storm suddenly swept over the area. Whole trees were

uplifted. Lightning struck repeatedly all around the house. When morning came, however, the man was still alive. He went back to Swami Shankara, who, on seeing him, hurried back with him and prostrated himself before Babaji. It was then that he asked for initiation, and Babaji taught him Kriya Yoga.

How could past karma be so exacting in its demands as to make Shankara so certain of that man's fate? How did Babaji protect his servant? What drew the servant to visit Swami Shankara? (The latter's reputation, yes, but it may have been something more.) What drew Shankara to the feet of Babaji? The fact of that servant's still being alive—all right—but Shankara was a master. It must have been more than those mere facts that led him, seemingly out of the blue, to accept Babaji as his guru.

Some of the above questions may seem trivial, and easily answerable by that convenient catchall word, "coincidence." I ask them because the preceding story suggested them as a possible bridge to my next subject. For one thing is very certain: Many events in our lives cannot be explained away as mere coincidences. One of these puzzles is the mystery of ongoing discipleship. A saying in the Hindu scriptures goes, "When the disciple is ready, the guru appears." One need not search the wide world for his guru. Nor need the guru necessarily be seeking a disciple, consciously. But even if the seeker will sit in his meditation room and call deeply for help, when the time comes, that meeting will occur.

Jerry Torgerson met an old man in a shop in Los Angeles who told him the following strange story:

"When I was young," the old man said, "I decided to seek God. I rented a small cabin in the mountains, and did my best there to meditate deeply.

"One day, I returned from a short walk to find an old man, from India, seated outside my cabin. 'I am your guru,' he said. 'I have come to help you.' We went inside, and he taught me certain yoga techniques. From then on, I went deeper and deeper into the Self. My guru visited me from time to time, and he continued his instructions.

"One day I returned again from a walk, but this time, when I entered the cabin, I found there, waiting for me, the most beautiful woman I had ever seen. We became lovers. Alas! after that first encounter, she disappeared! My guru stopped coming. And I found myself a prisoner of this most powerful of delusions. All I have left now is the wonderful, aching memory of my youthful search for God!"

What is the secret behind all the incredible-seeming occurrences in our lives? There is one all-uniting word for it: *magnetism.*

There was a disciple of Sri Yukteswar's who, though sincere in his commitment to celibacy, could not get out of his mind the desire for a perfect mate. One day, his guru said to him, "Today, God is going to do something for you."

They went on a short train journey. While their train was stopping briefly at a station, another train, traveling in the opposite direction, pulled in beside them and stopped. As that train came to a halt, Sri Yukteswar said, "Look in the window of that train next to us."

The young man looked, and saw in the compartment opposite to theirs a beautiful woman whose very appearance satisfied every longing he had ever felt for a balancing feminine perfection. The trains went their separate ways; he never saw that woman again. From then on, however, his longing for a partner was gone forever.

Magnetism, again! How else to account for my own birth in Romania, my guru's birth in India, my American home in New York state and his in Los Angeles, yet all of that ending in our coming together in 1948? I wasn't even consciously seeking a guru. Yet as soon as I read his book, I *knew* that I was meant to follow him.

Our partings from loved ones at death; our meeting of others with whom we feel an instant bond of affection: are the partings forever? and is there any accident in those meetings? By no means! Those whom we love in this life have been dear to us in other lives also. Yogananda said that this is also true of those whom we hate. Love and hatred: both form subtle magnets. "Sometimes," the Master said, "you see whole families that live in a turmoil of constant bickering. Their members are enemies from before, drawn together for the purpose of fighting it out, this time, at close quarters!" Magnetism is not only a property of certain metals.

In the present new age of Dwapara, when it is becoming widely understood that solid-seeming matter is actually a manifestation of innumerable vibrations of energy, the reality of magnetism is becoming more and more apparent on every level of cosmic manifestation. Gravity is a kind of magnetism. So also are the manifestations of karmic law.

Paramhansa Yogananda, who will, I believe, become known throughout the world as the guru of this Dwapara Yuga, devoted much of his teaching to explaining the importance of the concept of magnetism. For success in every field of endeavor, he said, including the spiritual, far more is needed than steadfast effort. Success depends at last on the power of magnetism one develops. The right, magnetic attitude can accomplish more than brow-furrowing hard work.

Magnetism, in its turn, is generated by the amount and quality of the energy one projects. And this energy depends on the strength of a person's will power. "The greater the will," was Yogananda's frequently iterated maxim, "the greater the flow of energy."

Success in every aspect of life depends on the strength of a person's magnetism to attract it. In future, the importance of magnetism will be taught in every school. People will consider it an obvious fact that knowledge itself is far less important to success than a person's magnetism to attract whatever he wants. He can even attract the right knowledge. Students in future will be taught that the very facts one needs can be attracted by right, magnetic expectation. If, for example, one is an archeologist seeking an ancient, lost city in a tropical jungle, his chances of finding it will be far greater if he attunes himself to the consciousness of those ancient people than if he studies only the supposed trade routes of those times. Intuition (which is itself magnetic) can guide one to the right conclusions far more unerringly than the piecemeal efforts of intellect.

Do those ancient people, then, in some way still exist? I had a friend some years ago who was from Yucatán, Mexico, and whose people were Mayans. Once, he told me, he spent a whole night in the ruins of an ancient Mayan temple. As he lay there on the temple stones, a whole scene came suddenly to life for him. Men and women, dressed in ancient garb, walked about freely, entering the temple, exiting it again, looking perfectly normal. I don't think they were ghosts. I think the vibrations left in that temple lingered on with sufficient strength to impress my friend with their continued reality.

I myself had an experience at least reminiscent of that one. It was in Capernaum, Israel. I had gone there as a pilgrim. Wanting to feel what the place had been like in the days of Jesus, I "dug down," mentally, through layers of history to discover that time. Suddenly, I felt with certainty that I had arrived! I could *feel* Jesus and his young disciples, and their enthusiasm for seeking God.

They were chanting together joyously. No, I didn't see them, but the feeling itself was, to me, very real.

Again and again throughout scholarly history, answers have come unexpectedly through psychic attunement. People usually scoff at this explanation, even when they themselves experience its truth (though in their homes, over a dinner table, they may regale their guests with the story of their "strange" insight). Once the phenomenon becomes widely known, however, and widely accepted, Dwapara Yuga will have truly come into its own, and mankind will be capable of feats that, today, seem miraculous.

How often are man's abilities hampered by his low expectations! It took many years for athletes to beat the four-minute mile. But once one man did it, and the accomplishment became widely accepted as a possibility, more and more runners began breaking it. Our possibilities are limited only by our own narrow mental horizons, drawn tightly around us by our timid expectations.

"Twenty years" Yogananda said about the acquisition of Mt. Washington, "for those who think twenty years; twenty months for those who think twenty months; and *three* months, for those who think three months!"

Among the priceless gifts he brought to mankind was the teaching that God *can indeed* be known. Spiritual greatness is not limited to a few rare souls whom God has graced especially. Nor is it given for any special merit of one's own. Nor, certainly, does it come because of some totally unaccountable whim on God's part. Spiritual greatness is for all. "God chooses those," Paramhansa Yogananda taught us, "who choose Him."

In the last years of his life, he drew to himself disciples who, later on, would carry on his work. I myself was a part of this inward flow. Not all who came to him remained faithful, for the spiritual path demands steadfastness—a quality often lacking in mankind. Still, their numbers grew steadily. "How many years I had to wait for you!" he lamented to us one evening. But now the true and deeper aspect of his mission began coming to flower: his training of direct and devoted disciples who would carry on his work, and who would display before the world the universal importance of his teachings.

He now found it possible to emphasize teachings that, in the beginning, he had felt free to discuss only vaguely.

Vegetarianism, for instance. During his early years he wasn't strict about this practice. He did strongly recommend that people avoid beef, veal, and pork. "I have been in slaughterhouses," he said, "and have watched as cancers were scooped out of the cadavers of cattle. Beef and veal are not physically safe to eat. And the reason for the sweet taste of ham is the pus with which that meat is permeated."

The main reason, however, for avoiding meat is that the higher animals are intelligent enough to know what is happening to them as they are being butchered. I have heard that cows on the way to the slaughterhouses emit anguished sounds that indicate they are already terrified. Emotions of fear, anxiety, and anger in the higher, more intelligent animals become implanted in their flesh. People who eat that meat ingest also those violent emotions.

Given that everyone on earth is seeking happiness, the eating of beef and pork, especially, is starkly counterproductive.

Meat-eating also reduces a person's magnetism, for it clogs his higher feelings with alien, animal emotions. Anything that interferes with the natural flow of energy, whether in the body or in the mind, weakens one's magnetism.

During his early years in America, Yogananda did not urge people strongly to embrace a vegetarian diet. He had other, and more important, principles to inculcate in people's minds. He did recommend, however, that people reduce their meat intake to lamb, fowl, and fish. He also recommended eating meat less frequently. Sheep, chicken, fish—these creatures are less intelligent than the ones he particularly recommended against; their emotions are less focused, and less strongly affected when they are butchered.

It is interesting to note that in countries where the intake of beef and/or pork is widespread, people in general are more choleric, more warlike, and more given to aggressive pride.

Above all, as I have just said, they are also less magnetic. Or perhaps I should say, correcting myself slightly, they are more magnetic in disharmonious ways (as in demonstrations of competitive pride), but less magnetic in ways that bring harmony into life, and into one's relationships with others. Beef-eating nations like England and Germany often direct great magnetism into deeds of competition with others, but have less magnetism for success through cooperation with others. Beef-eating, for them, interferes with the expression of their native spiritual magnetism.

I might say that the same is true for Americans. However, I think the American diet is changing, and leaning more toward the inclusion of more fruits and vegetables as Americans become increasingly health conscious. I admit I am less informed on this matter than I perhaps should be, but, having been a complete vegetarian now for over sixty years, I no longer give much thought to the "opposition." Moreover, I have never been a food fanatic. I incline to eat right and forget it. In this respect, as in all things—but in this one quite naturally—I follow Yogananda, who placed less emphasis on the fact that he was a vegetarian, and said to people instead, "I am a 'proper-eatarian.'"

An interesting story concerns (again) Dr. Lewis, who at one time during his youth developed a strange number of aches and pains. He went to physician after physician, seeking help. No one was able to alleviate his pains. Finally he asked the Master why his body was suffering in this way.

"It is because your body-cells have grown accustomed to eating meat," the Master responded. "Now that you've adopted a vegetarian diet, those cells are crying out for their customary diet. I suggest that, once a week, you eat a little lamb or chicken. The problem will then go away."

Doctor followed this advice, and the pains disappeared. After some time, he was able to give up even this once-weekly slip from the dietary ideal.

The rationale behind vegetarianism is not rooted (as one might expect it to be) in faithfulness to the practice of *ahimsa*, or harmlessness. One kills even vegetables when eating them, or at least when cooking them.

One may imagine (and I think this reasoning is true) that the lower life forms, in their urge to rise up the evolutionary scale, are happy to be of service to higher forms by offering up their lives to help sustain those forms. With this thought in mind, it is possible to eat also with an attitude of gratefulness, free from any thought that one is contributing toward the destruction of anything. If this thought seems fanciful, never mind. Kindly fancies make better sustenance, surely, than angry or bitter ones.

CHAPTER TWENTY-EIGHT

Renunciation

*P*aramhansa Yogananda, during his early years in America, did not stress the importance of renunciation. He gave people those spiritual teachings which they were ready to receive. In himself, however, he was firm in his commitment to renunciation. To know God, as he himself well understood, one must be dedicated completely to that highest search. Often, in fact, the Master quoted to us the words of Jesus, "Who is my father, mother, brother, or sister save those who love God?"

It is strange, he once said, that in the West, where Christianity is prevalent, Christians believe in a middle way of life—when Jesus himself was in many ways quite extreme in his teachings. He told people to "leave all and follow me." In India, on the contrary, where Krishna taught a middle way of life, Hindus since then have emphasized the importance of total renunciation. One might conclude that Christians have, in this sense, become more truly the disciples of Krishna, and Hindus, more truly the followers of Jesus Christ!

At any rate, Paramhansa Yogananda came to show the value of both ways. I said a moment ago, "In himself, however, he was firm in his commitment. . . ." Many people would have substituted, for "firm," the word, "stern." This is an unfortunate aspect of renunciation: it can make people too dour. Such an attitude unnecessarily takes the fun out of life! Self-righteousness does the same. Renunciates, alas, often don't see that the very goal of their renunciation is not suppression, but inner freedom. The hallmark of the *true* renunciate is his inner joy. This is what Paramhansa Yogananda came to bring to mankind in the present, higher age of Dwapara.

He told the story of a seeker who once went to a saint and asked to be taught how to meditate. "I want to find God *immediately*!" the young man declared. "How hard will I have to work at it?"

"Oh, you won't have to work at all," the saint assured him with a smile, meaning (though he didn't say so) that "work" wasn't the right word, since it implies tension; relaxation fits the case better. Therefore he added, "Simply banish thoughts from your mind, and focus your attention at the point between the eyebrows."

The new student was delighted; so little work, for such vast results!

Just as he reached the door, and was about to leave the room, the saint called out to him, "Oh, by the way, there's something I forgot to add: While doing this practice, be sure not to think about monkeys."

"Don't worry, Master," the other replied. "I never think about monkeys!"

A week later he returned. "Take back your technique, Master. It has given me monkey-consciousness!"

"Tell me," the saint replied with a smile. "What happened?"

"Well, when I got home and sat to meditate, the first thing that came into my mind was the thought, I mustn't think about monkeys! From there I proceeded to think of every different kind of monkey that is to be found in India. By the second night, I'd exhausted all the Indian monkeys, so I went to an encyclopedia and researched the different kinds of monkeys in Africa, in South America, in Indonesia, in Malaya, in northern Australia. I've become an expert on monkeys, but meditation has not given me a moment's peace! Therefore I say, Master: Take back your technique. It is ruining my life!"

The saint laughed heartily. "You see? I was trying to teach you that, in order to go beyond mind, you don't need to work in the worldly sense at all. What you need to do is *relax* your mind from all restless thoughts. Deep meditation isn't *work*, as such, though it does take deep effort. Just *relax*, absorbing yourself deeply in what you are doing."

"I don't understand," said the young man. "How can I both try and not try?"

"When you try not to think about something, that's all you will be able to think about. Concentrate positively, instead—on the inner light; on inner peace and calmness; on love or bliss. I told you to concentrate at the point between the eyebrows. Try to bring your consciousness forward, from its natural center in the medulla oblongata, to its superconscious center, at the point between the eyebrows—which is to say, at that corresponding point in the frontal lobe of the brain.

"In meditation, try to focus positively on one thing at a time; don't try *not* to think of anything. Don't think of monkeys, for example! In daily life, try to do one thing at a time; finish it, and only then go on to give your attention to something else. Gradually, you will develop the ability to do more than one thing at a time, while still keeping your mind focused."

In ego-consciousness, everything one does has its center in, and proceeds from an awareness of, the medulla oblongata. A master, on the other hand, does everything from his superconscious center at the point between the eyebrows.

In true renunciation, too, the point is not so much to focus on what one is giving up as on the freedom that comes when one doesn't depend on anything outward.

A good technique, if thoughts of worldly desires and attachments keep entering the mind, is mentally to build a bonfire before going to bed every night. Gaze intently into its all-consuming flames. Then, think of your worldly impulses; throw them, one by one, into the fire. As you watch them being burnt to ashes, feel the joy of inner freedom from all outward attachments.

The main delusions are three in number: money, sex, and intoxicants of all kinds—alcohol, drugs, and any other thing that man in his ingenuity may discover as a means of achieving some sense of temporary exhilaration. Subsidiary delusions rest in the emotional nature, causing one to react with pleasure or displeasure to innumerable outer circumstances, and therefore binding one to those circumstances.

The final, and most important, delusion to be overcome is ego-consciousness itself.

Let me propose what I think are excellent ways to overcome each of the major delusions. How much of this comes directly from my guru I am unable to say. I have arrived at these perceptions on my own, but as his disciple, and I believe I state truthfully that they must, therefore, come from him to some extent at least.

1. Money. This delusion is, I think, best overcome not violently—for example, by throwing it into the flames—but rather by relaxing the mind. Money is, of course, a necessity of life. The important thing is not to become addicted to its possession. Money, in itself, has no meaning. Owning it is only a path to some further goal,

usually vague, unidentified, and therefore capable of infinite multiplication. The craving for money creates in the mind a vision of oneself as sitting, figuratively, in a vast hall with innumerable shiny though indistinct objects that seem to mumble, each in turn, "You'll have to have me if you're ever to find true happiness." "And me!" "And me!" The mind becomes bewildered, and ends up saying, "Don't bother me with all that. Just let me, for now, have more and more money so I can buy you *all*. I want to be *rich*!"

The best way to achieve inner peace is simply to withdraw from all that tangle of imaginary fulfillments, and to concentrate on feeling completely fulfilled, right now, in the inner Self.

2. Sex. The yearning people feel for oneness with another person is, ultimately, the soul's yearning for oneness with God. Between two people it can never be satisfied. For one thing, there are these obstructing walls of flesh, which enclose us all. Even on the astral plane, there remains still the insuperable barrier of ego.

Sex is a way of trying to achieve perfect union with one other person. It can never happen. For one thing, the pleasure of sex lasts only a few seconds, and is followed by a lassitude that, finally, leads to revulsion. (The saying, "He looks like a man on the last day of his honeymoon," suggests the reason for that lassitude!) For another thing, sex takes the mind into the lower chakras— away from true happiness! For a third thing, sexual desire, more than any other, takes one's consciousness outward, away from the inner self.

Well, it is pointless to speak too strongly or too long against a delusion that is so strongly embedded in human nature! But if it weren't for the fact that sex is necessary to repopulate the world, one would have to say that it is, quite simply, satanic!

Two ways, particularly, can be proposed for overcoming sex:

a) When the desire seizes one, inhale and exhale deeply. In

this way the lungs become a magnet, drawing the energy up from that lower center to the heart region. Then sit to meditate. Concentrate at the point between the eyebrows: The magnetism there will draw the energy up to the spiritual eye, and wholly away from the sex region.

b) If you must surrender to the impulse, withdraw your mind from the thought of finding pleasure in it. Observe yourself with detachment and tell yourself, "This is not I." This is a tantric method, and dangerous to practice, but necessary when delusion becomes too strong.

Yogananda said that mankind, in the beginning, created children by the conjoining of a couple's energies at the spiritual eye. This, he said, is the true meaning of the Garden of Eden. Adam and Eve were told to enjoy everything, avoiding only the tree "at the center of the garden"—the latent sex impulse, in other words, memories of which lingered in the subconscious mind from past lives in animal bodies. The serpent represented outward stimulation by the serpent force in the spine: the kundalini.

Yogananda once spoke with a Christian fundamentalist who insisted that everything in the Bible is literally true. "Many of the teachings there," Yogananda said, "are deeply symbolic, not actual facts."

"No, they are meant literally!" reiterated the fundamentalist.

"What about the serpent in the book of Genesis?" inquired the Master. "We read that it *spoke* to Eve."

"In those days," declared the fundamentalist staunchly, "serpents could speak."

The Master took off his hat and, bowing deeply, said with a little smile, "I bow before the temple of colossal ignorance that I behold before me!"

In those pristine days—let me repeat—human reproduction

was accomplished simply by inviting souls from the astral world to come into earthly families, the invitation being extended by focusing two minds at the point between the eyebrows. Even today, this is the best way to create works of inspiration: paintings, books, inventions, etc. This kind of creativity may not require the union of couples, though there is the well-known saying, "Behind every great man, there is a woman's inspiration."

3. Intoxicants. People's reason for taking intoxicants is that they think, by numbing their senses, to experience even briefly a little diminution of the pains of life. The practice of drinking alcoholic beverages is so widespread that the common question one faces today, on entering a person's home as a guest, is, "What's yours?"— meaning, what would you like to drink: whiskey? scotch? brandy? tequila? vodka? My goodness, the number of ways man has found to grease his downhill slide! I reply to that question, "I'd like a cup of tea."

For every up, there must be a down. Every gleeful binge is followed by a depression, whether a hangover or a bad mood.

Even so, there is this much good to be said for alcohol, as opposed to drugs like cocaine: People usually drink alcoholic beverages simply for that "glow" they associate with being sociable. Drugs, however, have a different association. One takes them in order deliberately to get "high," or "stoned out of his mind." The effect is different, but one that is even more satanic. People who take "hallucinogens" think their minds become clearer during the drug experience, but I can only say that, to me, their minds at such times seem exceptionally fuzzy. It is difficult even to reason clearly with such people. They have some sort of logic of their own, a language in which they can communicate only with others who are on the same drugs. I lived in San Francisco during the "hippie era," and got to see many people in this "spaced-out" condition. I always felt, in their midst, as if a satanic presence hovered over them.

Yogananda's renunciate order really began to flourish only toward the end of his life. Women came first; then, many years later, men. The first woman (well, girl to be exact) was Faye Wright at the age of seventeen, in 1931. He called her his "nest egg" because he saw that, through her, others would be drawn. Kamala Silva came before her, but he saw that it was Kamala's karma to be married. Laurie Pratt once told me, "In those days, he hadn't yet any high expectation of creating a monastery. One day I came to his interview room. He greeted me with a smile, and asked, 'So are you thinking of getting married?'" (She was.) Durga had no wish to be married, but she was more concerned for her own salvation. Faye (Daya), therefore, was the one he depended on, if a monastic order was ever to get off the ground.

And even so, the Master's focus was still on the work he himself had to do in order to fulfill his mission. Michael Krull came seven or eight years after Faye. Bernard came at about the same time as Michael. Other men came, too, but our guru once said to us, "They couldn't seem to understand why they shouldn't go dancing on Saturday nights!" It was only around the time I arrived that men began coming with the wish to become monks.

Thus, before my time, no actual monastic order had ever been established. There were indeed monks and nuns, but no rule, no way of life, no group spiritual effort. Speaking of the group I knew, there had been men in charge of the monks, but this charge had no clear meaning in anyone's eyes; it seemed more or less to suggest a channel through whom the Master could transmit his wishes to one monk or another.

In 1949, a year after my arrival, he placed me in charge of the monks. I too, however, first viewed my duty as more titular than significant. And then a great exodus occurred.

It began in January, 1950. Our guru asked me to come out to the desert, to help him with his editing. Laurie Pratt was, of course, his chief editor, but he wanted preliminary help also, to lighten her task. I myself went through a great test during the months of ensuing seclusion at the monks' retreat. Meanwhile, the monks and nuns at Mt. Washington were also being assailed from within by a strong impulse to leave the spiritual path altogether.

The Master, when I got to spend many hours daily with him (this was after he'd finished dictating his commentaries on the Bhagavad Gita), explained to me what had been happening. "Satan has been testing the organization," he said.

"Is *that* what's been happening!" I exclaimed.

"Yes," he replied sadly. "Quite a few heads will roll." I myself had been feeling that it was quite hopeless to be on the spiritual path: I'd never amount to anything. My saving grace at the time was the simple thought: "What is the alternative? There is *no* alternative!"

A comparable "house cleaning" took place near the end of the life of Jesus Christ. He seems to have been testing his disciples, for he said to them, "You must eat my flesh and drink my blood." And the Bible goes on to state, "From this time forward, many walked with him no more." His true meaning, my guru explained, had been (speaking from Christ consciousness, not from ego), "You must become one with the Cosmic Vibration, and feel running through it the omnipresent Christ consciousness." But he left it to the disciples to figure out his meaning. The true ones solved this difficulty as I myself did (for this is what saved me, after months of agony): by knowing only that they loved him, and he, them. As Peter said, "Where else would we go?" And (to repeat) as I said to Master, "For me, there is simply *no* alternative!"

"That's the spirit!" he replied, lovingly.

In 1950 I resolved to take my position seriously of being the head monk. With so many leaving, it was, I saw, high time they were organized. I consulted with him occasionally, but mostly he worked through my attunement with him, while I insisted on his principles being applied by everyone. This book is not the place to recount my difficulties and triumphs in this field. Suffice it to say that my efforts evolved, over years, into a new expression of the monastic spirit: less world-rejecting, and more God-affirming; less ego-suppressing, and more ego-expanding in sympathy for all. Our renunciate order for the new age is, I believe, in complete accord with his wishes.

This new order also embraces those who are married, but who want now to live for God above all. Moreover, it is not limited to the followers of my guru's path, but is open to everybody. When it first began, a priest in Italy asked me, "How many are there in your new order?"

"One," I replied with a smile. Now, however, the number is upwards of six hundred, and is climbing rapidly.*

Yogananda never wanted to concentrate on one aspect of society alone. His mission was to show all mankind how to prepare for a higher level of consciousness by living together cooperatively, not competitively; by making business methods a process of sharing, not of taking; by treating life itself as an opportunity to find commonality with others, and not considering anyone an outsider to one's sympathies.

---

* For more information about this new renunciate order, including the book I wrote to describe it (available both in print and for free online), see www.nayaswami.org.

Yogananda standing with two brothers of Therese Neumann,
Konnersreuth, Bavaria, 1935.

CHAPTER TWENTY-NINE

True Christianity and True Hinduism

A member of my congregation at Hollywood Church told me how she had first met the Master. She said she was praying one morning in her home, when suddenly she heard a voice declare strongly: "Christ is coming today!"

The day was Sunday. Later that morning, a friend took her to the SRF Hollywood Church, and she heard Paramhansa Yogananda speak.

An important part of the Master's mission on earth was to show the underlying unity between the teachings of Jesus Christ and of Krishna, and also the *deeper* teachings beneath both those religions. He told us several times that Jesus himself, and Krishna through his present incarnation as Babaji, had sent this mission through him. He explained, further, that Jesus Christ had actually materialized before Babaji in the Himalayas, and had said to him:

"What has happened to my church? They are still doing good works, but they've forgotten the importance of direct, *inner* communion with God. Let us send an emissary to the West to promulgate my original message once again."

It is important to understand that no truly great prophet will tell people, "My way alone is right"—unless indeed, by this, he means, "The way I am showing you is the one true path for everyone, regardless of his religion," and then goes on to make it clear that he is talking about the inward path to God which lies already in every man: the highway of the spine, where alone the ego can be offered up into oneness with the Eternal Self. True masters, in other words, speak of *principles*, not of *personalities*. Jesus Christ didn't come on earth to tell people how great *he* was. He came to show them how great they too are, potentially, in their souls. His central message was, "What I have done, you can do, too. What I am, you can become."

"God," Yogananda used to say, "never creates unique manifestations of Himself labeled, 'GOD.' All His direct human manifestations are divinely awakened sons who have gone the whole gamut of countless incarnations. They themselves have suffered the sorrows of delusion. They themselves, by steadfast, undaunted effort have achieved final victory in oneness with God. They are all, equally, one with the 'only begotten Son of God,' the Christ consciousness, even as Jesus was."

It will of course be impossible for me to present all of Yogananda's teachings here regarding the Christ. I must do my best, however, to encapsulate them within the pages of a short chapter, for this aspect of his mission was fundamental to everything he accomplished in his life. It wasn't only that he turned the minds and hearts of countless thousands of people to God. It's that he did so within a tradition into which he was commissioned to inject new life.

Toward the end of his life he prayed to Jesus, "Lord, have I been giving them *your* teachings? I have not wanted to introduce anything foreign to them." He told us what happened then:

"I beheld a wonderful light, and Jesus Christ appeared above me. The Holy Grail passed from his lips to mine, and I heard his voice say, 'The cup from which I drink, thou dost drink.'" His editor (Laurie), later, thought it irreverent to quote those words. In his autobiography she would only let him say, ". . . words so sacred that I keep them locked in my heart." The Master, however, quoted them to us frequently. I myself see no need here, therefore, for such unnecessary scruples.

Let me list, as succinctly as possible, those teachings of Jesus Christ's on which Yogananda focused primarily.

1. He said that our first duty in life is to love God, and that, in our awakening divine love, we should love all beings in His name. Our neighbors, he said (again quoting Christ), are those who are in tune with us, wheresoever they may live. To them we should give more, for they have shown themselves capable of receiving more. In other words, don't waste energy in giving too much to people who are not receptive. ("Throw not your pearls before swine.") Concentrate especially on people who are open to what you have to give.

2. Seek God first, and everything else that you require will be given to you.

3. Don't settle for lesser fulfillments: become perfect in your Self, even as God Himself is perfect.

4. It is not enough to pray to God. We must also listen for His answer, in deep meditation.

5. The "keys to the Kingdom" of which Jesus spoke are meditation techniques which help one to prepare for divine enlightenment.

6. Belief is no proof of anything. Faith alone matters. People believed for centuries that the world was flat, but that belief

didn't make it so. I may believe in you as my friend, but only after our friendship has been tested by the experience of years can I say that I truly have faith in you.

7. Man's destiny is not to live for eternity in a self-limiting body. The kingdom of God lies within. Man's true destiny is to realize his oneness with the Infinite.

8. Christ's true teachings can never be confined within the walls of any institution. Anyone, anywhere, who fulfills his commandment to live for God, and to love Him with one's whole heart, is as much his follower as anyone who ever declared himself a Christian.

9. We can find God only through the Christ consciousness, which pervades all Creation.

10. "Living for God is martyrdom." This was a favorite saying of my guru's. Tests, suffering, opposition, misunderstanding—yes, persecution too: all these attend the spiritual journey, for God wants to be quite sure of our love. But if we meet every test with an attitude, not of forbearance, but rather of joyful, willing acceptance, God will never let us down. In the end, the devotee infallibly finds that these tests of God's have pointed him, always, toward his highest soul-happiness in the Lord.

11. We must forgive everyone who tries to harm us, for all men, in their heart of hearts, want only bliss. Everything they do, whether wise or foolish, kind or unkind, unselfish or self-ish, is done with the "ulterior motive" of achieving bliss. If others try to harm one, it is only this desire surfacing in them in a distorted way. No matter how they treat you, therefore, accept that treatment gratefully. View it as a blessing from God, sent to free you from ego-bondage.

12. Never be passive in your dedication. Even Jesus drove the moneychangers out of the temple, so commit yourself fearlessly to the truth, always. We cannot be responsible for the actions of others, but we can and must accept responsibility before God for our own actions.

13. We should consider our true family members to be those above all who love God.

14. We should go through life joyfully, knowing that God loves us. Suffering itself should be embraced joyfully, as a blessing from God meant to purge us from all delusion. The popular image of Jesus as "a man of sorrows and acquainted with grief" misses the point by many miles. Jesus showed us how, by loving God, we can rise above all sorrow forever.

15. We should never accept the thought that we are sinners, except perhaps as a playful expression of humility. But seriously to call oneself a sinner is to identify oneself with sin. The worst sin before God, then, is to say in all seriousness, "I am a sinner." To say "I have erred" is different. This admission is necessary, if one truly wants to change. But to say, "I err, because it is my nature to err," is to give oneself all the excuse he needs to keep on erring. To say, "I am a sinner," is actually to justify one's own sinfulness!

The teachings of Krishna in the Bhagavad Gita are, point for point, the same as those of Jesus. The so-called "idol worship" of Indians is really only "ideal worship." Krishna's teachings and those of Jesus are, in every essential point, identical. The only difference is Krishna's emphasis on achieving freedom through desireless action. This teaching can be understood on many levels. His teaching on right action also permits one to focus one-pointedly on the task at hand. It is, therefore, a good lesson on how best to succeed in life. But Jesus emphasized rather the need for devotion. His people had become too much preoccupied with understanding, in all its ramifications, the Law of Moses. Moreover, in their insistence on God as being One the Jews had excluded others, rather than *including* everyone, for they were unable—remember, this was during the depths of Kali Yuga, the dark age—to see that everything, literally *everything*, was, is, and ever shall be a part of God.

Bernard, Rev. Stanley, Dr. Lewis, Paramhansa Yogananda,
and the author at the Lake Shrine dedication, 1950.

CHAPTER THIRTY

The Lake Shrine

In 1950, Paramhansa Yogananda dedicated his last and most beautiful property, the SRF Lake Shrine in Pacific Palisades. Formerly a movie set, the lake is situated in a steep-sided bowl within the large loop which is formed by Sunset Blvd., an important Los Angeles "artery," as it makes its final curve, swooping down to the Pacific Ocean. The property contains a windmill, a houseboat, and a quaint old mill house. Over the years it has become a showcase of great beauty. Even when it was first acquired, however, its potential, though it had been neglected for some fifteen years, was obvious.

We monks worked hard, under our guru's supervision, to prepare the place for its grand opening ceremony.

I remember standing on the steep hillside with another monk, trying to position a palm tree. Master stood below us.

"A little to the left," he called out; then, "a little higher up. No, now a foot to my right."

At a certain point we were a little rough in handling the tree. (The hillside was *very* steep!) "Careful," our guru called out. "Can't you *feel*? It's *alive*!" Gingerly we moved the tree a foot to the right.

"There! Plant it there," he called up.

The place was beautiful. But alas! it was infested with gnats! They would get into our ears; tickle our skin; bother our eyes. Truly, the law of duality was hard at work here: great beauty, offset by the nearly complete ruin of our ability to enjoy that beauty!

"Master," I cried, "why must so much beauty be paired with so much nuisance?"

With a smile he replied, "That is God's way of keeping us always moving toward Him."

On one of the work days, a large group of us monks gathered with the Master in the boathouse. It was more weight than the boat could handle; the boat began to sink. To prevent it from sinking altogether, the Master had it shored up. Now it is no longer a genuine, floating house, but it still looks like one.

On our first visit there, our guru had us monks don bathing suits and go with him into the lake. As we stood around him there, he waved his hands through the water for a few minutes.

"I have sent my light throughout this lake," he then declared. "It is now holy water. Whoever comes here in future will be blessed by Godly vibrations."

I have said that Yogananda, nearing the end of his life, referred more openly to the loftiness of his state of consciousness. His former reticence about these matters was now gone, though he never spoke boastfully, nor in such a way as to draw attention to himself. Rather, he was so completely relaxed about his own true greatness that he sometimes even joked about it.

There was a statue we all thought of as the Buddha. A Buddhist later told me that it was of someone else in that line, but I forget which one. Anyway, thinking of this statue as the Buddha himself, I asked Master, "Where do you want the Buddha to sit, Sir?" He himself was standing nearby.

With a quiet smile he replied, "The Buddha prefers to remain standing."

The SRF Lake Shrine has become a place to which people come from far and near. Most of them, perhaps, are completely unconnected with Paramhansa Yogananda, and perhaps even quite unaware of his existence. They are drawn to enjoy the amazing beauty of this place, and its deeply inspiring vibrations. Disciples have lovingly, continuously over many years, not only maintained its beauty but contributed to it.

Rev. Stanley, a young man whom Master first placed in charge there, added a wonderfully creative spirit from the beginning. He placed a statue of Jesus Christ on top of a little hill, where a waterfall, made possible by a pump, sends water cascading down the hill.

Chuck Jacot, a plumber's son who had become an SRF monk, was trying one day to fix that pump, when he realized that this job was beyond him. He reflected, and then remembered that the Master had written in *Autobiography of a Yogi*, quoting Lahiri Mahasaya, "Whenever anyone utters with reverence the name of Babaji, that devotee attracts an instant spiritual blessing." Chuck immediately sat down, and called to Babaji in meditation. Instantly that great master appeared before his inner gaze. When Chuck came out of that meditation, the pump was working perfectly again!

Later, Yogananda explained, "I asked Babaji to give Chuck that special blessing."

Stanley was virtually alone at the Lake Shrine. After the Master's passing, the same thing happened that occurs all too often after a founder's death. In this case, the women at Mt. Washington, who were in charge of the organization, tried to tell Stanley what or what not to do, without sufficient knowledge of the conditions he faced. It was painful for me to see him struggle with this interference. But he rebelled in a way that I would never have done. For example, they didn't want Jesus on that hilltop, thinking the weather might spoil the statue, but it was too perfect, standing exactly there. Stanley created protection for the statue—perhaps by sheathing it in a coat of plaster—and insisted on placing it exactly where he did.

As I said, I myself would never have rebelled. But in time I faced the same troubles he had faced with "officialdom," and was eventually forced out, much against my own will.

A survey was made, some years ago, of the fate of organizations after their founders' death. It was found that very few of them ever survived that loss. Those institutions which did survive continued from then on in a very different spirit.

The Roman Catholic Church has departed very far from the teachings of Christ. It survives because, long ago, it encased itself in ideological concrete.

SRF determined that it would go the same route. Both institutions are doing good work, but both have so encased themselves in dogmas as to lose the freedom of spirit which their founders expressed. Is this a good thing, given that there may have seemed to be no alternative? I don't know. What I do know is that I've done my best to develop Ananda so as to prevent it from happening again. Whether I succeed or not remains to be seen.

There are at present eight Ananda communities in the world: near Nevada City, CA; in Sacramento, CA; Palo Alto, CA; Portland, OR; Seattle, WA; near Assisi, in Italy; in Gurgaon in North India; and near Pune in the village of Watunde, South India; with a budding ninth community in Los Angeles. In these communities about a thousand devotees live lives of harmony, cooperation, and very noteworthy happiness. We have our own businesses to help sustain the communities, schools, private quarters for residents, retreat facilities, farms and orchards. These communities were begun in 1968, and have well proved themselves as an ideal for the future.

"The Last Smile," Paramhansa Yogananda
on the night of his *mahasamadhi*.

CHAPTER THIRTY-ONE

🌿 His Final Years

*P*aramhansa Yogananda left his body on March 7, 1952. His last years were spent mostly in seclusion. The monastic order was now well established, and running smoothly. He still had a few books to complete.

In January, 1950, he went out to his desert retreat to work on his Bhagavad Gita commentaries. He asked me to go with him. Before a group of monks he said to me, "I asked Divine Mother whom I should take to help me with my work, and your face appeared, Walter (his name for me). I asked twice more to make sure, and each time your face appeared. That's why I am taking you."

Our first evenings there, I had a chance to be with him while he dictated. Dorothy Taylor, his secretary, wrote out everything on a typewriter. Master sat still and turned his eyes upward, gazing at the point between the eyebrows. Then he began dictating. Rarely did he pause or correct himself. Concepts poured through him effortlessly. For me it was an amazing experience.

Since I just mentioned Dorothy Taylor, let me tell a little story about something the Master said to me.

"I gave Michael much work. It was what he needed. But Dorothy felt sorry for him—oh, it wasn't serious, but a little something to be nipped in the bud—and Michael was a little affected by her pity. I said to him one day, 'There is a saying in Bengal, "Anyone who loves you more than your own mother is a witch!" I am your mother. Don't you think I want only what is for your best?' He was all right from then on.

"But Dorothy is too soft. One day I said to her, 'You must be more firmly outspoken in your loyalties. If someone were to come to you and say, "I saw Yogananda dead drunk, lying in a gutter on Main Street," you'd answer, wide eyed, "Is that so?" I know you wouldn't believe him, but—don't you see?—it's an important principle to stand up for certain things very firmly—like loyalty to one's own.' And so, although I don't ask anyone to create turmoil, one simply *must* stand up strongly for what he believes in, and for those to whom he has given his loyalty."

I myself saw the quality of loyalty strongly exemplified in my guru.

He often asked me to go to the house of Laurie Pratt, his editor, taking over her mail and messages, and bringing messages back from her. One day he told me he expected his Gita commentaries to come out by December of that year. I mentioned this statement delightedly to Laurie the next time I brought over his mail. She laughed.

"By *December*! It won't be ready *nearly* so soon!" I quoted her answer to Master when I returned to him.

"Delays. Delays! Always more delays!" was his answer. "I will write her a letter. You take it over to her."

When he gave me that letter, I assumed (I think fairly naturally) that it contained a scolding. As I gave it to her, therefore, I said, "I'm sorry. It's my fault."

Well, the letter didn't contain any scolding at all! An exhortation, perhaps (I never saw it), but Laurie only got a notion of his displeasure from me, because I had tried to take the blame for any misunderstanding onto my own shoulders. Instead of defusing such a possible misunderstanding, I had *created* it! Laurie realized immediately what had happened, and reacted in emotional protest. I had tried to quench what I saw as a potential fire, but had only, in effect, blown on the coals and set them aflame!

Nevertheless, it took another forty years for that book to see the light of day. When it did come out, moreover, I myself was not at all happy with it. It contained very little of the original brilliance I remembered so well. Eventually I put out my own version, and was amazed to find that I could remember every stanza of what he'd written—not word for word, but concept for concept. I wrote the whole 600 pages of this book in less than two months. It is named, *The Essence of the Bhagavad Gita*.

The days I spent with my guru at Twentynine Palms contain many of the happiest and most enlightening times I ever got to spend with him. They could not last, however. We had to return to Los Angeles to prepare for the grand opening of the SRF Lake Shrine, in August. Lieutenant-Governor Goodwin J. Knight and his wife were the guests of honor.

A student of the Master's had attended Gandhi's cremation, in India, and had rescued a portion of those ashes, which he sent to Yogananda in America. To the best of my knowledge, no other portions of Gandhi's ashes exist anywhere. It was never meant that *any* of them be saved! Nevertheless, Yogananda had them. They were enshrined in a sacred stone structure—imported, I believe, from Tibet—and Master created a place for this sarcophagus at the SRF Lake Shrine. The dedication of the sarcophagus was made part of that dedication ceremony, August 20.

Our guru had begun telling us that his work was almost finished. He had a few writings to do: that was all. He went back into seclusion at the desert. I remained at Mt. Washington to finish organizing the monks. By the time he left his body, my own work on this project was almost finished.

He seldom expressed approval in spiritual matters, for he wanted us to continue unceasingly until we'd reached the top of the mountain. One day, however, when we were alone together, and shortly before he left his body, he looked at me lovingly and said, "You have pleased me very much. I want you to know that." What a weight he lifted from my mind with those few, simple words! I had been unsure in myself as to whether anything I did would ever please him. (The misery of emotional immaturity!) Those words were consolation for a lifetime. Ever since then, I have never doubted that he was pleased—at the very least, by my intentions.

He left his body only days later. I asked him during those few days whether all those whom he had seen in his vision at Ranchi had already come.

"Most of them," he replied. "I am waiting for only one or two more."

Two more came to him during those few remaining days.

I put my heart into recounting the story of those days, in my book, *The New Path*. I simply don't want to relive them again. To me, now, he is an ever-living presence. I want to think of him in my heart, and not as lying there on the floor at the Biltmore Hotel, after his address at the banquet in honor of Binay R. Sen, India's new ambassador to the United States.

Two of his disciples in India were planning to come over, and his body was kept unburied for their arrival. As it happened, their coming was delayed. After twenty-one days we had to tell the officials at the Forest Lawn Mortuary that they might seal the coffin.

A few days later, an official letter came from Harry T. Rowe saying that, at the time the coffin was sealed, there was no reason to say there had been *any* change in the state of Yogananda's body. "As far as we know from mortuary annals, this state of perfect preservation in a body is unprecedented."

William the Great, in England and Normandy; Fernando el Santo, in Spain; and now Yogananda, in America: was the incorrupt state of their bodies a condition that would always attend this soul?

The death of Paramhansa Yogananda was a shattering blow to countless devotees around the world. Many of them expressed that they grieved more at his passing than they had at the deaths of their own family members. His aura of love will prove—so I fervently believe—to have cast its spell over the whole world, and in time to have made our whole planet a better place in which to live.

Daya Mata had asked him years earlier, "Sir, what can ever replace you, after you have gone?"

With the tenderest smile he had answered her, "When I am gone, only love can take my place." Love God, in other words, not only for Himself, but also in others. Treat all lovingly who come to you.

Toward the end of his life, Master said to a group of us monks, "Respect one another, as you respect me."

People are a very important part of any life of spiritual service. Our first duty is to love and respect them, as images of God.

Finally, out at Twentynine Palms, I once said to him, "Sir, after you are gone, will you be as close to us as you are now?"

"To those who think me near," he replied, "I will be near."

His proximity was indicated to us poignantly years later, by what happened to the mother of one of our Ananda members, Irene Schulman.

"My mom sometimes visited Ananda," she said. "One time, she saw Master here. She told him, among other things, how many people were coming to Ananda, and how many new homes were being built here. She then expressed a desire that Ananda always be what he, himself, wanted it to be. At some point she asked him, 'Do you often come here?'

"Yogananda replied with a smile, 'I am always here.'"

Paramhansa Yogananda and his guru, the second-floor dining patio
of Sri Yukteswar's Serampore hermitage.

CHAPTER THIRTY-TWO

His Legacy

I said earlier that several historians have written that William the Great's (I prefer that to the epithet, "The Conqueror") legacy has had an impact on the history of the entire Western world. I used to wonder why Yogananda had spoken to us repeatedly of his incarnation as William of England. After all, there must have been other and less controversial lives that he lived. Yes, this was one incarnation we'd all recognize, but if he had to mention it at all, why didn't he do so only briefly—as it were, in passing?

Over the years, I've come to understand that he made sure we never forgot that incarnation, because his present lifetime, too, was destined to have a similar impact on the world—indeed, a much greater impact, for now the world has, in a sense, shrunk in size. To circle the globe, now, requires less time and effort than it did in those days merely to travel from one country to another.

Paramhansa Yogananda's legacy is destined in many respects to be world-transforming. His influence will go infinitely beyond the borders of his own little organization. His disciples have gone to great effort to confine that legacy within the walls of that one organization. Tara (Laurie Pratt) accused me of megalomania for thinking I should take his message farther afield. But then, it was also she who had said to me, "What do they need with more books?" She herself never even tried to finish the editing of some of his most important works, including his commentary on the Bhagavad Gita. Of her it was that Yogananda said, "When I first got Mt. Washington, in 1925, Laurie's only comment to me was, 'Now your troubles begin!'" As for megalomania, I don't consider that I myself even exist. I live only to make *his* message known.

He *wanted* us, however, to "think big." He encouraged me, personally, to do so—to the point of insisting urgently: "And you *mustn't* disappoint me!" And I have tried to see all the ways in which his work is meaningful for everyone. What is his legacy? What were the specific gifts he brought to mankind? Let me list those I know. There may be others I don't know.

1. He encouraged people to come together in communities. This he did, repeatedly and sometimes fervently, almost from the very beginning. I myself have built eight such communities so far, in which altogether about a thousand people live.

The Master spoke sometimes fervently, as I said, of the need for such communities. In 1949, at a garden party put on by a Mrs. Myers in Beverly Hills, he was invited to speak toward the end as the guest of honor. Far from offering the few, gracious acknowledgements that are customary on such occasions, he gave the most powerful speech I have ever heard in my life.

"This day," he thundered, "marks the birth of a new era! I am sowing my thoughts in the ether, and my words *shall not die*!" He went on to say, "Thousands of youths must go north, south, east, and west to spread this concept of world brotherhood colonies." He then stated, still very forcefully, that this idea would solve countless social and personal problems that would arise in the future, particularly with worldwide economic depression.

In his "aims and ideals" he wrote that this ideal was central to his very mission on earth. That "aim and ideal" was later changed to read, ". . . to spread a *spirit* [italics mine] of brotherhood." The statement had actually read, ". . . to help form brotherhood colonies."

The Master also spoke a great deal about the world's future: about a worldwide economic depression, "much worse than the one in the thirties." He spoke of wars of massive destruction. The image I have formed in my mind is of cities everywhere vanishing from the face of the earth, and of little, intentional communities springing up everywhere. People who live their beliefs and ideals together would constitute a force that, gradually, would uplift the world.

At one point during a Sunday sermon the Master paused a moment, then cried out with great power, "You don't know what a *terrible* cataclysm is coming!" Cataclysm? This word suggests something greater than man himself is capable of producing. A comet, perhaps, striking the earth? a polar shift? the approach of some body from outside the solar system? At any rate, communities will help to offset any such calamity.

As for wars, there are over 30,000 known atomic weapons stockpiled in the world—and this number, I should point out, includes only the *known* weapons, not the unknown ones. Is it likely that no country will resort to dropping one? If such a bomb were ever to be dropped on the west coast of America, which, do you imagine, would be the more likely target: Mt. Shasta? or the sprawling city of Los Angeles? The question doesn't even beg an answer.

Yogananda's legacy will come into its own particularly after those hard times are over. It will point the way for all men to a new and better way of life.

2. Schools everywhere are causing anxiety among parents, who feel their children are being overburdened with knowledge. A serious problem is that children are taught, whether explicitly or implicitly, that life has no meaning. In fact, modern education is basically atheistic. In consequence, there are many adolescent suicides.

The ideals Yogananda held for child education could not be perfected during his lifetime. At Ranchi, the school ended up being controlled by the government, which imposed its own constrictive ideas of education in conveyor-belt fashion. In America, the ground was not yet fertile for initiating his educational ideas. My guru said to me, "Our way works better for the present: mature adults, eager to come to us for training, instead of boys with varied karma going off, after graduation, in countless different directions, and most of them to a worldly life." I have been able, however, to create his type of schools on three continents, and their impact promises to be enormous, at a time when people everywhere are losing faith in modern educational methods.

3. Paramhansa Yogananda's writings embrace a wide array of important topics, and are bound to become greatly influential.

a) His book, *The Science of Religion*, makes the simple but all-clarifying statement that everyone on earth is seeking only two things in life: to avoid pain, and to find happiness. On the basis of this simple truth will be found a clue to a new system of ethics; a new definition of success; a new approach to social upliftment. I myself rewrote this book, which had been pompously edited—to the point of obscurity—by Swami Dhirananda. I wasn't allowed to give it the same title, so I called it: *God Is for Everyone*.

b) Another book the Master wrote was *Scientific Healing Affirmations*. In this book he taught people how to use their mental power to cure any number of physical ailments. More and more, already, people are coming to understand the healing power of the mind. Affirmations help to focus that healing power, and to increase its effectiveness enormously.

c) He wrote *Whispers from Eternity*, which shows the right and best attitudes for approaching God.

d) He wrote commentaries on the actions and teachings of Jesus Christ. I believe these commentaries are destined, in time, to eliminate the innumerable sects of Christianity, and to convince everyone that the essential message of Jesus lies far beyond any organization, far beyond any system of mere beliefs, in the inner communion of the soul with God. The fact that he came from *outside* the Christian tradition made it easier for him to show that Christianity, like a diamond, has many facets. His explanations are fresh with new insights, made possible partly by the fact that he didn't need to participate in or respond to the endless internal debates that have developed over centuries within traditional Christianity.

e) He also wrote what was, in some ways, his most important scriptural commentary, on the Bhagavad Gita, which outlined for everybody an entirely new and transforming way of life.

4. I believe his life will also change society in far-reaching ways. It will make businesses in general aware that success is most surely theirs who put service ahead of gain. Our

Ananda bookstores, as an example, at a time when book-shops across the country are closing their doors, and even major bookstore chains are failing, thrive because they put their customers' needs ahead of gain. Dwapara Yuga will bring, and is bringing, a more fluid and less fixed attitude toward life. Yogananda taught people to depend less on dog-mas and more on experience. This flexibility is also helping to keep our bookstores afloat as they broaden their inventory, beyond books, to compatible items that attract customers.

5. Home life everywhere has been suffering, as new life di-rections divide couples that once would have walked in the same direction, together. Yogananda brought so much clarity to the very purpose of life that these forks in life's road will become less and less frequent.

6. Governments, usually, are whirlpools of power-seeking. Thus, governments themselves grow larger and larger, as people with that mentality attempt to do as much as possible to control people, while seeking always to win the popular vote. Government in future will become smaller, as politi-cians come to see their role as being, primarily, one of service.

7. Prisons will become places not of punishment, but of supportive correction.

8. Armies will focus more on defense than on aggression.

9. Policemen will become conditioned to expect cooperation from people, rather than opposition, for the people them-selves will understand better that, since the true goal of life is happiness, one can find more of what he really wants by sharing with others than by taking from them. Of course, I do not expect all criminal types to lay down their switch-blades and guns! People with strongly negative karma will

continue to express negativity, and the police will have to keep themselves in readiness against malefactors. Over-all, however, basic social attitudes will change, and will bring greater harmony to mankind everywhere.

"Whenever virtue declines, and vice is in the ascendant, I incarnate myself as an *avatar*. Appearing from age to age in visible form, I come to destroy evil and to reestablish virtue." (Bhagavad Gita 4:7,8)

Such, finally, is the legacy of Paramhansa Yogananda. The world will become a better place, because he lived.

CHAPTER THIRTY-THREE

How Will That Legacy Spread?

*P*aramhansa Yogananda once said to his close disciple, Faye Wright (later known as Daya Mata): "How you all will change the work after I am gone! I just wonder, were I to come back in a hundred years, whether I would even recognize it." It is a matter of historic record that every great master's teachings have been diluted in time: misunderstood, altered (both subtly and blatantly) to suit human convenience, and tailored to accommodate prevailing perceptions of the truth. What humanity is not ready to accept, it alters to what it considers more palatable. God has seen fit, therefore, to send His awakened sons back again and again to this world to bring His still-sleeping children patiently back to the central truth of their own being.

It would be naive to imagine that Yogananda's legacy will be spared this universal fate. He founded an organization, Self-Realization Fellowship, to promulgate that legacy, but he also made it clear that faithfulness to the legacy would depend, finally, on the dedication of individuals.

In *Autobiography of a Yogi*, he wrote that virtue must begin in the bosom of the individual before it can flower in civic virtue.

And to us renunciate disciples he once said, "You must *individually* make love to God." Merely to belong to a spiritual work, even as the direct disciples of a great master, does not guarantee anything.

It is important to understand that, where the perpetuation of a divine legacy is concerned, what counts is neither the organization nor the formal status of the individuals representing it, but the legacy itself. Since the rise of democracy in modern times, people have come to look upon truth itself as something that can be voted into or out of existence. "Power to the people" is a slogan greatly overused. Divine teachings are not declared for the convenience of man, but for his soul-upliftment, and for his eventual absorption in divine bliss. Such teachings cannot but go against innumerable ideas that human beings hold as necessary to their happiness and convenience: for example, the satisfaction of their material desires; their attachment to possessions; their self-satisfaction.

Jesus Christ taught: "And every one that hath forsaken houses, or brethren, or sisters, or father, or mother, or wife, or children, or lands, for my name's sake, shall receive an hundredfold, and shall inherit everlasting life." (Matthew 19:29) Mark, after ". . . shall receive an hundredfold . . . ," adds (in 10:30), ". . . with persecutions." (Yogananda often quoted this saying from St. Matthew, adding almost as frequently these further words from St. Mark.)

Jesus taught also: "He that loveth father or mother more than me is not worthy of me: and he that loveth son or daughter more than me is not worthy of me." (Matthew 10:37)

How many Christian churches today preach these essential sayings—so inconvenient socially!—of their own master?

Jesus said, again, "Be ye therefore perfect, even as your Father which is in heaven is perfect." (Matthew 5:48) How many Christians emphasize this teaching? How many even accept it as possible? Virtually none! Instead, modern versions of the Bible substitute, for that word "perfect," something more acceptable and "realistic"—for instance: "Be ye therefore *good*." Well, of course translators must work from the text in Greek, since the original Aramaic is either unavailable or too arcane for general recognition. Nevertheless, Yogananda taught that the soul's ultimate destiny *is* to become one with God, and therefore as perfect as He is.

God's way of sending "the eternal religion" to earth again and again, expressed ever newly to meet humanity's changing needs, has always been through His enlightened sons. They have brought people back to their true Source, in Him. Yogananda's legacy will surely have to surrender, in time, to the fate of every such mission. The fault will lie, not in the mission, but in human nature, which inevitably dilutes whatever it accepts of the divine teachings—even if it does so with enthusiasm.

Jesus spoke of that same destiny of oneness with God, but Christians today believe that the soul's highest destiny is a life eternally separate from God, encased forever in a little, ego-centric (if transcendent) body. Yet, surely, anyone so imprisoned would eventually come to consider this fate a living hell! For there is something about spiritual awareness which longs to reach out expansively toward oneness with all life.

How can a divine legacy be perpetuated best to ensure its purity and endurance? In Christendom, the accepted answer has been, "Through church organizations." In Islam, it has been by absolute rule—preceded by *Jihad*, or "Holy War." Both religions have tried to stamp out all opposition, sometimes by dogmatic denunciation, and—almost as frequently—by force. In any case, the idea has been to enforce one interpretation, and one interpretation only.

Organizations undeniably serve a good purpose. They help to promulgate a new teaching. They also serve as safe bastions for

316 · PARAMHANSA YOGANANDA: A Biography

people in need of the security of being surrounded by others on whom they can depend to agree with their views. Organizations are not, however, the guarantee they claim to be for the purity of a teaching. And why not? Simply because their first priority cannot be service, whether to mankind or to an ideal. It has, rather, to be the simple Darwinian principle of survival.

Tara Mata (Laurie Pratt), Yogananda's chief editor, put it with characteristic bluntness: "In every situation, our primary consideration must be, *What is best for the work?*" By *work*, she meant the organization.

This statement should be contrasted to the Mosaic commandment: "Thou shalt have no other gods before Me." For what it did was violate that ancient dictum. In simple fact—which is to say, in practice—it set up "the work" as a new god. It became a means of justifying meanness, lack of kindness, lack of charity, and total indifference not only to the rights, but even to the valid needs of individuals. Political considerations, not human ones, were made the "bottom line," the supreme guideline.

Tara insisted that this principle be enforced unilaterally, even ruthlessly, and even if it meant betraying the very teaching our guru insisted was fundamental to the harmonious development of his mission. As he had said to Daya Mata, "When I am gone, only love can take my place."

I have borne some of this treatment, myself, and I have also, with grief, observed it inflicted on many others.

The need for self-preservation is only one disadvantage of religious institutions. Another one is that, inevitably in every organization, those who rise to positions of authority are not its saints, or those, even, of saintly nature who also possess more down-to-earth skills, but those who possess the best heads for administration. This is not to say that saints never rise to the top, for sometimes they, too, have the right practical aptitudes. But if there is a choice between a saintly person who lacks that aptitude, and someone who is only relatively good but institutionally competent, the latter invariably receives preference. An institution may survive a compromise in its virtue, but it cannot survive incompetence. It cannot, in other words, survive bankruptcy.

Thus, even the most spiritual organizations tend, in time, to become top-heavy with leaders of bureaucratic mentality. And then the principle, "Birds of a feather flock together," comes to the fore. Persons of bureaucratic temperament cannot but feel more comfortable with others of similar temperament. Certainly, when they face even a choice between saintly "competents" and unsaintly ones, they feel more at ease with that new candidate for a position who is not *too* saintly. Indeed, they may settle, in time, for one whose qualifications are *only* his bureaucratic efficiency.

Thus, organizations, whether spiritual or worldly, develop a bias toward competence and efficiency—and *away from* such ideals as kindness, truthfulness, and adherence to high principles. In this sense, it must be said that, although religious organizations do offer some assurance, at first, of preserving the purity of their original teachings, that assurance must be offset from the outset by the conflicting principle of self-interest. Their teaching, therefore, cannot but become greatly diluted, in time, by the inevitable process of humanizing—that is to say, of de-spiritualizing—the loftiest teachings of their founding *avatar*.

In time, the process cannot but result in a kind of morality which is basically good, but hopelessly compromised—one which leaves people more or less where they were before they even began going to church.

In the Roman Catholic Church, the custodians of its teachings have been the true (as opposed, often, to the institutionally recognized) saints. In the Protestant churches, saints are given little or no credence—all their loyal members being dubbed, saints—and the high teachings of Jesus the Christ are portrayed as little more than an assurance that Jesus himself will do most or all of the work of saving those who believe in him, no matter how badly they live.

The counterpart to this teaching is, of course, that all who don't believe in Jesus Christ will be damned forever—no matter how virtuously they live!

Obviously, something better is required than the Protestant Way. Once religious truth has become so diluted as to require no more of one than a supportive badge and a few shouted slogans, it is time for God to send another *avatar* who will remind people of what the soul's destiny is really all about.

If organizations have their drawbacks, so also (of course) have individuals. Both are needed in this world. Indeed, they serve as "checks and balances" to one another. Individuals, however, are at least not motivated by any need for compromise as a means to self-preservation. They can state the truth as they themselves honestly understand it. Even here, of course, the problem may be that their own understanding is faulty—as Martin Luther's was in his declaration that scripture itself would guarantee the correctness of one's understanding. (Luther then went on to engage in a controversy with Zwingli, a fellow Protestant, on the meaning of an important scriptural teaching.)

The danger that ego may intrude itself on one's understanding is, of course, equally present in both individuals and institutions. But it is noteworthy, at least as the suggestion of a guideline, that saviors, or avatars, are sent singly to earth, not in committees.

I was standing one day outside the main building at Mt. Washington with Herbert Freed, a fellow disciple. The Master was on the point of leaving by car, but he took the time to give Herbert a few last-minute words of advice for his new assignment as minister of the SRF church in Phoenix, Arizona. After doing so he paused a moment, then added, "You have a great work to do."

I turned to Herbert to offer my felicitations.

"It's you I'm talking to, Walter," Master corrected me. He said nothing more on the subject at that time.

On later occasions—always, however, when we were alone—he made the same statement to me. Once, out of doors at his Twentynine Palms retreat, he said to me (as I have partially quoted him doing earlier), "Apart from Saint Lynn, every man has disappointed me—and *you MUSTN'T disappoint me!*" He spoke these last words almost fiercely, as if to make sure they entered deeply into my consciousness. I knew he didn't mean that all his male disciples had disappointed him spiritually, for some of them were spiritually deep. Their interest, however, had always been primarily in their own salvation. My own interest, from the start, had been a deep desire also to see his message reach out to and embrace all mankind.

Masculine and feminine energies, in this respect, are different from one another. Men's tends to be more outward; women's, more inward. For the Master's message to reach out to and embrace all mankind, masculine energy was essential. I alone seem to have manifested this particular trait. This must have been the reason he devoted so many hours to explaining to me in great detail so many of the subtler aspects of his teachings. He also said to me, "Your job is lecturing, writing, and editing."

"Sir," I objected on that occasion, "haven't you already written everything that is needed?"

"Don't say that!" He seemed almost shocked by my suggestion. "*Much* more is needed!"

Yet Tara wasn't interested in even completing the editing of the books he himself had written. "What do people need with more books?" she demanded of me once, rhetorically. "They have everything they need for their own salvation!"

Imagine, then, the likelihood that any of my own writings would be published within SRF! Nothing was ever published without Tara's editorial approval. Indeed, then, imagine my being permitted even to write a serious book.

Why, I sometimes asked myself, did I come to him so late in his life? I understand, now. Obviously, it was to ensure that I lived long enough to complete this aspect of his mission.

My own firm belief for many years was that I would always work in concert with my fellow disciples. They themselves, however, had very different ideas. My suggestions were dismissed, almost as a matter of routine, as "impractical." In time, they began to ask one another with increasing concern, "Why can't he just wait to be told what to do?"

In the end, I was simply dismissed from the organization. I will not go into that painful period of my life story, or into the years of uncertainty it entailed. I will say only that it proved, in the end, to be the greatest blessing of my life, freeing me as it did to accomplish whatever I have done in my life to make my guru's message known to the world.

I feel deeply blessed to have been able to render this service, in which I have not really figured at all. It is my guru's work. I have simply done my very best to give it full outward expression. Nothing of what I've done is important except as it has been what he himself wanted me to do.

An important question remains: What about Ananda? I founded it to fulfill aspects of his mission in which SRF was self-declaredly not interested—notably, the formation of residential communities. Will the Ananda communities adhere always to his high principles? I'd be naive to think so! Yet I have at least done my best to ensure their endurance for as long as possible. I have reduced the temptation of pride in its leadership by decentralizing as much as possible; by making the communities themselves autonomous; by appointing those to leadership positions who had no desire for it; by appointing those as ministers who showed a desire only to share our guru's teachings; and by having both a spiritual director and a general manager—positions to which people are appointed, not elected. Yogananda provided against insurrection from below by appointing a self-generating board of directors. The result, unfortunately, has been a growing insensitivity to the needs and valid interests of others. I have not in any case been able in this respect to follow his example; it simply would not have worked. The Ananda communities are created by those who will then constitute the membership. Thus, probably, the dilution will come from below rather than from above. But who can tell? Delusion is a hydra-headed monster. I have simply not been able to imitate Hercules and cut off all its heads at once. This feat one may be able to accomplish for himself, by a supreme act of love, but no one can ever impose such a thing on others. Nor would it be desirable, even if it were possible.

So, yes, Ananda too will in time follow the well-beaten path and betray its ideals. The best we can insist on is that individuals be empowered to maintain their own integrity and follow their own star, regardless of the common opinion. Communities, too, will work as long as enough of their members think, "What can I give?" and not, "What can I get?"

As in religion, the saints alone are its true custodians.

Yoganandaji during a public satsang at Mt. Washington. Swami Kriyananda is standing in the back to the far right with the other monks.

Index

A

advaita (non-duality), 182, 262
Agastya, 107, 108
Agatha (daughter of William the Conqueror), 133. *See also* Daya Mata
Agra, 40
ahimsa (non-violence), 50, 52, 159–60, 187–88, 242–44, 249, 272
Ainslie, Grant Duff Douglas, 118
Alaska, *56*
Alexander the Great, 123
Alfonso X, 134, 134 n. *See also* Swami Kriyananda
America (U.S.A.), 169, 271. *See also* Alaska; Boston; Deep South; Encinitas; Los Angeles; Miami; Minneapolis; New York City; Philadelphia; San Francisco; Santa Rosa; Seattle; Washington, D.C.
    Dwapara Yuga in, 73
    future of, 73, 125, 126
    the Great Depression, 174
    karma of, 136
    racism in, 106
    Yogananda's mission in, 73, 224–26
American Unitarian Association, 60, 65
Ananda
    bookstores (East-West), 309–10
    communities, 55, 174, 175, 197, 295–96, 302–3, 306, 320–21
    retreat, 212, 224
    Sangha, 103, 125, 320–21
    Yoga, 241–42
Ananda Moyi Ma, 170, 171, *263*
Ananta (older brother of Paramhansa Yogananda), *11*, 12, 14, 40
Anderson, Andy, 209
Antony, Mark, 124
Aristotle, 192
Arjuna, 93–94, 128, 129, 196, 221, 257
Arnold, Benedict, 124
Aryans, 57, 106
astral entities, 146
astral world, 125, 169, 256, 262, 278, 280
astrology, 199–200, 264
attunement, with the guru, 195, 196, 225, 253
AUM (Cosmic Vibration), 20, 67, 96–102 *passim*, 183, 282
    experienced in meditation, 39, 101–2

AUM technique, 102–3. *See also* "Doors of Silence"; "temple of silence"
aura, 126–27
Aurangzeb, 168
Autobiography of a Yogi, 34, 118, 171, 176, 197, 230, 252
    "The Blissful Devotee and His Cosmic Romance," 18 n
    quoted, 40, 108, 238, 287, 294, 313
    "The Resurrection of Sri Yukteswar," 169–70
    "Samadhi," 145, 169, 198–99, 238
    stories, 39, 49, 117, 130, 164, 169–70
    "Two Penniless Boys in Brindaban," 40, 237
    Yogananda, as author of, 1, 2, 63, 129, 267
avatars, 3, 162, 313, 315, 317, 318. *See also* Agastya; Babaji; Buddha; Jesus Christ; Krishna; Lahiri Mahasaya; Paramhansa Yogananda; Sri Yukteswar

B

Babaji, 128–29, 285, 294
    and Shankara, 264–65
Bagchi, Basu. *See* Swami Dhirananda
Bannerji, Gurudas, 167–68
Bareilly, 9, 31
Beda Byasa, 189
Benares, 39, 40, 93, 230, 264
Bengal, 161, 165, 258
Bengali, 7, 69, 141, 159, 161–62
Bengal-Nagpur Railway Company, 12
Bernadette Soubirous, St., 96
Bernard (disciple of Yogananda), 253–54, 281, 290–*91*
Beverly Hills, 306
Bhagavad Gita, 50, 129, 257, 289, 309
    quoted, 3, 108, 110, 123, 137, 162, 221, 311
Bhajan (Calcutta college teacher), 60
bhakta (saint of devotion), 7, 29
Bhrigu, 107, 108
Bible, 70–71, 96, 279, 290
    New Testament, 65, 128, 195. *See also* Jesus Christ; John the Baptist; Judas Iscariot; Mary Magdalene; Virgin Mary
    Old Testament, 191, 279, 316. *See also* Elias; Ten Commandments
Bimal (Ranchi student), 59–60

The original 1946 unedited edition of
Yogananda's spiritual masterpiece

AUTOBIOGRAPHY OF A YOGI
by Paramhansa Yogananda

Autobiography of a Yogi is one of the best-selling Eastern philosophy titles of all time, with millions of copies sold, named one of the best and most influential books of the twentieth century. This highly prized reprinting of the original 1946 edition is the only one available free from textual changes made after Yogananda's death. Yogananda was the first yoga master of India whose mission was to live and teach in the West.

In this updated edition are bonus materials, including a last chapter that Yogananda wrote in 1951, without posthumous changes. This new edition also includes the eulogy that Yogananda wrote for Gandhi, and a new foreword and afterword by Swami Kriyananda, one of Yogananda's close, direct disciples.

THE NEW PATH
My Life with Paramhansa Yogananda
by Swami Kriyananda

This is the moving story of Kriyananda's years with Paramhansa Yogananda, India's emissary to the West and the first yoga master to spend the greater part of his life in America. When Swami Kriyananda discovered *Autobiography of a Yogi* in 1948, he was totally new to Eastern teachings. This is a great advantage to the Western reader, since Kriyananda walks us along the yogic path as he discovers it from the moment of his initiation as a disciple of Yogananda. With winning honesty, humor, and deep insight, he shares his journey on the spiritual path through personal stories and experiences. Through more than four hundred stories of life with Yogananda, we tune in more deeply to this great master and to the teachings he brought to the West. This book is an ideal complement to *Autobiography of a Yogi*.

THE ESSENCE OF THE BHAGAVAD GITA
Explained by Paramhansa Yogananda
As Remembered by his disciple, Swami Kriyananda

Rarely in a lifetime does a new spiritual classic appear that has the power to change people's lives and transform future generations. This is such a book. This revelation of India's best-loved scripture approaches it from a fresh perspective, showing its deep allegorical meaning and its down-to-earth practicality. The themes presented are universal: how to achieve victory in life in union with the divine; how to prepare for life's "final exam," death, and what happens afterward; how to triumph over all pain and suffering.

"A brilliant text that will greatly enhance the spiritual life of every reader."
—**Caroline Myss**, author of *Anatomy of the Spirit* and *Sacred Contracts*

"It is doubtful that there has been a more important spiritual writing in the last fifty years than this soul-stirring, monumental work. What a gift! What a treasure!"
—**Neale Donald Walsch**, author of *Conversations with God*

REVELATIONS OF CHRIST
Proclaimed by Paramhansa Yogananda
Presented by his disciple, Swami Kriyananda

The rising tide of alternative beliefs proves that now, more than ever, people are yearning for a clear-minded and uplifting understanding of the life and teachings of Jesus Christ. This galvanizing book, presenting the teachings of Christ from the experience and perspective of Paramhansa Yogananda, one of the greatest spiritual masters of the twentieth century, finally offers the fresh perspective on Christ's teachings for which the world has been waiting. *Revelations of Christ* presents us with an opportunity to understand and apply the scriptures in a more reliable way than any other: by studying under those saints who have communed directly, in deep ecstasy, with Christ and God.

"This is a great gift to humanity. It is a spiritual treasure to cherish and to pass on to children for generations."
—**Neale Donald Walsch**, author of *Conversations with God*

"Kriyananda's revelatory book gives us the enlightened, timeless wisdom of Jesus the Christ in a way that addresses the challenges of twenty-first century living."
—**Michael Beckwith**, Founder and Spiritual Director, Agape International Spiritual Center, author of *Inspirations of the Heart*

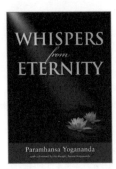

WHISPERS FROM ETERNITY
Paramhansa Yogananda
Edited by his disciple, Swami Kriyananda

Many poetic works can inspire, but few, like this one, have the power to change your life. Yogananda was not only a spiritual master, but a master poet, whose verses revealed the hidden divine presence behind even everyday things. This book has the power to rapidly accelerate your spiritual growth, and provides hundreds of delightful ways for you to begin your own conversation with God.

CONVERSATIONS WITH YOGANANDA
Recorded, Compiled, and Edited with commentary by his disciple Swami Kriyananda

This is an unparalleled, first-hand account of the teachings of Paramhansa Yogananda. Featuring nearly 500 never-before-released stories, sayings, and insights, this is an extensive, yet eminently accessible treasure trove of wisdom from one of the 20th Century's most famous yoga masters.

"A wonderful book! To find a previously unknown message from Yogananda now is an extraordinary spiritual gift. Open up at random for an encouraging word from one of the century's most beloved spiritual teachers."

—**Neale Donald Walsch**, author of *Conversations with God*

THE ESSENCE OF SELF-REALIZATION
The Wisdom of Paramhansa Yogananda
Recorded, Compiled, and Edited
by his disciple Swami Kriyananda

With nearly three hundred sayings rich with spiritual wisdom, this book is the fruit of a labor of love that was recorded, compiled, and edited by his disciple, Swami Kriyananda. A glance at the table of contents will convince the reader of the vast scope of this book. It offers as complete an explanation of life's true purpose, and of the way to achieve that purpose, as may be found anywhere.

Six volumes of Paramhansa Yogananda's timeless wisdom in an approachable, easy-to-read format. The writings of the Master are presented with minimal editing, to capture his expansive and compassionate wisdom, his sense of fun, and his practical spiritual guidance.

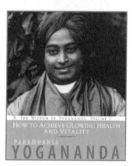

HOW TO BE HAPPY ALL THE TIME
The Wisdom of Yogananda Series, VOLUME 1

Yogananda powerfully explains virtually everything needed to lead a happier, more fulfilling life. Topics include: looking for happiness in the right places; choosing to be happy; tools and techniques for achieving happiness; sharing happiness with others; balancing success and happiness; and many more.

KARMA & REINCARNATION
The Wisdom of Yogananda Series, VOLUME 2

Yogananda reveals the truth behind karma, death, reincarnation, and the afterlife. With clarity and simplicity, he makes the mysterious understandable. Topics include: why we see a world of suffering and inequality; how to handle the challenges in our lives; what happens at death, and after death; and the purpose of reincarnation.

SPIRITUAL RELATIONSHIPS
The Wisdom of Yogananda Series, VOLUME 3

This book contains practical guidance and fresh insight on relationships of all types. Topics include: how to cure bad habits that can end true friendship; how to choose the right partner; sex in marriage and how to conceive a spiritual child; problems that arise in marriage; the Universal Love behind all your relationships.

HOW TO BE A SUCCESS
The Wisdom of Yogananda Series, VOLUME 4

This book includes the complete text of *The Attributes of Success*, the original booklet later published as *The Law of Success*. In addition, you will learn how to find your purpose in life, develop habits of success and eradicate habits of failure, develop your will power and magnetism, and thrive in the right job.

HOW TO HAVE COURAGE, CALMNESS, & CONFIDENCE
The Wisdom of Yogananda Series, VOLUME 5

~ Winner of the 2011 International Book Award for Best Self-Help Title ~

This book shows you how to transform your life. Dislodge negative thoughts and depression. Uproot fear and thoughts of failure. Cure nervousness and systematically eliminate worry from your life. Overcome anger, sorrow, over-sensitivity, and a host of other troublesome emotional responses; and much more.

HOW TO ACHIEVE GLOWING HEALTH & VITALITY
The Wisdom of Yogananda Series, VOLUME 6

Paramhansa Yogananda, a foremost spiritual teacher of modern times, offers practical, wide-ranging, and fascinating suggestions on how to have more energy and live a radiantly healthy life. The principles in this book promote physical health and all-round well-being, mental clarity, and ease and inspiration in your spiritual life. Readers will discover the priceless Energization Exercises for rejuvenating the body and mind, the fine art of conscious relaxation, and helpful diet tips for health and beauty.

THE RUBAIYAT OF OMAR KHAYYAM EXPLAINED
Paramhansa Yogananda, edited by Swami Kriyananda

The Rubaiyat is loved by Westerners as a hymn of praise to sensual delights. In the East its quatrains are considered a deep allegory of the soul's romance with God, based solely on the author Omar Khayyam's reputation as a sage and mystic. But for centuries the meaning of this famous poem has remained a mystery. Now Yogananda reveals the secret meaning and the golden spiritual treasures hidden behind the Rubaiyat's verses, and presents a new scripture to the world.

THE BHAGAVAD GITA
According to Paramhansa Yogananda
Edited by Swami Kriyananda

This translation of the Gita, by Paramhansa Yogananda, brings alive the deep spiritual insights and poetic beauty of the famous battlefield dialogue between Krishna and Arjuna. Based on the little-known truth that each character in the Gita represents an aspect of our own being, it expresses with revelatory clarity how to win the struggle within between the forces of our lower and higher natures.

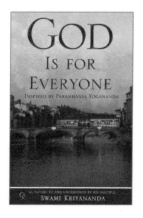

GOD IS FOR EVERYONE
Inspired by Paramhansa Yogananda
by Swami Kriyananda

This book presents a concept of God and spiritual meaning that will broadly appeal to everyone, from the most uncertain agnostic to the most fervent believer. Clearly and simply written, thoroughly non-sectarian and non-dogmatic in its approach, it is the perfect introduction to the spiritual path. Yogananda's core teachings are presented by his disciple, Swami Kriyananda.

AWAKEN TO SUPERCONSCIOUSNESS
by Swami Kriyananda

This popular guide includes everything you need to know about the philosophy and practice of meditation, and how to apply the meditative mind to resolve common daily conflicts in uncommon, superconscious ways. Superconsciousness is the hidden mechanism at work behind intuition, spiritual and physical healing, successful problem solving, and finding deep and lasting joy.

THE ART & SCIENCE OF RAJA YOGA
by Swami Kriyananda

Contains fourteen lessons in which the original yoga science emerges in all its glory—a proven system for realizing one's spiritual destiny. This is the most comprehensive course available on yoga and meditation today. Over 450 pages of text and photos give you a complete and detailed presentation of yoga postures, yoga philosophy, affirmations, meditation instruction, and breathing techniques. Also included are suggestions for daily yoga routines, information on proper diet, recipes, and alternative healing techniques. The book also comes with an audio CD that contains: a guided yoga postures sessions, a guided meditation, and an inspiring talk on how you can use these techniques to solve many of the problems of daily life.

MEDITATION FOR STARTERS
by Swami Kriyananda

If you have wanted to learn to meditate, but never had a chance, this is the place to start. Filled with easy-to-follow instructions, beautiful guided visualizations, and answers to important questions on meditation, the book includes: what meditation is (and isn't); how to relax your body and prepare yourself for going within; and techniques for interiorizing and focusing the mind. Includes a 60-minute companion CD with guided visualization and meditation instruction.

CRYSTAL CLARITY PUBLISHERS

Crystal Clarity Publishers offers additional resources to assist you in your spiritual journey including many other books, a wide variety of inspirational and relaxation music composed by Swami Kriyananda, and yoga and meditation videos. To see a complete listing of our products, contact us for a print catalog or see our website: www.crystalclarity.com

Crystal Clarity Publishers
14618 Tyler Foote Rd., Nevada City, CA 95959
TOLL FREE: 800.424.1055 or 530.478.7600 / FAX: 530.478.7610
EMAIL: clarity@crystalclarity.com

ANANDA WORLDWIDE

Ananda Sangha, a worldwide organization founded by Swami Kriyananda, offers spiritual support and resources based on the teachings of Paramhansa Yogananda. There are Ananda spiritual communities in Nevada City, Sacramento, and Palo Alto, California; Seattle, Washington; Portland, Oregon; as well as a retreat center and European community in Assisi, Italy, and communities near New Delhi and Pune, India. Ananda supports more than 75 meditation groups worldwide.

For more information about Ananda Sangha communities or meditation groups near you, please call 530.478.7560 or visit www.ananda.org.

THE EXPANDING LIGHT

Ananda's guest retreat, The Expanding Light, offers a varied, year-round schedule of classes and workshops on yoga, meditation, and spiritual practice. You may also come for a relaxed personal renewal, participating in ongoing activities as much or as little as you wish. The beautiful serene mountain setting, supportive staff, and delicious vegetarian food provide an ideal environment for a truly meaningful, spiritual vacation.

*For more information, please call 800.346.5350
or visit www.expandinglight.org.*